E
F
1
2
3
4
Zhoujiazui Rd.
周家嘴路
九龙路
Hanyang Rd.
汉阳路
Jiulong Rd.
东长治路
东大名路
Tanggu Rd.
Wuchang Rd.
Wusong Rd.
Huangpu Rd.
黄埔路
The Bund Tourist Tunnel
外滩观光隧道
BinJiang Ave.
Fenghe Rd.
明珠公园
Mingzhu
Lujiazui
陆家嘴站
陆家嘴西路
Lujiazui Rd. (W.)
银城中路
Central Yincheng Rd.
陆家嘴绿地
Lujiazui Green Land
Yincheng Rd. (E.)
陆家嘴东路
昌邑路
Changyi Rd.
钱仓路
Qiancang Rd.
Pudong Ave.
浦东大道
Lujiazui Rd. (E.)
Jimo Rd.
即墨路
Zhongshan No.1 Rd. (E.)
Yan'an East Rd. Tunnel
延安东路隧道
银城西路
Yincheng Rd. (W.)
富城路
Fucheng Rd.
滨江大道
世纪大道
浦东南路
栖霞路
Xiaxia Rd.
崂山西路
崂山东路
Laoshan Rd. (E.)
福山路
Rushan Rd.
Fushan Rd.
源深路
Rushan Rd.
乳山路
ShangCheng Rd.
桃林路
Taolin Rd.
Dongchang Rd.
东昌路站
Zhangyang Rd.
浦东体育公园
Pudong Sports Centre
Yincheng Rd. (S.)
银城南路
Dongchang Rd.
东昌路
Yincheng Rd. (E.)
Shangcheng Rd.
浦明路
商城路
Laoshan Rd. (W.)
Dongfang Rd.
东方路站
Century Avenue
潍坊路
Fushan Rd.
Yuanshen Rd.
Jinling Rd. (E.)
Renmin Rd.
民路
Central Sichuan Rd.
中山东二路
Zhongshan No2. Rd. (E.)
Puming Rd.
张杨路
Weifang Rd. (W.)
Central Fangbang Rd.
Fuxing Rd. Tunnel
复兴路隧道
潍坊西路
Pudong Rd. (S.)
Pucheng Rd.
Henan Rd. (S.)
Fuxing Rd. (E.)
中华路
白渡路
Baidu Rd.
中山南路
外马路
Waima Rd.
Zhongshan Rd. (S.)
Pudian Rd.
浦电路
Yanggao Rd. (S.)
Dongjiadu Rd.
Zhonghua Rd.
董家渡路
Dongfang Rd.
塘桥新路
Tangqiaoxin Rd.
东绣路
Lujiabang Rd.
浦建路
PuJian Rd.
Dongxiu Rd.
锦绣路
Nanpu Bridge
南浦大桥
龙阳路
南浦广场公园
Nanpu Park
龙阳路立交桥
Longyang Rd.
Zhongshan Rd. (S.)
Huangpu River
Dongfang Rd.
杨高南路
严中路
Jinxiu Rd.
浦三路
Yanzhong Rd.
博文路
Bowen Rd.
Pusan Rd.
Yanggao Rd. (S.)
Bei'ailianyuan Rd.
下南路
上南路
Chengshan Rd.
Xianan Rd.

Shanghai Downtown Mape

Upscale Restaurants

C3 1. Ambrosia 仙炙轩
C3 2. Grand Hall 大公馆
B4 3. La Villa Rouge 小红楼
E2 4. M on the Bund
C3 5. Paulaner Brauhaus 宝莱娜餐厅
C3 6. Sasha's 萨沙餐厅
E2 7. Sens & Bund
E2 8. Three on the Bund 外滩 3 号
B3 9. The Yongfoo Elite 雍福会

Shopping

E2 10. Cangbao Lou Antiques Market 藏宝楼古玩市场
C3 11. Changle Lu 长乐路旗袍店
D2 12. Dimei Shopping Mall and Hong Kong Branded Street 迪美百货与香港名品街
D3 13. Dongtai Lu Antiques Market 东台路古玩市场
C3 14. Huaihai Zhonglu 淮海中路
B2 15. Jingan Xiaoting Market 静安小亭市场
D2 16. Nanjing Lu 南京路
D1 17. Qipu Lu Wholesale Clothing Market 七浦路服装批发市场
E3 18. South Bund Cloth Market 南外滩面料市场
D3 19. Taikang Lu Art Stores 泰康路艺术店
B4 20. xujiahui Commercial Center 徐家汇商圈
E2 21. Yuyuan Shopping City 豫园商场

Around the Bund 外滩

E1 22. Architecture on the Bund 外滩
E1 23. Bund Sightseeing Tunnel and the Shanghai Wing of the Chinese Museum of Sex Culture 性文化博物馆
D2 24. FuzhouLu 福州路
E1 25. Huangpu Park 黄浦公园
E1 26. Lovers Wall 情人墙

Around People's Square 人民广场

D2 27. Mu En Methodist Church 沐恩堂
D2 28. Park Hotel 国际饭店
D2 29. People's Square 人民广场
D2 30. Shanghai Art Museum 上海美术馆
D2 31. Shanghai Museum 上海博物馆
D2 32. Shanghai Urban Planning Centre 上海城市规划展示馆

Around Lujiazui 陆家嘴

E2 33. Jin Mao's 88th floor Observation Deck 金茂 88 层观光厅
E2 34. Lujiazui 陆家嘴
E1 35. Oriental Pearl Television Tower 东方明珠
E1 36. Shanghai International Convention Center 国际会议中心
E1 37. Shanghai Natural Wild Insect Museum 上海野生昆虫馆
E1 38. Shanghai Ocean Aquarium 上海海洋水族馆

Around The City God Temple 城隍庙

E2 39. Cangbao Lou Antiques Building 藏宝楼
E2 40. Chenxiang Ge Temple 沉香阁
D3 41. Confucian Temple and Secondhand Book Market 文庙
E3 42. Dongjiadu Catholic Church 董家渡天主教堂
D2 43. Shangh 上海自
E3 44. Little 小桃园
E2 45. The Ci
D3 46. The D 东台路
D3 47. The O
E2 48. The Sl 上海老
E2 49. Yu Ga

Around Jiang

B3 50. Kadoo Childre
B3 51. Jingan
B3 52. Jingan

Around Huar

C3 53. Fuxing
C3 54. Reside
C3 55. Rui Jir
C3 56. St Nicl 圣尼古
C3 57. The Dr 孙中山
C3 58. The M Taiyua
D3 59. The Si Comm 中共一
D3 60. Xintiar

Around Huai

C3 61. Easter 东正大
C2 62. Moller
C3 63. Xingya

Shanghai Outskirts Mape

Around Jiading District 嘉定区

1. Eastern Paris Golf Village Club 东方巴黎高尔夫球俱乐部
2. Fahua Pagoda 法华塔
3. Guyi Yuan Garden 古猗园
4. Jiading Confucian Temple 嘉定孔庙
5. Pool of Convergent Dragons 汇龙潭
6. Qiuxiapu Garden 秋霞圃
7. Yunxiang Temple 云翔寺

Around Fengxian District 奉贤区

8. Eryan Temple 二严寺
9. Fengxian Bay Tourist Area 奉贤海湾旅游度假区
10. Huatingdong Stone Embankment 华亭东石塘
11. Tongjin Bridge 通津桥
12. Wanfo Ge Pavilion 万佛阁

Around Songjiang District 松江区

13. Heavenly Horse Mountain 天马山
14. Square Pagoda 方塔
15. Songjiang Mosque 松江清真寺
16. She Shan National Holiday Resort 佘山国家级
17. The Toroni
18. Yi Garden
19. Zuibai Chi

Around Chon

20. Chongming 崇明学宫
21. Dongping N 东平国家森
22. Jin'ao Moun
23. Shou'an Ter

ai Natural History Museum
然博物馆
Peach Orchard Mosque
清真寺
y God Temple 城隍庙
ngtai Lu Curio Street
古玩市场
d City Wall 大镜阁
anghai Old Street
街
den 豫园

an Temple 静安寺
'e Residenc—Shanghai
n's Palace 嘉道理公馆
Park 静安公园
Temple 静安寺

gpi Nanlu 黄陂南路
Park 复兴公园
nce of Zhou Enlai 周公馆
Guest House 瑞金宾馆
olas Church
拉斯大教堂
Sun Yat-sen Residence
故居
arshall Residence—The
n Vill 马歇尔公馆
e of the First National
unist Party Congress
大会址
di 新天地

ai Lu 淮海路
n Orthodox Church
教堂
Villa 马勒别墅
ng Park 襄阳公园

Around Hengshan Lu 衡山路
B3 64. Ai Lu 爱庐
C3 65. Director of the French Concession Chamber of Industry Mansion 总董官邸
B3 66. Shanghai Library 上海图书馆
B3 67. Song Qingling Residence 宋庆龄故居
B3 68. The Shanghai Community Church 国际礼拜堂
B4 69. Xujiahui Catholic Church — St. Ignacious Cathedral 徐家汇天主教堂
B4 70. Xujiahui Library 徐家汇藏书楼

Around Sichuan Beilu 四川北路
D1 71. Duolun Lu 多伦路
D1 72. Lu Xun Museum 鲁迅纪念馆
D1 73. Lu Xun's Residence 鲁迅故居

Around the City
B1 74. Art Archives and Warehouse—50 Moganshan Lu 大库艺术工厂
B2 75. East China University of Politics and Law 华东政法学院
E1 76. Fudan University 复旦大学
B4 77. Hanghai Film and Television Amusement Park 上海影视城
B1 78. Jade Buddha Temple 玉佛寺
C4 79. LonghuaTemple 龙华寺
C4 80. Shanghai Botanical Garden 上海植物园
A3 81. Shanghai Zoo 上海动物园
E1 82. Tongji University 同济大学
A2 83. Zhenru Temple 真如寺

东游度假区
utra Stela 唐经幢
园
白池

gming Island 崇明岛
Palace of Learning

tional Forest Park
林公园
ain 金鳌山
nple 寿安寺

24. The Eastern Shore 东滩

Around Qingpu District 青浦区
25. Ancient Town of Zhijiajiao 朱家角古镇
26. Grand View Garden 大观园
27. Qushui Yuan Garden 曲水园
28. Sun Island Golf and Resort 太阳岛俱乐部
29. The Bridge town Jinze 金泽
30. Wanshou Pagoda 万佛阁

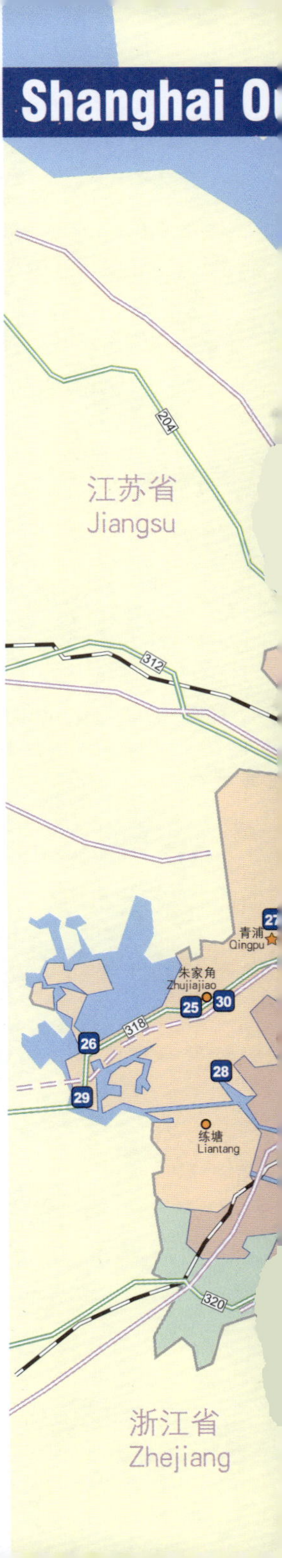

C D

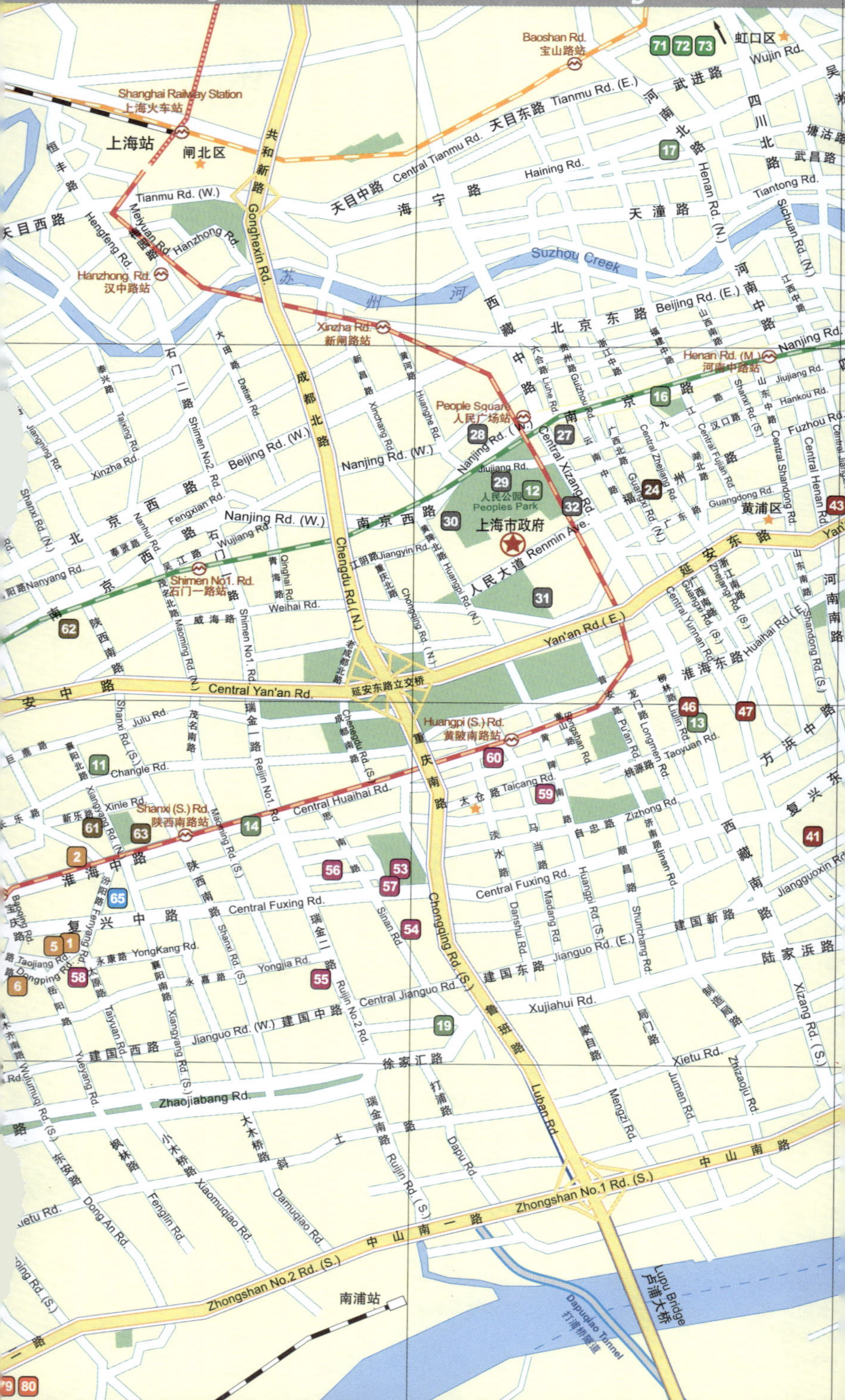

Baoshan Rd.
宝山路站
71 72 73
虹口区
Wujin Rd.
武进路
Shanghai Railway Station
上海火车站
上海站
闸北区
Tianmu Rd. (E.)
天目东路
Central Tianmu Rd.
天目中路
共和新路
Gonghexin Rd.
河南北路
Henan Rd. (N.)
四川北路
塘沽路
武昌路
Tiantong Rd.
Sichuan Rd. (N.)
17
Haining Rd.
海宁路
天潼路
Tianmu Rd. (W.)
天目西路
恒丰路
Hengfeng Rd.
Meiyuan Rd.
梅园路
Hanzhong Rd.
Hanzhong Rd.
汉中路站
Suzhou Creek
苏州河
Xinzha Rd.
新闸路站
西藏中路
北京东路
Beijing Rd. (E.)
河南中路
Nanjing Rd.
Henan Rd. (M.)
河南中路站
People Square
人民广场站
南京东路
16
Jiujiang Rd.
Hankou Rd.
Fuzhou Rd.
Central Henan Rd.
Central Shandong Rd.
Central Fujian Rd.
Central Zhejiang Rd.
Guangxi Rd. (N.)
Guangdong Rd.
黄浦区
43
Yan'an
28 27 29 12 24 32 30 31
人民公园
Peoples Park
上海市政府
人民大道
Renmin Ave.
Central Xizang Rd.
Liuhe Rd.
Guizhou Rd.
石门二路
Shimen No2. Rd.
Dalian Rd.
大田路
成都北路
Xinchang Rd.
新昌路
Huanghe Rd.
黄河路
Nanjing Rd. (W.)
Beijing Rd. (W.)
北京西路
Fengxian Rd.
Wujiang Rd.
吴江路
Nanjing Rd. (W.)
南京西路
泰兴路
Taixing Rd.
Xinzha Rd.
Jiangning Rd.
Shanxi Rd. (N.)
Nanhui Rd.
泰兴路
Nanyang Rd.
Shimen No1. Rd.
石门一路站
Qinghai Rd.
Jiangyin Rd.
江阴路
Huangpi Rd. (N.)
黄陂北路
Chongqing Rd. (N.)
重庆北路
Chengdu Rd. (N.)
Weihai Rd.
威海路
Shimen No1. Rd.
Maoming Rd. (N.)
62
陕西南路
Yan'an Rd. (E.)
延安东路
Central Yan'an Rd.
延安中路
延安东路立交桥
淮海东路
Huaihai Rd. (E.)
Central Yunnan Rd.
Zhejiang Rd. (S.)
Shandong Rd. (S.)
河南南路
Julu Rd.
Shanxi Rd. (S.)
茂名南路
瑞金一路
Reijin No1. Rd.
Chengdu Rd. (S.)
成都南路
Huangpi (S.) Rd.
黄陂南路站
重庆南路
Songshan Rd.
Pu'an Rd.
Longmen Rd.
Liulin Rd.
46 13 47
人民路
方浜中路
Taoyuan Rd.
桃源路
60
11
Changle Rd.
Xiangyang Rd. (N.)
Xinle Rd.
新乐路
Shanxi (S.) Rd.
陕西南路站
61 63 14
Maoming Rd. (S.)
Central Huaihai Rd.
淮海中路
Taicang Rd.
太仓路
59
马当路
淡水路
自忠路
Zizhong Rd.
顺昌路
Jinan Rd.
济南路
西藏南路
复兴东路
41
Jiangguoxin Rd.
2
65
56 53 57
Central Fuxing Rd.
复兴中路
Sinan Rd.
54
Chongqing Rd. (S.)
Central Fuxing Rd.
Danshui Rd.
Madang Rd.
Huangpi Rd. (S.)
Shunchang Rd.
建国新路
陆家浜路
Baoqing Rd.
宝庆路
5 1 6
Taojiang Rd.
Dongping Rd.
58
YongKang Rd.
永康路
Fenyang Rd.
Yongjia Rd.
永嘉路
Shanxi Rd. (S.)
瑞金二路
Ruijin No.2 Rd.
55
Central Jianguo Rd.
Jianguo Rd. (E.)
建国东路
Xujiahui Rd.
Xizang Rd. (S.)
Taiyuan Rd.
太原路
Xiangyang Rd. (S.)
襄阳南路
Jianguo Rd. (W.)
建国中路
建国西路
19
鲁班路
蒙自路
局门路
Xietu Rd.
Zhizaoju Rd.
Wulumuqi Rd. (S.)
Yueyang Rd.
徐家汇路
打浦路
Zhaojiabang Rd.
大木桥路
斜土路
瑞金南路
Ruijin Rd. (S.)
Dapu Rd.
Luban Rd.
Mengzi Rd.
Jumen Rd.
中山南路
Zhongshan No.1 Rd. (S.)
中山南一路
Dong An Rd.
东安路
枫林路
Fenglin Rd.
小木桥路
Xiaomuqiao Rd.
Damuqiao Rd.
Zhongshan No.2 Rd. (S.)
南浦站
Dapuqiao Tunnel
打浦桥隧道
Lupu Bridge
卢浦大桥
80

C D

utskirts Mape

Shanghai Downtown Mape

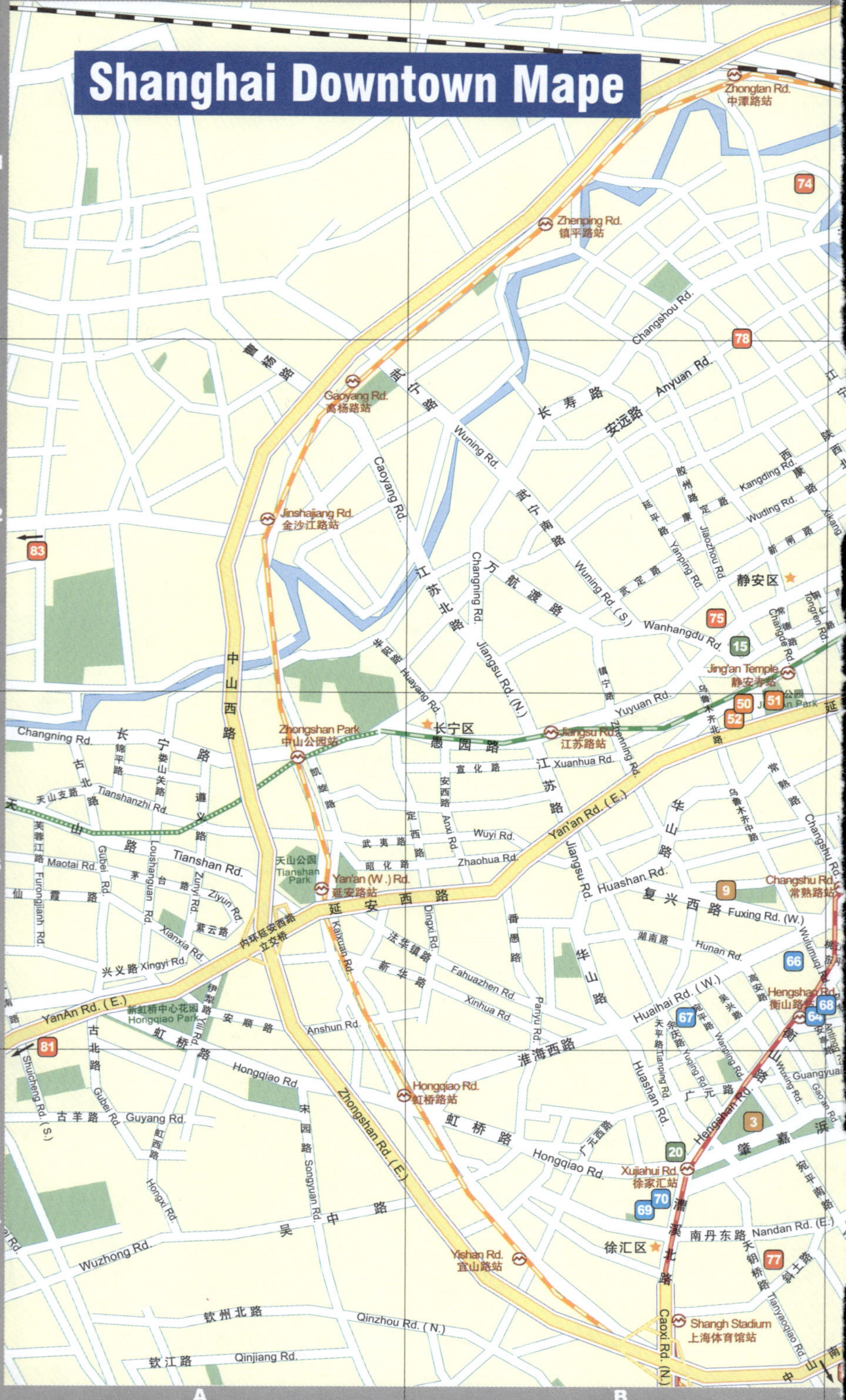

Shanghai Travel Guide

Daya
Jonathann Giammarco

CHINA TRAVEL & TOURISM PRESS

Contents

Shanghai

7 Ten Things to do on a Shanghai Day
8 Travel Itineraries
12 History
17 Shanghai's Administrative Structure
17 Geography
18 Climate
19 What to Pake
19 Currency
20 Banking
21 Communications
22 Staying Healthy
24 Safety
25 Local Services and Information
25 Foreign Consulates in Shanghai

Transportation

30 Long Distance Transportation
30 Air
31 Train
32 Long Distance Bus
33 Boat
34 Citywide Transport
34 Subway
35 Bus
36 Taxi
37 The Maglev

Accommodations, Food, Drink, Entertainment

40 Accommodations
41 Exclusive Luxury Hotels
49 High-end Options
55 Middle Level Accomodations
57 Budget Hotels: 300 RMB and Less
59 Renting Houses and Apartments
60 Food and Drink
62 Upscale Restaurants

71 Local Shanghai Fare
76 Shanghai Snacks
81 Classic Shanghai Favorites
83 Vegetarian Cuisine
86 **Entertainment**
86 Nightlife
96 Theaters and shows
97 Cinemas
100 The Performing Arts
103 Go-cart Tracks
104 Massage
104 For the Children

Shopping

110 Best Places to Shop
115 Markets
118 Books
119 Camera & Film

Downtown

122 Around The Bund
144 Around People's Square
152 Around Lujiazui
158 Around The City God Temple
174 Around Jingan Temple
180 Around Huangpi Nanlu
196 Around Huaihai Lu
204 Around Hengshan Lu
216 Around Sichuan Beilu

Around the City

228 Temples
236 Universities
242 Others

Outside the City

250 Around Jiading District
258 Around The Fengxian District
266 Around Songjiang District
278 Around Chongming Island
286 Around Qingpu District

296 language
300 index

Shanghai

Shanghai
(shànghǎi, 上海)

One of the world's leading international metropolises, today's Shanghai is a glittering marvel of modernity. At the same time, Shanghai has not sacrificed any of its Chineseness or the Haipai (Shanghai) character that makes it unique from other urban centers around the world. Part of Shanghai's charm lies in its cultural and architectural diversity, with the Bund's famous turn of the century western architecture facing modern skyscrapers across the Huangpu River. The sounds of hymns drift out of the Xujiahui Catholic Church, mixing in the Shanghai air with wisps of incense fluttering out of the Jade Buddha Temple. Older Shanghai folks play mahjong in the street while the young kick soccer balls in Shanghai's meandering lanes and alleys, and the urban masses turn out at local opera houses to see the Shanghai Opera, farcical Chinese plays, and the Shanghai Grand Theater to listen to the symphony and watch ballet. When you are hungry you can look for Little Shaoxing's Three Yellows Chicken and or a bucket of dark meat at the omnipresent KFC. Enjoy a quiet cup of chrysanthemum tea in one of the old tea houses on the Shanghai Old Street or a Heineken in a bar on Hengshan Lu. Shanghai is a true combination of east and west, warmly welcoming the new and deeply nostalgic for the old. When night draws on, neon lights glow and Shanghai assumes an air of regality. Jazz at the Peace Hotel and the soothing music of bamboo instruments at Yu Yuan Garden will help you reawaken the Shanghai dream of the 1920's and 30's as the coffee shops, nightlife, and pace of modern life keep you grounded in the twenty first century.

This city of dreams and illusions awaits your exploration.

Ten Things to do on a Shanghai Day

1. The Bund

This is Shanghai's most famous waterfront. Stretching about one mile along the west shoreline of the Huangpu River, here on Zhongshan Dong Yi Lu you can stroll through the beautifully restored colonial buildings of old Shanghai. Afterwards, head across the street to the Bund Promenade. Early morning weekdays are the best time to go avoid the crowds of tourists and souvenir vendors. You can join the masses of local residents in their tai chi exercises and Western ballroom dancing. Return to the Bund in the evening for the glittering night lights.

2. Oriental Pearl TV Tower

Climb to the top of the twin towers, the Oriental Pearl Television Tower and the Jin Mao Tower, for unforgettable views of Puxi and the Bund.

3. Shanghai Museum

Known as China's finest museum, its four floors hold 11 galleries, three exhibition halls and 120,000 historic artifacts. In the heart of People's Square, it's accessible by Metro Lines 1 and 2. Consider buying a People's Square Combo Ticket if you're planning to visit one of its other attractions such as the Grand Theatre or the Shanghai Urban Planning Exhibition Center.

4. Admire Landscaping Artistry in the Yu Yuan Garden

Yu Yuan will take your breath away with its exquisitely crafted and finely manicured arrangements. Spring and winter are both fine seasons to visit the garden, but winter is most ideal. This is the season when the plum blossoms bloom, creating this most quintessential Chinese scene.

5. Munch on Shanghai Snacks at the City God Temple

Chenghuang Miao — the City God Temple — is a fine representation of old Shanghai life. Home of Shanghai's city guardian who has protected generations of Shanghai people, the area around the temple also happens to be a gathering spot for dozens of snack shops and stalls. Come with an adventurous mind and try a little bit of everything. You are guaranteed to come away satisfied. After feasting on Shanghai delights, wash it all down with a cup of tea or two at a teahouse on Shanghai Old Street.

6. Xintiandi

This is Shanghai's most extravagant downtown development. Xintiandi has become the top spot for people watching, and the lines of restaurants and bars here are some of the trendiest in the city. The shops are posh and the price tags prove it. The exterior design is a unique mix of traditional and modern, western and Chinese. When it becomes too much, head down to the Shikumen buildings and revel in the culture of the past.

7. Nanjing Lu

This fabulous shopping street is a must stop if only to check out the pre-revolutionary department stores, hotels and shops here. Be careful not to get lost in the crowds upon crowds of fellow shoppers.

8. Explore Shanghai's Old Cathedrals

With the arrival of Christian missionaries in Shanghai over a century ago, churches began springing up around the city. Xujiahui Catholic Church, Dongjiadu Church and the Shanghai Community Church on Hengshan Lu, make up just a small sampling of the religious architecture that can be found around the city. You may also have the opportunity to interact with members of the Chinese Christian Community, many of whom were alive during the early twentieth century.

9. Visit Buddhist Temples and Sample Vegetarian Cuisine

Shanghai is home to some of the most famous Buddhist temples in China, including the Jade Buddha Temple and Jingan Si Temple. In both complexes, you will find ancient traditional Chinese temple architecture and crowds of people who flock to these locations to pray and burn incense. Many temples also have their own vegetarian restaurants. Serving only food that adheres to Buddhist dietary principles, the "meat" dishes in these restaurants are made with tofu and ground taro root. Temple cuisine is cooked in the local Shanghai style.

10. Zhujiajiao

Head to Zhujiaojiao, the "village of rivers and streams" found just outside the Shanghai metropolis. Stroll through the mysterious Ming Dynasty alleys, and interact with locals inside their ancient courtyards. If feel down on your luck, you can release a fish or two at the Fangsheng Qiao Bridge.

Travel Itineraries

Overview

Three Day Plan

If you are in town for only three days,

you definitely want to dive right in and get the most out of your Shanghai experience. Hotels near the People's Square, the Bund, or Huaihai Lu are all excellent jumping off points for Shanghai's most quintessential sites. Transportation is also convenient.

Seven Day Plan

Seven days in Shanghai is more than enough time to carefully explore Shanghai's essential tourist sites and check out a few other places as well. The seven day plan will allow you to add a great deal of variety to your trip. Hotels around the People's Square, Nanjing XiLu, Xizang ZhongLu, and Huaihai Zhonglu are all excellent locations to set up home base.

Ten Day Plan

Ten days give you ample time to really dig below the city's surface. After making your way through the 10 activities listed above, you can spend a day or two touring the sites outside of town like the Longhua Si Temple, Zhujiajiao, or She Shan Mountain. Take a full day to stroll along the Bund, Chenghuang Miao, Fenyang Lu, or a half day on Shaoxing Lu, Tongren Lu and Xintiandi. Fully explore the Moller Villa, Grand Hall, Rui Jin Guest House, and sip coffee in Face Cafe. Do not forget to see a Shanghai-style melodrama at the Yifu, Lyceum or Majestic Theaters. If feel so inclined, you can also sneak in a circus performance at the Shanghai Circus World.

With the amount of time you have, there is no need to get up early in the morning and come home too late. Stay in transportaion-friendly People's Square, Nanjing XiLu, Xizang ZhongLu, or Huaihai ZhongLu. Or,

you may want to consider a hotel at Xujiahui, Hengshan Lu, Zhongshan BeiLu, or Yan'an Lu.

Two Week Plan

Two weeks in Shanghai will allow you to really settle in and enjoy the city. Be sure to make detailed travel plans and thoroughly explore Shanghai's hidden corners and small alleys. Before you leave, it is suggested you read up on Shanghai's history and learn a little bit more about the places you are going to visit. This will add an extra element of depth to your trip, and turn your vacation into a journey of discovery that will leave you with a lifetime of memories.

Photography buffs should take advantage of the more relaxed schedule. The stretch around Chenghuang Miao and Dongjiadu has great old alleys worth shooting. You also need to check out the Sinan Lu, Fuxing XiLu, and Duolun Lu. Danshan Lu, Sichuan ZhongLu, and Suzhou River offer photogenic old resident architecture and villa-style garden residences.

Living accomodations should be booked according to your plans. You may choose to find a place near Xujiahui, Hengshan Lu, Zhongshan BeiLu, or Yan'an ZhongLu. Hotels in these sleepy residential areas tend to be quieter and relatively inexpensive. It will also give you a better opportunity to see how the local Shanghainese live.

The Plans

Three Day Plan

Day One

Morning: Tour the Bund architecture first thing in the morning, and take a stroll down Nanjing Lu and Fuzhou Lu. From there you can walk, take a bus, or cab to Chenghuang Miao (City God Temple) and sample some local snacks like a basket of small Nanxiang-style stuffed steamed buns (南翔小笼包子).

Afternoon: Visit Chenghuang Miao and than go see the Yu Yuan Garden and Chen Xiang Ge Pavilion. On weekends, you can buy discounted books at the Wenmiao Confucian Temple book fair, before heading over to the Shanghai Old Street and Cangbao Lou curio market. If you still have time and want to check out more curios, then quickly move on to the Dongtai Lu Curio Market. Keep in mind that the Dongtai Lu curio market closes at 5 pm.

Day Two

Morning: First, go visit the Jade Buddah Temple and then take a cab over to Moganshan Lu to tour the art exhibits at the Art Warehouse. From there you can move on to Duolun Lu and the Lu Xun Residence before sitting down to lunch in one of the restaurants along Sichuan ZhongLu.

Afternoon: Take a bus or a taxi to the Rui Jin Guest House and then walk to Sinan Lu. After visiting the Sun Yat-sen and Zhou Enlai Residences, move on to Xintiandi to visit the site of the first National Communist Party Congress. Have dinner in a local Shanghainese restaurant near Shikumen. After dinner you can relax in one of the nearby bars or cafes. Prepare your camera for some splendid nighttime photography at Shikumen, and than go to Fuxing Park's Park 97 to witness the parade of Shanghai's fashionable people at play.

Day Three

Morning: Go to Xujiahui Catholic Church and the Xujiahui library first thing in the morning before moving on to the Xujiahui Commercial Street. Afterwards, you can take a car or bus to Huaihai Zhonglu to visit the Song Qinling Residence and the Shanghai Library, before moving on to Fenyang Lu and Dongping Lu. Have lunch in one of the eateries along these two roads and snap a few pictures of the old houses nearby.

Afternoon: Head to Huaihai Lu for some shopping and then stop in at the Moller Villa for a cup of coffee. Finally, end your trip with dinner at Xijia Huayuan, Ouyue Niandai or one of the other restaurants along Julu Road.

Seven Day Plan

Day One

Morning: Tour the classic architecture along the Bund and go for a walk along Nanjing Lu and Fuzhou Lu. Be sure to have lunch at Laobanzhai, Laozhengxing, or one of the traditional restaurants along Fuzhou Lu.

Afternoon: First, take a stroll through the People's Square and then go check out some of the attractions nearby such as the Daguangming Movie Theater, Shanghai Grand Theater, Shanghai Museum and the Shanghai Art Museum. Afterwards you can pay a visit to the Shanghai Concert Hall. As evening approaches, take a bus or a cab to Lujiazui. For a spectacular sunset view, ride the elevator up to Jin Mao Tower's Cloud Nine Bar or the obeservation deck on the 88th floor.

Day Two

Morning: Spend the morning at Chenghuang Miao, Yu Yuan Garden and Shanghai Lao Jie (Shanghai Old Street). Have lunch near Chenghuang Miao or on Shanghai Lao Jie.

Afternoon: Shop for curios on Dongtai Lu and then visit the Dongjiadu Catholic Church.

There is a fabric market on the South Bund *(nánwàitān miànliào shìchǎng, 南外滩面料市场)* where you can have clothes custom made.

Day Three

Morning: Stroll through the East China University of Politics and Law's western campus and then burn some incense at Jingan Si Temple. From here you can go on to visit the residence of legendary author, Zhang Ailing, before heading to Nanjing XiLu or the Jingan Xiaoting Pavilion. Have lunch along Tongren Lu or Jingan XiLu.

Afternoon: Visit the Moller Villa and then walk over to the Orthodox Eastern Church. From here you can catch a film at the Cathay Theater and go shopping on Maoming NanLu. Maoming NanLu is a great place for dinner and spend the rest of the evening.

Day Four

Morning: Tour the Taiyuan Villa and then go to the White House at 79 Fenyang Lu. When you are finished there, move onto Aihu on Dongping Lu. Lunch at Sasha's is recommended.

Afternoon: Go see Rui Jin Guest House and walk over to Sinan Lu. From there you can visit the Sun Yat-sen and Zhou Enlai residences and continue on to Xintiandi, and the site of the first National Communist Party Congress. Have dinner nearby and then relax in a Xintiandi bar or cafe. You may also want to head to Fuxing Park's Park 97 to party with the fashion set.

Day Five

Morning: First tour the Community Church on Hengshan Lu and then move on to the Xujiahui Catholic Church and church library.

Afternoon: Pay a visit to the Song Qingling Residence and then have a look at the Shanghai Library. Have dinner on Huaihai ZhongLu and catch a melodrama at the Lyceum or Majestic Theaters.

Day Six

Morning: Explore the Jade Buddha Temple and have lunch at the temple's vegetarian restaurant.

Afternoon: Tour art galleries at the Moga--nshan Lu Art Warehouse and along the Suzhou River.

Day Seven

Go out to visit Fudan University, Duolun Lu and the Lu Xun Residence. From here you can continue on to explore Sichuan Beilu. Use the rest of your time in one of the city's famous shopping centers looking for souvenirs and gifts to take home.

History

As it is commonly understood, the history of Shanghai extends back only as far as the nineteenth century. Cultural traces found in modern Shanghai life are falsely considered to be nothing more than the vestiges of colonial influence and bland homogenizing forces of urban living. However, if you could travel through time, you would discover that this piece of land off the East China Sea has seen human habitation as early as six thousand years ago. The beginnings of urban Shanghai appeared as early as the first half of the tenth century. This region's most ancient culture was excavated in 1957 in the northern end of Qingpu County's Songze Village. With characteristics representative of Tai Hu Lake Neolithic culture, the Songze discovery has proved to be the earliest culture to have lived in the Shanghai regions, and its archaeological significance runs deep. The Neolithic peoples living downstream of the Wusong River mouth survived on a lifestyle of fishing and hunting, and developed a fishing tool called a "hu", which was particularly suited for Shanghai's rising and falling tides. Local regions eventually came to adopt "hu" as a place name, which is still used today as an abbreviated way of writing "Shanghai". The Huangpu River can be traced back to the China's Chunqiu and Warring States Period (777 B.C.-221 B.C.). At that time, the area comprising modern Shanghai was once the estate of the Chunshen Sovereign, Huangxie. The stretch of Huangpu River from Longhua to the Songjiang River was originally called "Huang Xie Pu" in memory of the ruler, and has been since simplified to "Huangpu". The word "Shen" is used like "hu", an abbreviated form of the word Shanghai.

Qin Dynasty

In 223 B.C., several years after the Qin state defeated the Chu, the Huiji Prefecture was created and the seat of the local gov-

ernment was established in Suzhou. The Huiji Prefecture administered Miao Xian, Youquan Xian, and Haiyan Xian counties. Miao Xian County included territory making up today's Jiading and Shanghai counties, most of Qingpu and Songjiang counties, and some of urban Shanghai.

After Qin Shihuang (China's first Emperor) had united the six states into China's first empire, a wide imperial highway was built running from Xianyang through Hubei, Hunan, Jiangsu and Shanghai. According to historical records, the highway was fifty paces wide, with trees planted at every 10 meters, and ran through the northwest of Shanghai's Songjiang. In 210 B.C., the Emperor Qin Shihuang led a group of civilian ministers and military officers south on an inspection of Heng Shan, the Xiaokun Mountains, and Sanmao along the eastern border of Songjiang and the southern border of Qingpu. Records show that the region had a wealth of natural resources, and the busy populace could be seem bustling around, with people conducting trade on the river. Urban Shanghai, at this time, was clearly a long time coming.

Jin Dynasty

During the Jin Dynasty, the Shanghai regions relied upon fishing and harvesting salt to develop a strong economy. In 585, the first year of Southern Dynasty Emperor, Liang Datong, Haiyan Xian County was divided up into Qingpu and Qianjing Counties.

Tang Dynasty

During the Tang Dynasty, the southern part of Kunshan, the east of Jiaxian, and the north of Haiyan were combined into the new Huating County which then formed a county seat in today's Singjiang County.

In 746 A.D., Qinglong Zhen Town was founded in the northeast of today's Qingpu under the southern bank of Wusong River. Originally an anchoring point for the Three Kingdoms-era King of the Wu, Sun Quan's warships, Qinglong Harbor is the starting point of the Wusong River's downstream region, and was a thriving port of trade during the Tang Dynasty. Boats that stopped here not only moved on to important coastal and inland towns, but also to destinations in Japan and the Korean Peninsula. At this time, Shanghai was still nothing more than a seaport and fishing village in Huating County.

There were two rivers in eastern Shanghai that emptied into the Huating Sea in the northwest. The easternmost of the two rivers

was called Xaihaipu, and the westernmost of the two rivers was called Shanghaipu. This small fishing village derived its name from the closer of the two rivers — the western Shanghaipu River — and thus was called Shanghai.

Song Dynasty

At the beginning of the Song Dynasty, Huating Xian County was taken in by Zhejiang's Luxiu Zhou Prefecture. Huating's beach in its east was then an important salt producer. The river's commerce increased by the day as it became thick with people and incoming boats. With the Songjiang channel's dredging in 1119, Qinglong Zhen Town saw even more rapid development. According to Song Dynasty poet, Mei Yanchen, Qinglong Zhen had twenty-two bridges, thirty six workshops, three pavilions, seven pagodas, thirteen temples, and crowds of people. Mei Yanchen's contemporaries referred to this thriving town as "little Hangzhou". While Qinglong Zhen enjoyed its prosperity, Shanghai remained desolate.

Silt build-up in the Wusong River gradually led to a change of fortunes in Qinglong Zhen as the river became shallower and river traffic had more difficulty passing through. Eventually, its harbor became less accessible and Qinglong Zhen's status fell as it sunk into rapid decline. During the reign of Song Emperor Xi Ning (1068-1077), Huating's trade center shifted to Shanghai in its northeast, attracting more residents, and allowing this small fishing village to grow into a town. In 1267, during the Southern Song Dynasty, a town government and military garrison were established in the western part of Shanghaipu, and the town was officially given the name Shanghai Zhen. A

seaport customs office was set up in Shanghai in 1277, and it became one of the seven largest official seaport offices in China.

Ming & Qing Dynasty

Shanghai really began to prosper in the Ming Dynasty. A forest of commercial taverns sprang up around town, and Shanghai came to be known as "the southeastern city".

At the end of the Ming and the beginning of the Qing Dynasties, the Shanghai administrative region continued to develop, and its dimensions grew to approximately those of modern Shanghai. In 1840, on the eve of the Opium War, Shanghai had already turned into a big town with 63 streets and lanes, a forest of shops, and was a pivotal center for ocean traffic.

Colonial Times

After suffering defeat in the Opium War, the Qing Dynasty government ordered capitulators, Shi Ying and Yi Libu, along with British envoy, Sir Henry Pottinger, to sign the infamous Treaty of Nanking. The treaty established Britsh extraterritoriality in China and opened the five ports of Guangzhou, Fuzhou, Xiamen, Ningbo, and Shanghai to free trade.

Under the guise of reparations, the Qing Government signed the Treaty of Humen which stipulated that the British were able to establish homes in certain areas of the five newly-opened commercial ports.

According to the original terms of the treaty, local Chinese authorities had to work together with the British to define the terms of each plot and locale before allowing the British to lease out a property. But, on November 8 of that year, the first British Consul of Shanghai, Captain George Balfour, approached Mu Jiu, the official in charge of Shanghai and demanded that a special "settlement" be drawn up exclusively for British use. Mu Jiu surprisingly acquiesced to Bafuer's demands, reasoning that separating the British from the Chinese would help avoid trouble. As a result, on November 14, Baufour released an announcement declaring that as of November 17, 1843 Shanghai opened for business.

After the Shanghai port was finally forced open, there was a one hundred year period where colonials from different countries poured into Shanghai, vying with each other to develop their own concession areas. The British were first to set up their settlement area in 1845, and they were quickly followed by the United States (1848) and France (1849). The British and American Concessions eventually merged to form the International Settlement. Over the course of the century, Shanghai was turned into the "playground of adventurers".

Today

The May Fourth Movement shook the country to its roots in 1919 when Shanghai workers and students went on a general strike. On July 7, 1921, the Chinese Communist opened its first party congress in Shanghai. In January 1925, the "Feng Jun" troops from the northeast marched into Shanghai, and the Beijing government temporarily changed Shanghai's name to Songhu City. Shanghai's temporary city government was set up in 1927. Finally, the Shanghai People's Government was founded in 1949, and General Chen Yi became its first mayor.

Shanghai's Administrative Structure

Shanghai is a municipality directly under the central government, and is China's largest financial center. The city includes fifteen administrative districts including: Huangpu, Jingan, Changan, Luwan, Nanshi, Putuo, Hongkou, Zhabei, Yangpu, Xuhui, Baoshan, Minhang, Jiading, Jinshan, and Songjiang. There are also four administrative counties, Qingpu, Fengxian, Nanhui, and Chongming, and the Pudong New District. Shanghai has 13.5 million permanent residents and a floating population of 2.5 million.

Geography

At 31.14 degrees latitude and 121.29 degrees longitude, Shanghai sits in the middle of China's eastern coastline. To the direct east is the Pacific Ocean, while Hangzhou Bay sits to Shanghai's south; the Jiangsu and Zhejiang provinces are to Shanghai's west and an estuary of the Yangtze River sits to the north.

Shanghai is part of the Yangtze River Delta flatlands. Aside from the mountains in the southwest, the rest is broad lowland alluvial plane, averaging four meters above sea level. Within Shanghai's boundaries are three of China's biggest islands: Chongming Island, Changxing Island, and Hengsha Island. Shanghai's total area measures at 6,340.5 square kilometers, accounting for 0.06% of China's total area, stretching 120 kilometers from north to south and 100 kilometers from east to west. Shanghai's territory includes 643.06 square kilometers of urban area, 3,697.44 square kilometers of suburban area, and 122 square kilometers of water cover. Shanghai's Chongming Island, China's third largest island, has a total area of 1,041 square kilometers.

Pudong New District, which includes a triangle-shaped piece of urban Shanghai east of the Huangou River and southwest of the Yangtze River Estuary, has an area of 523 square kilometers. It is right across the river from the 350 square kilometer Puxi District.

Huangpu River

This is Shanghai's main body of flowing water. Orginally called Dongjiang or the "East River", the Huangpu River originates at Dianshan Lake, but only carries the name "Huangpu" after passing through Songjiang. Before 300 A.D., Huangpu River was extremely short, heading south and emptying into Hangzhou Bay. After changing course several times, the river current settled on a new direction, now heading northeast, effectively stretching the length of the river. The river solidified its new direction around the fifteenth century, becoming the Huangpu River we know today.

At 114 kilometers long, the Huangpu River flows past the five counties of Qingpu,

Songjiang, Fengxian, Shanghai, and Chuansha, and flows into urban Shanghai where it merges with the Suzhou River, and then dumps into the Yangtze River. Also called the Wusong River, Suzhou River is the Huangpu River's biggest tributary. Beginning in the Jiangsu Province's Tai Hu Lake, the river heads east across the province and through urban Shanghai before merging with the Huangpu River near Waibaidu Qiao Bridge.

Suzhou River

In the past, the Suzhou River nurtured Shanghai's prosperity. Boats and sampans began turning up on its waters during the reign of Qing Dynasty Emperor, Xian Feng. With the opening of Shanghai's ports and the development of the city, farmers from Jiangsu and Zhejiang began flooding into the city. With hearts full of hope, they headed up the Wusong and Suzhou Rivers on rocking boats, bringing along building materials, raw cotton, grains, and agricultural chemicals. Although their sampans were narrow and small, whole families often lived on them, and adults churned the boats' sculls to the chants of their family as they paddled into Shanghai, chasing their dreams.

In the 1920's and 30's, small steamships became popular along Suzhou River and slowly took over river traffic from the scull boats. Pulling freight for Chinese and foreign businesses, the steamships would come and go at fixed times from Shanghai to ports along China's inland rivers. With this new quick and efficient transport, national enterprises began investing in factories, and within a short period of time, dozens of national enterprises sprung up along the Suzhou River.

The Shanghai Western Industrial District eventually became the birthplace of China's national industry. Located to the west of modern day Hengfeng Lu Qiao Bridge, the industrial area stretched along Putuo, Changning, and Jingan. In recent years, the Suzhou River has become a popular shooting location for modern directors. Well-known films such as Zhang Yimou's Shanghai Triad and Lou Ye's Suzhou River have done much to increase the profile of the location. Today, Suzhou River still has 27 well-preserved bridges, the oldest of which, Waibaidu Qiao Bridge, was built in 1907. It is located at the head of the Suzhou River and is connected to Zhongshan Dong Yi Lu.

Climate

Shanghai sits on both the ocean and the river, is situated at a central latitude, and has a northern subtropical monsoon climate. Mild and wet throughout the year, Shanghai has four seasons, plenty of sunshine, and significant amounts of rain.

Seasons

Shanghai's spring and fall tend to be short, and its summers and winters long, presenting monsoon, oceanic, and local cli-

mate characteristics. With its large urban area and dense population, Shanghai can become a real hot box in the summertime.

Temperatures

Temperatures in Shanghai average 15.8 degrees Celsius annually, and tend to be coldest in January with an average of 3.8 degrees Celsius and hottest in July with an average of 27.8 degrees Celsius.

Rainy & Dry Periods

Rainfall averages 1149 millimeters a year, and it rains 132 days (36%) annually. 70% of all rainfall occurs during the flood season between May and September. Every year has three rainy periods and three dry periods with the rainy periods coming in the spring, fall, and flood season, and the dry seasons coming in midsummer, post-fall, and winter.

What to Pack

Shanghai is most comfortable in the spring, summer, and fall; sweatshirts, shirts, and short-sleeved shirts are all appropriate choices to pack.

During the summer's rainy season, be sure to bring an umbrella and raincoat. Nevertheless, Shanghai should still have plenty of sunny clear days.

Shanghai's winter is not unbearable. In Shanghai's coldest moments, long underwear, a sweatshirt, and a wind breaker should be enough to keep you warm. Indoor temperatures are definitely cold in the winter, so when you choose a hotel, be sure to pick one that provides central heating or an air conditioning unit.

Currency

rénmín bì

The Chinese currency is the *rénmín bì* (RMB, 人民币), also known as the *yuán*

(元) or *kuài* (块) as it is referred to on the street. Originally fixed at 8.27 to one against the dollar, over the past year or so the RMB has been given a small amount of room to shift, so small fluctuations against the dollar are not unheard of. Expect the RMB to remain at about the current exchange rate of about 7.99 to one against the dollar, and 10 to one against the Euro.

Bank Notes

Chinese currency comes in 1, 2, 5, 10, 20, 50 and 100 paper Yuan bills. Smaller bills and coins come in denominations of one Yuan, five Jiao, one Jiao and five Fen. Have plenty of smaller bills on hand, especially 10's and 50's, for small purchases and taxis. Shop owners and taxi cab drivers will whine and complain if you try to give them a 100 RMB bill. 20RMB bills and under are helpful for buying tickets at the metro. Collect 1 RMB coins for use in certain busses.

Banking

You can change money, traveler's checks, and use ATM's at most branches of Bank of China, Industrial and Commercial Bank of China, and China Construction Bank--China's national banks. Local Shanghai banks such as China Merchants Bank, Bank of Communications, and Shanghai Pudong Development Bank can often but not always change money. Most banks are open Monday through Friday 9 am through 12 pm and 1pm through 4:30 pm. Aside from Bank of China, China Commercial Bank and China Construction Bank, most banks are closed on the weekend.

Bringing your Money to China

If you have a credit card or a debit card affiliated with a major credit card company, then you can make cash withdrawals from ATM's at most of China's large national banks, large branches of some of Shanghai's local banks, some foreign banks like Citibank and HSBC, airports, and even large hotels and shopping centers.

ATM

Visa and MasterCard are definitely the most widely accepted of all credit cards, but you should be able to find ATM's that accept American Express and other credit cards regularly. Before you make a withdrawal, first confirm that the machine you are using can accept your card. The types of cards that an ATM accepts are usually labeled on a panel overhead or on the ATM's introductory screen.

Be sure to enquire about your credit card's withdrawal fees before you leave

home, so that you are not shocked by hidden fees when you receive your bill. As with anywhere, take caution when making an ATM withdrawal. Do not make huge withdrawals alone at night, be discrete with your password, and do not forget to retrieve your card when your transaction is completed.

Credit Card

If you want to pay directly with a foreign credit card, you can freely do so at expensive hotels, restaurants, and large shopping malls. Keep in mind that in most places, including smaller hotels and many middle range shopping centers, cash is the only accepted form of payment. Cash advances from major credit cards can be made at major branches of Bank of China, and a handful of national banks.

Traveler's Check

Traveler's checks are still a much safer option than cash. They can be changed at most branches of the Bank of China, at airports, and in many in larger hotels. Change money as you need it. Pickpockets are not unknown in China, especially on crowded busses or trains, so the inconvenience of changing money may be offset by your added feeling of security. If something happens to your checks, be sure to have handy the local contact number of the issuing company, so that you can be issued replacements.

Special Note

If you leave urban Shanghai for the countryside or the suburbs, then all bets are off regarding credit cards and traveler's checks. When you leave town, bring a good supply of local currency with you and be very careful.

Communications

Country code: +86
City code: 021
Post code: 200000

Long Distance Telephone Calls

Making a long distance call from Shanghai is the same as it is all over China. Calls from within the hotel are extremely expensive, running up to 20-30 RMB per minute. If you make international calls regularly, then you better buy a local Shanghai IP telephone card. IP card rates are about 80% cheaper than standard international rates. It is also possible to buy IP cards with substantial discounts. Expect to pay about 30 RMB for a 100 RMB IP card. International rates are often written on the back of the card. Calls to Hong Kong and Macao tend to run 1.2 RMB per minute and calls to North America 2.8 RMB per minute. Calls to other international locations can be as expensive as 3.6 RMB per minute.

You call also use IP card telephone booths found at the Shanghai telecommunications office and along the street. Most of these places use a network IP telephone system and prices are pretty reasonable.

Cell Phone

The China Telecom network is compatible with most telephone networks worldwide. If you take your cell phone to China, and do not mind astronomical roaming charges, then you can use it anywhere in the country.

If you plan to stay in Shanghai for a long time and want access to cellular telephone service, then you can buy a local telephone SIM card. Cards can be found almost everywhere including newspaper stands, the Shanghai telecommunications office, and cellular telephone stores. A China Telecom card costs between 60 RMB and 100 RMB, and includes a limited amount of telephone credit. China Unicom sells cheaper cards. You will need to buy special cell phone cards to increase the balance on your phone. Expect to pay about 0.6 RMB per minute for local calls. China Telecom generally has better coverage and special deals such as 10 RMB for 500 minutes of answered calls and 20 RMB for 1,000 minutes of answered calls.

Internet

Most hotels and hostels provide free internet service,and many hotel rooms, bars, and cafes also provide wireless internet access. To access wireless internet you will need your own laptop computer and LAN card.

Internet cafes — wang ba — provide internet access for locals and travelers. It can be hard to find a wang ba on Shanghai's main streets, but you should be able to find plenty in Shanghai's more residential areas. Wang ba provide cheap internet access, usually 2 to 3 RMB per hour.

Staying Healthy

Shanghai holds one of the country's highest hygiene standards, and although travelers have no need to worry about major health concerns, precautions should still be taken here. To minimize upset stomachs, do not drink unboiled tap water; instead opt for bottled water. Wash your hands frequently; eat freshly cooked food, and peel or wash fruit well. Try to eat at clean-looking restaurants, and if you are in town for a short while, you probably do not want to be too adventurous with cooked meat sold on the street.

Over-the-counter remedies can be easily found at drugstores and supermarkets. If you have any preferred brands or if you suffer from allergies, than be sure to jot down the names and chemical names of the medicines you use so that a pharmacist can help you

locate them. You definitely want to bring along a good supply of all essential medications and prescription drugs from home as well as a few over-the-counter treatments for upset stomachs and diarrhea, which are commonly suffered by international travelers. If you come during the winter months, then take along some nighttime cold medicine.

If you do come down with a serious illness, you can go to clinics that cater to foreigners. Also you may see some locals wearing cloth or gauze masks. Do not worry. They are not privy to any special information. Masks are generally worn to protect against pollution, and were commonly seen on the streets during the SARS crises of 2003. These masks do nothing to protect from either airborne pathogens or pollution, so you do not need to wear one unless you are into the look.

Immunizations

You are not required any vaccinations before entering China and Shanghai, although a vaccine for hepatitis A is highly recommended. You should also consider updating inoculations against polio, typhoid, tetanus, cholera, hepatitis B and meningococcal meningitis, if you do not have them already. Speak to your doctor if you have special medical needs. For more on the latest updates for infectious diseases and travel risks, consult the World Health Organization (who.org) and look for health updates on your country's embassy or consulate website.

Healthcare

There are many clinics available in Shanghai with English-speaking and foreign-trained doctors. You can find international standards of healthcare provided here, but fees will be similar to that of those in the West.

Huashan Worldwide Medical Center Foreigner's Clinic: Located on the 18th Floor

12 Wulumuqi Lu; telephone: 021-62483986 and 021-62489999 ext. 2531

Huadong Hospital Foreign Clinic: Located at 221 Yanan Xilu; telephone: 021-62484867 and 021-62483018 ext. 3160

International Peace Maternity Hospital: Located at 910 Hengshan Lu; telephone: 021-64070434 ext. 1105

International SOS: Located inside the Guangdong Development Bank Tower at 555 Xujiahui Lu; telephone: 021-62959951; fax: 021-63901428; website: www.internationalsos.com

Pediatric Hospital, Foreigner's Clinic: Located on the second floor of the Shanghai Medical University at 183 Fenglin Lu; telephone: 021-54524666; fax: 021-64038992

Ruijin Hospital of Shanghai Second Medical University: Located at 197 Ruijin Er Lu; telephone: 021-64370045; fax: 021-64333548

Shanghai Dental Medical Center Cooperative Co., Ltd.: Located on the 7th Floor of the main building at 639 Zhizaoju Lu; telephone: 021-63133174 and 63133174; fax: 021-63139156

Shanghai East International Medical Center: Located at 551 Pudong Nan Lu; telephone: 021-58799999

Shanghai First People's Hospital International Medical Care Center: Located at 585 Jiulong Lu; telephone: 021-63243852 and 021-63240090 ext. 2101; fax: 021-63069484

United Family Hospitals and Clinics: Located on the ground floor of the Shanghai Racquet Club 555 Jinfeng Lu; telephone: 021-51331900 and 021-22010995; 24-Hour Hotline: 021-51331999

World Link Medical Centres, Portman Clinic: Located inside the Shanghai Center's Suite 203 West at 1376, Nanjing Xilu; telephone: 021-62797668 and 021-62798678; fax: 021-62797698

Zhongshan Hospital: Located at 180 Fenglin Lu; telephone: 021-64041990 ext. 2718; fax: 021-64037187

Safety

Shanghai has an extremely low crime rate compared to other major metropolitan cities of its size, and you can feel quite secure here. Violent crime is extremely rare, but it happens, so when you head out for the day take the necessary precautions. Although Shanghai is considered a safe destination for female travelers, women should avoid heading out alone at night. Trust your instincts regarding the safety of strangers or late-night cabs.

Pickpockets

Pickpockets are a nuisance in crowded streets, bus, subway and train stations, airports, and crowded shopping centers and markets. Thieves tend to work in teams, so be aware of your belongings when crowds of people begin to surge on the bus or subway. Leave your valuable belongings in the hotel safe if you can, and wear a money belt inside your clothes. Report any theft to the district Public Security Bureau and save the report for insurance claims when you return back home.

Traffic

Traffic may cause you the biggest annoyance. Seat belts are rarely worn and are sometimes even ripped out of the taxi seats. Speed limits are often ignored, and do not be surprised to see cars going the wrong way down a one-way street or even driving up onto the sidewalk. Check all directions several times before and while crossing the street, and when you are at crosswalks, do not take the green walk signal at face value. You can go only when the drivers decide to stop, not when the light turns green. Try to cross the street with packs of people, or follow someone else's lead when the light turns green.

Do not emulate the daring Chinese risk-takers who dart their way through the moving traffic. Besides cars and taxis, be careful of the countless numbers of mopeds and bikes sailing down the streets.

Local Services and Information

Police: 021-110
Local Telephone Number Inquiry: 021-114
International Enquiries: 021-116
Weather Inquiries: 021-12395
Emergencies: 021-999, 120

Foreign Consulates in Shanghai

Argentina

Consulate General of the Argentina Republic in Shanghai
Chancery: 4F West Tower, Sun Plaza, No.88 Xianxia Lu
Telephone: 021-62780300
Fax: 021-62958539

Australia

Consulate General of Australia in Shanghai
Chancery: 22F, CITIC Square, 1168 Nanjing Xilu
Telephone: 021-52925500-210
Fax: 021-52925267

Brazil

Consulate General of the Federative Republic of Brazil in Shanghai
Chancery: 10F, Qihua Tower, 1375 Huaihai Zhonglu
Telephone: 021-64370110
Fax: 021-64370160

Canada

Consulate General of Canada in Shanghai
Chancery: Suite 604, Shanghai Center, 1376 Nanjing Xilu
Telephone: 021-62798400
Fax: 021-62798401

Egypt

Consulate General of the Arab Republic of Egypt in Shanghai
Chancery: 19A/B, Qihua Tower, 1375 Huaihai Zhonglu
Telephone: 021-64331020/64330622/6433 0502
Fax: 021-64330049

France

Consulate General of the Republic of France in Shanghai
Chancery: 12F, United Plaza,.1468 Nanjing Xilu
Telephone: 021-62897414
Fax: 021-62792249

Germany

Consulate General of the Federal Republic of Germany in Shanghai
Chancery: No.118 Yongfu Lu
Telephone: 021-34010106
Fax: 021-64714448

India

Consulate General of the Republic of India in Shanghai
Chancery: Room 1008, Shanghai International Trade Center, 2201 Yan'an Xilu
Telephone: 021-62758882/62758885/6275 8886
Fax: 021-62758881
E-mail: cgisha@public.sta.net.cn

Iran

Consulate General of the Islamic Republic of Iran in Shanghai
Chancery: 296 Xinhua Lu
Telephone: 021-62814666
Fax: 021-62810502

Italy

Consulate General of the Republic of Italy in Shanghai
Chancery: 11A, 11B, Qihua Tower, 1375 Huaihai Zhonglu
Telephone: 021-64716980
Fax: 021-64716977

Japan

Consulate General of Japan in Shanghai
Chancery: No.8 Wanshan Lu
Telephone: 021-52574766
Fax: 021-62788988

Malaysia

Consulate General of Malaysia in Shanghai
Chancery: Room 1101, CITIC Square, 1168 Nanjing Xilu
Telephone: 021-52925424
Fax: 021-52925951

Norway

Royal Norwegian Consulate General in Shanghai
Chancery: Room 321, 12 Zhongshan Dong Yi Lu
Telephone: 021-63239988
Fax: 021-63233938
E-mail: cons.gen.shanghai@mfa.no

Pakistan

Consulate General of the Islamic Republic of Pakistan

Chancery: Suite O, 7F Hongqiao Business Centre, 2272 Hongqiao Lu
Telephone:021-62377000
Fax: 021-62377066
E-mail: pakrepshanghai@yahoo.com

Philippines
Consulate General of the Republic of Philippines in Shanghai
Chancery: Suite 368, Shanghai Center, 1376 Nanjing Xilu
telephone: 021-62798337
Fax: 021-62798332
E-mail: pcg@philcongenshanghai.org

Korea
Consulate General of the Republic of Korea in Shanghai
Chancery: Room 402, Shanghai International Trade Centre, 2200 Yan'an Xilu
Telephone: 021-62196420
Fax: 021-62196918

Russia
Consulate General of the Russian Federation in Shanghai
Chancery: 20 Huangpu Lu
Telephone: 021-63248383 and 63242628
Fax: 021-63069982
E-mail: gkshanghai@mail.ru

Singapore
Consulate General of the Republic of Singapore in Shanghai
Chancery: 89 Wanshan Lu
Telephone: 021-62785566
Fax: 021-62956038
E-mail: singcg_sha@sgmfa.gov.sg

South Africa
Consulate General of the Republic of South Africa in Shanghai
Chancery: Room 2706, the Bund Center, 220 Yan'an Zhonglu
Telephone: 021-53594977
Fax: 021-63352980
E-mail: sacgmkt@yahoo.com

Spain
Consulate General of Spain in Shanghai
Chancery: 12 Zhongshan Dong Yi Lu
Telephone: 021-63213543
Fax: 021-63211396

Thailand
Royal Thai Consulate General in Shanghai
Chancery: 3F, 7 Zhongshan Dong Yi Lu
Telephone: 021-63234095/63219371/63219406
Fax: 021-63234140

U.K.
Consulate General of the UK of Great Britain and Northern Ireland in Shanghai
Chancery: Suite 301, Shanghai Center, 1376 Nanjing Xilu
Telephone: 021-62798103
Fax: 021-62798254
E-mail: visa.shanghai@fco.gov.uk

U.S.A.
Consulate General of the United States of America in Shanghai
Chancery: 1469 Huaihai Zhonglu
Telephone: 021-64336880
Fax: 021-64334122

Transportation

Transportation

Shanghai is located at the intersection of China's eastern coastline and the great Yangtze River. As a result, land and water transportation is extremely convenient. Two international airports, three train stations, and a number of long distance bus stations and passenger wharfs create a dense transportation network that connects to every mid to large sized city in China and most countries in the world.

Long Distance Transportation

Air

Shanghai has two airports. Pudong Airport (airport code PVG) has an average of 560 incoming and departing flights a day, and has flights connecting to 73 international and 62 national cities. Hongqiao Airport (airport code SHA) has an average of 540 arriving and departing flights per day. The name of the airport should be clearly printed on your plane ticket. When flying out of Shanghai, be sure that you are going to the

correct airport or you could miss your flight. If you plan on changing planes in Shanghai make sure that your incoming and departing flights are leaving from the same airport; otherwise, leave yourself plenty of time to switch airports between flights.

Pudong International Airport

(pǔdōng guójì jīchǎng, 浦东国际机场)

There are airport busses running to Pudong Airport from the central Shanghai and from certain major hotels. You can also take subway line number two to the Longyang Lu stop and transfer onto the Shanghai Maglev Train that runs daily from 7am to 9pm. Trains leave every fifteen minutes and arrive at the airport in just seven minutes. Tickets are 50 RMB each, and cost 40 RMB when you show a valid airplane ticket of same-day departure. A 30 minute cab ride to the airport can cost up to 80 RMB, but it remains a good option if you can split the fare between a few people. Pudong Airport also has a long distance bus running to and from Hangzhou, Nanjing, Wuxi, and Suzhou.

Hongqiao International Airport

(hóngqiáo guójì jīchǎng, 虹桥国际机场)

Located about 13 kilometers from the city center, it costs about 40 RMB to take a taxi from central Shanghai. If you plan on going to the airport during the morning and evening rush hours, than you would be wise to first take the subway number two line to the Jiansu Lu station or lines 3 or 4 to the Yan'an station, before switching over to a taxi for the final stretch of the journey. Hongqiao Airport also has long distance busses running to and from Hangzhou, Nanjing, Suzhou, and Wuxi.

Airlines

Air Canada: 021-62792999
Air China: 021-52397227
Air France: 021-62688817
China Eastern Airlines: 021-62472255
Dragon Airlines: 021-62798099
Japan Airlines: 021-64723000
Lufthansa: 021-58314400
Northwest Airlines: 021-62798088
Qantas Airlines: 021-62798660
Russian Airlines: 021-64156700
Shanghai Airlines: 021-62550550
Singapore Airlines: 021-62798000
Thai Air Ways: 021-62797170
United Airlines: 021-62798009

Train

Urban Shanghai has three railway stations: Shanghai Zhan Railway Station (Xinkezhan); Shanghai Xizhan, the western railway station; and Shanghai Nanzhan, the southern railway station. The Huning and Huhang rail lines leave from Shanghai Zhan and travel to locations nationwide. Every day over 70 passanger trains leave from Shanghai Station to large and mid-sized cities all over the country.

Trains leave from Shanghai Xizhan for cities like Yantai, Zaozhuan, Hengyang, Ganzhou (Jinggang Shan Mountain) Chengdu, Zhangjiajie, and there are several trains lines starting in other cities that make stops here. Shanghai Nanzhan has five trains that come and go from Hangzhou.

Shanghai Zhan Railway Station

(shànghǎi zhàn, 上海站)

Transportation to and from Shanghai Zhan is easy. You can take subway lines 1, 3, and 4 and get off at the Shanghai Zhan Railway Station, take bus lines 13, 41, 58, 63, 64, 69, 78, 95, 104, 106, 109, 113, 114, 115, 117, 213, 223, 234, 301, 302, 308, 315, 319, 322, 324, 328, 329, 332, 502, 506, 510, 563, 573, 584, 710, 722, 723, 741, 767B, 768, 801, the Suisan line, Nanxin line, Shenchuan line, Xinjia Line, Hutang line, Wusong line, and Jiwu line. In total over 70 busses pass by, start or finish their routes at Shanghai Zhan.

Shanghai Nan Zhan

(shànghǎinánzhàn, 上海南站)

Take the subway number 1 line toward Jinjiang Amusement Park otherwise known as the "Meilong Zhan Station". Turn left as you exit the station and walk forward about 100 meters. Cross the overpass bridge and the Shanghai Nanzhan will be sitting right in front of you. Take notice: The Shanghai South Railway Station stop on the subway's number 1 line does not actually lead to the train station. Keep this in mind when you are planning your route.

Long Distance Bus

There are many long distance bus terminals in Shanghai, the two major ones being the Long Distance Bus Station Main Ter-

minal and the Long Distance Bus Southern Station. You can find busses at these two stations that leave for basically every province in eastern China. Many of these busses are large comfortable luxury buses.

Tourist buses leave from two of Shanghai's tourist meeting centers, the Hongkou Football Stadium and the Shanghai Stadium, to famous scenic spots in and around Shanghai. Oftentimes, the tourist bus tickets include round trip fair and entry fees.

Boat

Although Shanghai is located in the middle of China's east coast, passanger boats only leave for Zhou Shan and Chongming Island. For boats heading to the Zhou Shan Archipelago first head to Shiliu Pu, and then transfer by bus to your wharf of departure. Make sure that you are getting on the right bus, as there are busses leaving for Luchao Gang Wharf and busses leaving for Jin Shan Warf. If you are heading to Chongming Island, make sure you know when to board the boat. Leave from Wusong Wharf if you are heading to Changxing or Hengsha Island.

Shanghai to Putuo Shan Mountian Ferry Schedule

Departing Station	Final Station	Departure Place and Time	Arrival Place and Time	Tickets
Shanghai	Putuo Shan	10:00/Shanghai Luchao Wharf	12:15/Putuo Shan Wharf	Normal Vessel 195 RMB Luxury Vessel 225 RMB
Putuo Shan	Shanghai	13:00/Putuo Shan Wharf	15:30/Shanghai Luchao Wharf	Normal Vessel 196 RMB Luxury Vessel 226 RMB
Dinghai	Shanghai	7:30/Dinghai Paseneger Wharf	9:45/Shanghai Luchao Wharf	Normal Vessel 110 RMB Luxury Vessel 145 RMB
Shanghai	Dinghai	15:45/Shanghai Luchao Wharf	18:00/Dinghai Passenger Wharf	Normal Vessel 110 RMB Luxury Vessel 145 RMB

Special Note

Tickets include free transportation from Shanghai's Nanpu Daqiao to Luchao Wharf. The trip takes 1.5 hours.

Ticket Purcheses and Bus Commute

1588 Waima Lu under the Nanpu Daqiao bridge, behind bus line 64's bus final stop. Tickets can be purchased at travel agencies like the Shanghai Travel Agency *(shànghǎi lǚxíngshè, 上海旅行社)* located at 739 Fuzhou Lu and Spring Travel Agency *(chūnqiū lǚxíngshè, 春秋旅行社)* at 342 Xizang Zhonglu.

Telephone

021-63135229 and 021-64869406

Citywide Transport

Shanghai has a fully developed public transportation system. You can buy an electronic traffic card from the ticket window of any subway station that can be used in taxi cabs, subway, and most busses instead of cash. Buying a card costs 100 RMB, which covers 70 RMB worth of transportation and a 30 RMB deposit. It can be refilled at any of the subway ticket windows. Using the electronic card is convenient and helps you to avoid scrambling for change every time you want to take a bus or subway. Unfortunately, you may discover that getting your deposit back is a real hassle. If you do not want to go through the trouble getting your deposit back, just consider it a nonrefundable souvenir card.

Subway

Shanghai's subway network has five separate lines. Line 1 runs from Gongfu Xincun past the Shanghai Zhan railway station and ends at Shen Cun. Line 2 runs between Zhongshan Park and Zhangjiang Gaoke; line 3, "The Peal Line", goes from Shanghai Nan Zhan to Jiangwan Zhen; line 4 from Damuqiao Lu to Pudong Jiancun Lu; and line 5 goes from Shen Zhuang to Minhang Kaifaqu. The base ticket price begins at 3 RMB (only 2 RMB on line five) and increases by 1 RMB past the first six kilometers and 1 RMB for each additional ten kilometers.

Shanghai's main urban attractions (the Bund, People's Square, Xujiahui, Longhua, Hongqiao, Hongkou, Lujiazui, and Huamu) and bustling commercial areas (Nanjing Lu, Huaihai Lu, Xujiahui, Buye Cheng, Babaiban) can be found right along the subway.

Subway Transfer Stations

Lines 1 and 2 can change trains at the People's Square; lines 1 and 3change at Shanghai Nan Zhan; lines 1 and 4 change at the Shanghai Indoor Stadium; lines 1 and 5 change at Shen Zhuang; lines 2, 3, and 4 change at Zhongshan Park; lines 3 and 4

move parallel along the same line between Baoshan Lu and Hongqiao Lu, and you can switch lines at any stop along this stretch. The line 3 subway cars are marked with a yellow line and the line 4 subway cars are marked with a purple line; keep this in mind so that you do not confuse the two when boarding the subway. If you want to switch between lines 1 and 3 at the Shanghai Zhan railway station, you have to leave the subway station and rebuy tickets.

Each subway station is outfitted with automatic ticket dispensers, which accept both coins and paper bills in small denominations. You can also buy tickets at the staffed ticket window. Each subway station also has a management office. If you are having trouble with your electronic traffic card, you can stop into the management office to ask for help.

Bus

Shanghai busses come in a number of varieties. There are the one RMB and one and a half RMB non air-conditioned busses, the two RMB air-conditioned busses, and busses with ticket prices that vary according to the distance of your bus ride. One route may often be serviced by both air conditioned and non-air-conditioned busses, each with a different ticket price. Air conditioned buses, kongtiao che, in Chinese are marked with the Chinese characters 空调 or with a ※ symbol. Bus lines of two-digit numbers or three-digit numbers beginning with 1 or 7 usually have no ticket salesperson, and expect customers to feed exact change into a money slot at the front of the bus. Bus line numbers beginning with the number two usually run during rush hour in the morning and the evening, and bus lines beginning with number three run in the evening. The

unnumbered Daqiao Xian bridge line and Suidao Xian tunnel line connect Pudong and Puxi. Expect heavy crowds on the trips from Pudong to Puxi in the morning and from Puxi to Pudong in the evening. The "XX Zhuan Xian" special line busses service Shanghai's suburbs. While there are not many of these special suburban lines, the ones that exist are comprehensive enough to take you to any sights you would want to visit outside the city.

Shanghai rail station, People's Square, Xujiahui, Zhongshan Park, and Wujiaochang are urban Shanghai's main bus transfer hubs. Bus stops can be particularly confusing, especially in these large transportation hubs. Stops are usually named according to the street they are located on, but you will frequently notice two or more bus stops with the same name located far apart from each other or two bus stops with different names right next to each other. If you are unsure of whether or not you are on the right bus, you may want to confirm with the ticket salesperson or the bus driver that you are heading in the right direction.

Sepcial Note

One more thing to be aware of is that Shanghai is full of one-way streets, so a bus line may make its return trip along a different path (with different stops) than its departure. When you set out for the day, make sure you know which bus line you need to take for your return.

Taxi

The majority of the cars in Shanghai's fleet of taxis are Volkswagon Santanas and Pasats, although there are a few Mercedes sprinkled in as well. Prices do not change according to the type of car you get, so if you manage to flag down a Mercedes, consider yourself lucky.

Taxi fares start at 11 RMB and increase 2.1 RMB for every kilometer past the third kilometer mark. If your journey surpasses ten kilometers then the per kilometer price goes up another fifty percent. During the evening (between 11pm and 5am) taxi fairs start at 13 RMB and increase by 2.6 RMB passed the third kilometer. Per kilometer prices still increase by fifty percent passed the tenth kilometer. There are no toll fees for any bridge, tunnel, or overpass in urban Shanghai. If you need to go to a far-away location or to a bustling area (like Hengshan Lu) in the evening, you can try to get the cab driver to give you a 20% discount or to run the meter at the daytime price. When you bargain, do it before and not after you have stepped into the cab.

To Reserve a Taxi Cab

Shanghai Taxi: 021-62580000
Tourist Taxi Co. : 021-64383420
Friendship Taxi Service Corp: 021- 62584584

The Maglev

The Shanghai Maglev Train runs between the Longyang Lu subway number 2 line station in the West and the Pudong International Airport in the East. The entire trip is 30 kilometers and takes about seven minutes and 20 seconds to complete. Over the course of the short journey, the train reaches a top speed of 431 kilometers per hour. It is the world's first commercial high-speed magnetic levitation railway.

Hours of operation: 8:30am-5:30pm. Trains leave every 20 minutes.

Address: Longyang Lu Station, 2100 Longyang Lu (near Baiyang Lu); take exits three and four from the Longyang Lu subway station. You can also get there on bus lines 983, 976, Daqiao Bridge line number five, Daqiao Bridge line number 6, and the Shenjiang Xian line.

Maglev airport address: Shanghai Pudong International Airport at the eastern end of the Houji Lou Building (connected by a three hundred meter walkway).

Tickets: Regular ticket One way: 50 RMB, Round Trip: 80 RMB; Children under 1.2 meters tall and accompanied by an adult ride for free.

VIP tickets: One Way: 100 RMB; Round Trip: 160 RMB

Hotline: 021-28907777

Special Note

All train passengers who plan to take a flight from Pudong Airport can receive a 20 percent discount on a one-way Maglev ticket when they show a valid same-day airplane ticket. The readjusted price for a normal ticket becomes 40 RMB and a VIP ticket becomes 80RMB.

Disabled veterans, retired cadres, and disabled peoples, and other special personnel also receive a 20 percent discount with valid ID.

All passengers with a valid ticket can visit the Maglev Technology Exhibition on the station's bottom floor.

Shangri-La

Accommodations Food, Drink, Entertainment

Accommodations

Since Shanghai is mainly a commercial city, hotels tend to not give low season rates. However, you can often get discounts between the months of December and February. Rates are at its highest in May through October.

Special Note

Bargaining is not only for the market place, it even works for hotels. Most hotels are never full during the year so the chance of you getting a good rate is much better if you bargain in person than booking in advance. It does not hurt to check out the room before paying to make sure it's what you've asked for. Don't be afraid to seem rude since this is standard practice at all Chinese hotels.

Helpful Websites for Hotel Reservations

Listed below are several travel websites offering hotel reservations and discounted fairs. These websites have agreements with a number of hotels and offer low prices on rooms and services. www.english.ctrip.com and www.elong.net in particular, have a virtual monopoly on the lowest hotel prices around China. If you book through one of these web sites, it would not be unusual to find hotel rooms for between forty and sixty percent under the listed price; they can even help you find discounted airline tickets during the peak travel seasons. Many expats and travelers refer to: www.tripadvisor.com, www.hoteltravelshanghai.com for online ratings and other hotel and travel information.

Exclusive Luxury Hotels

Grand Hyatt Shanghai

(jīnmào jūnyuè dàjiǔdiàn, 金茂君悦大酒店)

Located at 88 Shiji Dadao inside the Jin Mao Tower; to get there, take the subway to the Lujiazui station; telephone: 021-50491234; fax: 021-50491111; website: www.shanghai.grand.hyatt.com

Rates: A standard room runs 2,560 RMB; a business suite is 3,760 RMB; an executive suite 4,000 RMB; a VIP Suite: 4,320 RMB; a standard room with a view of the Bund will set you back a whopping 2,680 RMB. Expect to pay a fifteen percent service fee.

Without a doubt, this is one of the highest five star hotels in the world. The Grand Hyatt Shanghai is located between the 53rd and 87th floors of the Jin Mao Tower which towers over the city at 420.5 meters. The hotel lobby is on the 54th floor, and you need to take an elevator up here before you check in. If you choose to stay in a standard room over the Bund, you will be treated to spectacular views of Puxi.

JW Marriott

(wànháo jiǔdiàn, 万豪酒店)

Located at 399 Nanjing Xilu; to get there take the subway to the People's Square Station; telephone: 021-535949691; fax 021-63755988; Web site:www.marriott.com

Rates: double rooms run 2,700 RMB; executive rooms are 3,200 RMB; expect to pay about 4,100 RMB for a suite. Be sure to ask for a discount before you book a room.

If you are looking for an extravagant five-star experience in Shanghai than you could definitely do worse than the JW Marriott. Here you will find large rooms with all the amenities you could possibly desire, from satellite TV to cotton kimonos, dual phone lines, and high-speed internet access. Well-equipped bathrooms come with hydraulic massage showers. Rooms are intelligently designed, with the office areas at an appropriate distance from the bathroom and bed. Real coffee is there for your coffee pot, not a mix. There is even a special safe for your laptop. What is not intuitive is the location of the hotel gym and pool. The JW Marriott will have you running through a maze of elevators and stairs before you find it.

Of course this may all be old hat to the luxury business traveler, but the view and the location really set this hotel apart from the rest. JW Marriot is located on the top half of the iconic Tomorrow Square building. No matter what you think of the building's odd shape, there is no doubt that the oddly proportioned walls help create stunning views from the hotel guest rooms. Located in the heart of the action in Nanjing Xilu, the JW Marriot puts you at mere steps away from the People's Square, musuems, and Xintiandi.

Four Seasons Hotel Shanghai

(sìjì jiǔdiàn, 上海四季酒店)

Located at 500 Weihai Lu between Nanjing Xilu and Yan'an Zhonglu; to get there take the subway to the Shimen Yi Lu station; telephone: 021-625688881; fax: 021-62565678; website www.fourseasons.com

Rates: expect to pay up to 3,000 RMB for a superior double and up to 4,800 RMB for a suite; you will need to pay an addition fee for enhanced privileges at the executive lounge.

The Four Seasons has always been a top

name in luxury accommodations, and its new Shanghai incarnation more than lives up to the hotel chain's considerable reputation. Rooms are spacious and extremely well-equipped, with fully-loaded marble bathrooms, DVD players, internet access, safes and all of the other usual amenities. The Four Seasons gets huge thumbs up for its grand pool and fully-equipped gym, and most people appreciate the uncrowded layout of each floor, which helps keep the elevators from getting overcrowded and preserves a sense of privacy. The hotel's location near Nanjing Lu and Huaihai Lu gives you easy access to transportation, and puts you at a leisurely walk away from the Shanghai Exhibition Center. Most people save their greatest compliments for the Four Season's enthusiastic service, which is both courteous and efficient.

The Westin Shanghai

(shànghǎi wēisītīng dàfàndiàn, 上海威斯汀大饭店)

Located inside the Bund Center at 88 Henan Zhonglu; to get there, take to subway to the Henan Zhonglu station; telephone: 021-63351888; fax: 021-63352888; website: www.westin.com

Rates: Expect to pay about 2,500 RMB for a basic deluxe room and 3,500 RMB for a suite with Executive Club benefits. Ask for a discount before you book.

The Westin gets mixed reviews for its decidedly unsubtle lobby and atrium. Palm trees, garish colors and a glass staircase may give you the unsettling feeling that you have stepped not into a five-star hotel, but into the Emerald City. Rooms are up to five-star standards with great beds, work desks, high-speed internet, and decked-out bathrooms

with rainforest showers.

With its prime location on Henan Zhonglu, the Westin is only a hop skip and a jump away from Nanjing Lu, Yu Yuan Garden, the City God Temple, and of course, the Bund. Transportation is convenient. Be sure not to miss the Westin's award winning Banyan Tree Spa, which can help you relax after a long day of walking the pavement.

Regal International East Asia Hotel *(fùháo huánqiú dōngyà jiǔdiàn, 富豪环球东亚酒店)*

Located at 516 Hengshan Lu; to get there take the subway to Hengshan Lu; telephone: 021-64155588; fax: 021-64458899; website: www.regal-eastasia.com

Rates: A delux or premier room can run as low as 1,400 RMB in the low season, but may reach up to 2,000+ RMB in peak travel seasons; Regal Club rooms and basic suites usually run over 3,000 RMB. Be sure to ask about discounts before booking.

Located on Hengshan Lu, the Regal puts you within reach of the Xujiahui Commercial Street, the Xujiahui Cathedral, and La Villa Rouge. If you want to venture out further, the Hengshan Lu subway station is conveniently located nearby. Expect your rooms to live up to the five-star rating. They are well-appointed with functioning work areas, great deluxe bathrooms, coffee pots, and slippers. The Shanghai International Tennis Center offers outstanding athletic facilities including nine tennis courts (two indoor and seven outdoor) and a 25 meter indoor pool. All in all, the Regis is a solid luxury hotel, and is considered a "bargain" among hotels of this class.

Sofitel Hyland Shanghai

(suǒfēitè hǎilún bīnguǎn, 索菲特海仑宾馆)

Located at 505 Nanjing Donglu To get there

take the subway to Henen Zhonglu; telephone: 021-63515888; fax: 021-63514088; website www.sofitel.com

Rates: Expect to pay about 1,800 RMB for Club Sofitel Room and 3,600 RMB for a suite; prices vary widely depending on the season.

Sofitel's location on the Nanjing Donglu promenade is both its strength and its greatest weakness. If you love shopping, then you will not have to waste anytime getting down to business, as the hotel entrance leads right onto Nanjing Lu. If you plan to stay for more than a few days though, the crowds on the promenade can become claustrophobic, and you may well become tired of the unwelcome attention you receive from hawkers as you exit the hotel. Nevertheless, the subway do nearby transportation is extremely convenient, and the Sofitel is only a short walk away from the Bund, Yu Yuan Garden, and the People's Square. Rooms tend to be smallish, but are nevertheless extremely comfortable and well-stocked with all of the typical five-star amenities. Considering the star rating and the prime location, Sofitel is a relatively inexpensive choice among high-end Shanghai hotels.

Okura Garden Hotel Shanghai

(huāyuánfàndiàn, 花园饭店)

Located at 58 Maoming Nanlu, north of Huaihai Zhonglu; to get there take the subway to the Shanxi Nanlu station; telephone: 021-64151111; fax 021-64158866; website: shanghai.okura.com

Rates: expect to pay about 2,300 RMB for a standard double room and about 3,500 RMB for a suite. Expect heavy discounts in the off-season.

The Okura Garden Hotel is one of Shang-

hai's great old standbys. This Japanese-run hotel has been operating in Shanghai for over fifteen years, and continues to maintain its exceptionally lofty standards. When you come to Okura Garden, expect high efficiency and impeccable service. A favorite choice of Japanese business travelers, do not be surprised if the rooms run a smidgen smaller than those of competitors. Nevertheless, expect your rooms to be fully-appointed and immaculately clean. Okura Garden's exceptional bathrooms are outfitted with white marble. Renovations are underway, and they are much needed considering the hotel's age. However, the hotel is extremely well cared for, and is an exceptional choice for Shanghai accommodations.

Okura Garden Hotel offers easy access to the Sun Yat-sen Residence and Shanghai Exhibition Center. The subway is also nearby.

Hilton Hotel

(jìngān xīěrdùn fàndiàn, 静安希尔顿饭店)

Located at 250 Huashan Lu (south of Yan'an Zhonglu); to get there take the subway to Jingan Si; telephone: 021-62480000; fax 021-62483848; website: www.hilton.com

Rates: Expect to pay 2,500 RMB for a deluxe room; 3,300 RMB for an executive room; 4,200 RMB for a suite.

The Hilton plans to have all of its guestrooms renovated next year. Some of the rooms are finished already, and you can definitely see the difference. They are large and modern with great bathrooms, comfortable beds, and all of the bells and whistles you would expect with a five-star room. The rooms that have not yet undergone renovation, with out-of-date facilities and smallish bathrooms, definitely have a ways to go before they can compete with the likes of the JW Marriott and the Four Seasons. While the hotel restaurants are generally good, breakfast can be a drag at whopping 200 RMB. What saves this hotel, however, are its wonderful views and great location. Within walking distance of the Children's Palace, and a short bus ride to the Jade Buddha Temple, this is an excellent place to set up home base.

Pudong Shangri-La

(pǔdōng xiānggélǐlā jiǔdiàn, 浦东香格里拉酒店)

Located at 33 Fucheng Lu; to get there, take the subway to the Lujiazui station; telephone: 021-68828888; fax: 021-68826688; website: www.shangri-la.com

Rates: Expect to pay 2,700 RMB for a delux double and 3,200 RMB for a room with executive privileges.

If you are planning on staying in the Pudong area, then the Pudong Shangri-La is hard to beat. With some of the largest double rooms in Shanghai, each is elegantly decorated and outfitted with a five-star collection of facilities, including satellite television, executive desks, refrigerators, complimentary bottled water, and more. The bathrooms are also top-notch with a separated shower and bath, and an assortment of designer toiletries. Suites go several steps further with multiple desks, lavish sitting areas, and large plasma televisions. Many of the rooms have killer views of the Bund and Puxi. If that is not enough, Shangri-La also has a collection of fine restaurants, and serves an absolutely fabulous breakfast. Located in the heart of Lujiazui, the hotel is a short walk from the Lujiazui subway station. If you need to go over to Puxi on the other side of the Huangpu River, you can always zip under the Bund tourist tunnel. Put simply, Pudong Shangri-La is one of the best hotels in China if not all of Asia.

Crowne Plaza Shanghai

(shànghǎi huángguān jiàrì jiǔdiàn, 上海皇冠假日酒店)

Located at 400 Panyu Lu,right off of Xinhua Lu; to get there, take the subway to Yan'an Xilu. The hotel is a moderate walk away from the subway station. Bus line 946 will take you from the subway station to the hotel; telephone: 021-62808888; fax: 021-62803353; Website: www.shanghai.crowneplaza.com

Rates: Expect to pay about 1,500 RMB for a standard double; 1,800 RMB for a deluxe; and a 3,200 RMB for an 88 Suite.

Located right next door to the Shanghai International Film Arts Centre, but at least five kilometers away from the next closest site, the Crowne Plaza Shanghai does not have the most ideal location. The closest subway station, Yan'an Xilu, is within walking distance of the hotel, but the walk can be a drag if you are coming back late in the evening. That being said, there are some nice shops and restaurants to explore nearby, and the Crowne Plaza offers quick access to the Hongqiao Airport if you need to catch a domestic flight. Rooms are spacious and attractive with a full compliment of all the amenities you expect, and the hotel facilities are extremely well-maintained. Overall this is a solid choice and offers a decent value.

Shanghai JC Mandarin

(shànghǎi jǐncāng wénhuá dàjiǔ diàn, 上海锦沧文华大酒店)

Located at 1225 Nanjing Xilu; to get there take the subway number two line to the Jingan Si station; telephone: 021-62791888; fax: 021-62791314; website: www.jcmandarin.com

Rates: Expect to pay 2,200 RMB for a

deluxe double room and 3,600 RMB for an executive suite.

Another wonderfully located hotel in the heart of Shanghai, the JC Mandarin is mere steps away from some great upscale shopping at Plaza 66 and the CITIC Square, and a short walk from the Jingan Si Temple and the Shanghai Exhibition Center. Aside from its great location, the food here is fairly good, certainly as good or better than some of the offerings at Shanghai's other five-star hotels. There are excellent buffets in the morning and the evening. Despite recent renovations, the hotel still cannot really shake the kitschy early-nineties feel in its hallway and lobby. Rooms are fully decked out with all of the usual five star appliances and amenities, but certainly lack the extra polish that you would find in newer hotels. Service can be described as friendly, but not the most efficient. If you can get a good rate on the room, then stay here for the location.

Cypress Hotel

(lóngbǎi sēnlín huāyuán fàndiàn, 龙柏森林花园饭店)

Located at 2419 Hongqiao Lu just east of Hongqiao Airport; telephone: 021-62688868, fax: 021-62681878; website: www.cypress-hotel.com.cn

Rates: Expect to pay 1,330 RMB for a deluxe view with a garden view; 2,000 RMB for a suite.

If you need a break from the glossy five-star urban locales of Puxi and Nanjing Lu, than come to Cypress Hotel for a nice change of pace. Located well outside Shanghai's urban center in the Hongqiao Development Zone, Cypress Hotel sits on 40 acres of woods and gardens. Do you feel like going on a romp through the woods and taking an afternoon off to go fishing by the pond? You can do that here. There is also a great pool for lap swimming, three tennis courts, a well-equipped fitness center, and even a driving range. A property once owned by famed ultra-wealthy Shanghai businessman, Victor Sassoon, this is truly an oasis in the middle of this furious city. Transportation from here is a problem unless you are going to the Hongqiao Airport, which is less than a mile away. A cab into town will take about 20 minutes. Cypress Hotel offers a free shuttle into town, and a number of busses leave from the Shanghai Zoo, located to the Hotel's east and well within walking distance.

Peace Hotel

(hépíng fàndiàn, 和平饭店)

Located at 20 Nanjing Donglu; to get there, take the subway to Henan Zhonglu; telephone: 021-63216888; fax: 021-63290300; website: www.shanghaipeacehotel.com

Rates: Expect to pay 1,500 RMB for a deluxe room; 3,800 for a suite; always ask for discounts, and try to bargain the price down.

One of the most famous and historic hotels in Shanghai, the Peace Hotel was built in 1929 by the super wealthy Baghdadi-British businessman Victor Sassoon. Called the Cathay Hotel, it became worldwide symbol of opulence, with marble floors and stained glass, and catered to the richest and most powerful people in the world. Those days are long gone. Riding on the coattails of history, the Peace Hotel still attracts large numbers of guests from around the world. The hotel is extremely dark in its hallways and rooms. Despite recent renovations, the decor feels a bit dated, the bathrooms are somewhat disappointing, and the amenities do not live up to the hotel's five-star rating (or prices). Rooms are spacious though, and they have a very atmospheric feel to them. If you want to have the total Peace Hotel experience, and you have the money to burn, than you can try out one of the classic National Suites, which come in nine styles: Chinese, British, Indian, American, French, Japanese, Italian, German, and Spanish. Do not expect much from the service at the Peace Hotel, which is absent-minded at its best and surly at its worst. All that being said, the hotel has a beautiful lobby, and the rooftop bar is a great place to enjoy a drink. Located on Nanjing Donglu, this is probably the best location you could ask for, sitting right on the Bund, and with convenient transportation everywhere.

The hotel's South Building, originally called the Palace Hotel, is several decades older than the old Cathay Hotel. It is also a beautiful peace of work.

(Note: For more information about the

large and cozy and bursting with amenities. Rooms on the club floor, however, are newly renovated and completely up to Ritz-Carleton standards. If you come to the Ritz, be sure to ask to see your room first. Ritz supplies a top-notch pool and health facilities, and there is no doubt that the Portman Ritz-Carlton has one of the best locations in town, right on Nanjing Xilu with convenient access to transportation and high-end shopping outlets.

history of the Peace Hotel, please turn to the section on Bund architecture.)

Portman Ritz-Carlton Hotel

(shànghǎi bōtèmànlìjiā jiǔdiàn, 上海波特曼丽嘉酒店)

Located at 1376 Nanjing Xilu, part of the Shanghai Centre; to get there, take the subway to the Jingan Si station; telephone: 021-62798888; fax 021-62798800; website: www.ritzcarlton.com

Rates: Expect to pay 2,700 RMB for a deluxe room and 3,500 RMB for a club level room; an executive suite runs at 4,500 RMB. Be aware that prices vary per season.

The Ritz-Carlton name is more than enough to make this one of Shanghai's top-draw luxury hotels. Known around the world for their opulent rooms, extravagant suites, impeccable service, and top-notch facilities, on many fronts, the Ritz does not disappoint. The hotel lobby is grand, and the service is thorough and efficient. You may feel let down by the rooms, especially the ones on the lower levels, which seem dated with older televisions and outdated furniture. On the other hand, they are still

High-end Options

Jinjiang Hotel

(jǐnjiāng fàndiàn, 锦江饭店)

Located at 59 Maoming Nanlu; to get there, take the subway to the Shanxi Nanlu station; telephone: 021-62582582; fax: 021-64725588; website: www.jinjianghotel-shanghai.com

Rates: Expect to pay about 1,000 RMB for a double room and 2,400 RMB and up for a suite. You definitely want to enquire about discounts before booking your room.

Like Shanghai's other famous historical hotel, the Peace Hotel, Jin Jiang Hotel seems to suffer from a small degree of complacency. Banking on its history, its great art deco architecture, and its superb location, Jinjiang Hotel lets things go slack when it comes to its rooms and service. Comprised of three main buildings, North Building, South Building, and the Grosvenor House, the North Building is the oldest and most historically significant of the three. Built in 1929 as the Cathay Mansions, this was supposedly one of the first high-rise buildings to go up in Shanghai. Built in 1931 by the Cathay Land Company, the Grosvenor House is the most architecturally interesting of the

three, and is modeled after the Barclay-Vessey Building. When you stay at the Jinjiang Hotel, you are most likely to get a room in the North Building. Most of the rooms are spacious and well presented with desks, a sofa, internet, and decent sized bathrooms. Quality is definitely uneven between different rooms, so be sure to check out your room before you make a final decision. You especially want to look out for the walls and the carpets, which in some rooms can be ragged and dirty. If you can get a suite in the Grosvenor House, you will be better off for it with the large rooms and more efficient service. Service leaves much room for improvement. Jinjiang Hotel's location is tops, and puts you right next to Xintiandi. Transportation via subway is also quite convenient.

Novotel Atlantis Shanghai

(hǎishén nuòfùtè dàjiǔdiàn, 海神诺富特大酒店)

Located at 728 Pudong Dadao, east of Oriental Pearl TV Tower; to get here take the subway's number four line to the Pudong Dadao station: telephone: 021-50366666; fax: 021-50366677; website: www.accorhotels.com

Rates: 1,300 RMB for a double; 2,000 RMB for an executive room. Expect deep discounts in the off season.

A slick no-nonsense property in Pudong, this is typical Novotel with its shiny high-tech feel and its efficient service. If you have been to other Novotel branches before, the rooms here will not surprise you. This is a good thing. Clean and orderly, guest room has all the amenities you want and some neat high-tech gadgets as well. Views of Pudong and the Jin Mao Tower are fantastic from the rooms and restaurants on the upper floors. Many people stay away from the Pudong hotels because of their remote location, and that is fair, but the Novotel is close to the Pudong Dadao subways station (line 4), which really brings the rest of the city closer. Novotel is a solid choice for the unpretentious business traveler, and has plenty to offer the pleasure traveler as well.

Park Hotel

(guójì fàndiàn, 国际饭店)

Located at 170 Nanjing Xilu; to get there take the subway to the People's Square station; telephone: 021-63275225; fax: 021-63276958; website: www.parkhotel.com.cn

Rates: A standard room will runs around 1,100 RMB; an executive room 1,700 RMB; a suite usually runs 2,300 RMB. You can usually find 50 to 60 percent discounts through CTRIP and similar travel websites.

This art deco gem is plugged right into the brain of Shanghai's public transport system, located right across from the People's

Square subway station. Rooms are spacious, clean, and well furnished, but they will not blow you away. Beds are hard, as they are in many Chinese hotels, and there are reported rare mishaps with the air conditioners. Try to get a room higher up in the hotel as the noise sometimes drifts up street. The service level you get is generally a roll of the dice; it is sometimes great and sometimes not, but it never dips below mediocre. The buffet breakfast is terrific. Park Hotel provides atmospheric accommodations at a decent price, and puts access to entire city right at your fingertips. (For more information about the history of the Park Hotel, please turn to the section on the People's Square.)

Grand Pacific Hotel

(tàipíngyáng guójì dàjiǔdiàn, 太平洋国际大酒店)

Located at 288 Shaanxi Beilu; to get there take the subway to the Shimen station; telephone: 021-32184555; fax: 021-32184556; website: www.grandpacifichotel.com.cn

Rates: A standard suite runs 1,536 RMB and a luxury suite costs 2,366 RMB. These prices can usually be hammered down to the hundreds most times of the year.

With its great location and decent prices, it is hard to go wrong with the Grand Pacific Hotel. Here you will find suites and only suites, many of which can be had for the price of a standard double at another hotel. Do not let the unattractive lobby scare you away, the rooms here are nicely furnished with delightful Asian-themed decor, and the service is great. Be sure that you check out your room before you decide. Some of the suites are not suites in the traditional sense with strangely laid out sitting areas, and expect hard Chinese-style mattresses. Bathrooms are clean and wonderful with high-pressure showers. Avoid the hotel restaurant, which is not great, and dine in one of the many fantastic restaurants nearby. Just a short walk away from the Bund, and an even shorter walk from the subway. Grand Pacific Hotel offers an ideal place to start your tour of the city.

Renaissance Yangtze Shanghai Hotel *(shànghǎi yángzǐjiāng jiǔdiàn, 上海扬子江酒店)*

Located at 2099 Yan'an Xilu; the hotel is located four kilometers away from the Zhongshan Park subway station; bus line 57 will take you to Jingan Si; telephone:

021-62750000; fax 021-62750750; website: www.renaissancehotels.com

Rates: Expect to pay 1,400 RMB for a delux room and 2,100 RMB for an executive suite.

It is a real shame that the Renaissance Yangtze's location is so far from the major sites downtown, because otherwise this would be a top recommendation for travelers. The hotel has excellent food including wonderful French pastries, and a knockout breakfast. The hotel gym and spa are both in excellent condition. Rooms run a little small compared to some of the other luxury giants in town, but it has all of the amenities you could possibly desire. The bathrooms are also nice except for some occasional water pressure and temperature problems. Despite its distance from most major tourist sites, the hotel is still in a relatively commercial area and you should be able to find some decent shopping nearby.

Ramada Plaza Shanghai

(nánxīnyǎ huáměidá dàjiǔdiàn, 南新雅华美达大酒店)

Located at 719 Nanjing Donglu; to get there, take the subway to the People's Square; telephone: 021-63500000; fax 021-63506666; website: www.ramadaplazashanghai.com

Rates: A standard double generally costs 1,000 RMB; expect to pay 1,350 RMB for an executive room, and 1,650 RMB for a suite.

A fine four-star hotel located on Nanjing Donglu and across from the People's Square, the Ramada Plaza puts in you in the middle of the transportation network, and at walking distance from the Shanghai Museum and the Bund. The marble lobby is grand, and the many of the rooms look out onto the gigantic atrium. Expect a nice pool and a basic gym. The hotel's restaurants do not exactly shine, but you are better off finding a place on Nanjing Lu anyway. Rooms are generally spacious, clean, and well-appointed, and the general hotel staff is pleasant. For its top location and good facilities, the Ramada Plaza is a nice place to spend a holiday.

Miramar Apartment

(shànghǎi měilìhuá gōngyù, 上海美丽华公寓)

Located at number 11 Lane 1720, Hongqiao Lu; the closest subway station is the Zhongshan Park station. You can get there from the hotel via bus line 519; telephone: 021-62706921; fax: 021-62705463; website: www.miramar-group.com/h017.htm

Rates: Expect to pay 1,000 RMB for a two-bedroom suite and 1,300 for a three-bedroom suite.

Another hotel in the Hongqiao area, Miramar Apartments suffers from its location outside the city center. It is, however, a convenient distance from the Hongqiao Airport, and a short bus ride from the Zhongshan Park and Yan'an Xilu subway terminals, which will plug your right into the city. As its names suggests, Miramar Apartments only operates in two and three-bedroom suites. While pretty standard-looking, the suites are spacious, clean, and fully furnished with separate living and dining rooms, kitchenettes, terraces, and a range of amenities. The hotel's location puts you within walking distance of some interesting local stores and restaurants. If you are willing to put up with the location, Miramar gives a solid value and plenty of space to spread out.

Rui Jin Guesthouse

(ruìjīn bīnguǎn, 瑞金宾馆)

Located at 118 Ruijin Er Lu; to get there take the subway to Shanxi Nanlu; telephone: 021-64725222; fax: 021-64732277; website: www.shedi.net.cn/outEDI/Ruijin

Rates: A delux double room runs 1,320 RMB, but can usually be had on discount for 990 RMB; delux large wooden room costs 1,320 RMB, and it can probably also be obtained for 990 RMB. Breakfast is included.

A compound made up of five separate villas, the Rui Jin Guesthouse was once a series of disconnected properties owned by famed British newspaperman, gambler, and adventurer H. Morris. Like the other historical hotels in town, you have to cut Rui Jin some slack, and understand that you have to sacrifice some service and a few amenities in order to get the unique historical experience of staying here. The grounds are absolutely gorgeous with verdant grass yards and fountains. Get rooms in the older villas. The furniture may be a little bit worn, but it is clean and definitely luxurious. Rui Jin's building number three was once Morris's personal residence, and it has a terrific suite. Try not to get a room in the modern building in back. It has terrific rooms and amenities, but no one stays here for modern conveniences. Service is reasonable, and you will find that people are eager to please, even if some have trouble communicating in English. From Rui Jin you can step out of your door onto quiet tree-lined boulevards, and walk to and from Shikumen and Xintiandi. This is a luxury that makes the hotel's four-star price seem like a bargain.

(For more information about the Rui Jin Guesthouse, please turn to the section on Xintiandi.)

Taiyuan Villa — The Marshall Residence

(tàiyuán biéshù, 太原别墅)

Located at 160 Taiyuan Lu; to get here take the subway to the Huangpi Nanlu station and walk; telephone: 021-64716688; fax: 021-64712618

Rates: The deluxe double is listed at 1,320 RMB, although you can probably get

that discounted down to about 930 RMB. A deluxe suite can probably be yours for about 2,750 RMB, and it includes breakfast.

Another historical offering close to Huangpi Nanlu/Xintiandi area, the Taiyuan Villa is also known as the Marshall House, named after General George Marshall who stayed here during his failed attempt to mediate between the Chinese Nationalists and the Communists after World War Two. Built in the 1920's, this beautiful French-style chateau set in one of the more peaceful parts of town. Much later, the villa became the part-time residence of infamous Gang of Four conspirator and Mao Zedong's wife, Jiang Qing. Just as in the Rui Jin Guest House, expect to give a little in terms of service and luxury, for all that you are getting in history and atmosphere. That being said, rooms are large and comfortable, complete with replica 1920's era furniture and you should expect to have a more than pleasant stay. Do not miss the villa's splendid garden. (For more information about the Marshall Residence and General George Marshall, please turn to the section on Huangpi Nanlu.)

Hengshan Moller Villa

(héngshān mălè bíeshù fàndiàn, 衡山马勒别墅饭店)

Located in the Jingan District at 30 Shanxi Nanlu; to get there, take the subway to the Shaanxi Nanlu station; telephone: 021-62478881; Fax: 021-62891020; Website: www.mollervilla.com

Rates: A standard room runs 850 RMB; a deluxe double room 1,500 RMB.

All rooms come with a computer, and breakfast is included. During the off season you can expect large discounts. When you book a room be sure to ask for the lowest price — they will not give it to you automatically — and you will end up saving a lot of money.

Believe that in Shanghai, you will not find more attractive accommodations than in the Moller Villa. Built in 1936, this venerable piece of architecture is constructed in the image of a fairy tale castle. The main building is Norwegian in design, with a total of three floors, and rooms decorated and outfitted in the decadent early twentieth century Shanghai style. (To learn more about the Moller Villa, please turn to the section on Huangpi Nanlu.)

Middle Level Accomodations

New Asia Hotel

(xīnyà dàjiǔdiàn, 新亚大酒店)

Located at 422 Tiantong Lu, near Sichuan Lu; the closest subway stop is Baoshan Lu, which can be reached from the hotel on bus line 37; telephone: 021-63242210; fax: 021-63566816

Rates: Expect paying 400 RMB for a standard double; 500 RMB for a superior business room, and 700 RMB for a suite. Ask about discounts before you book.

Yet another historical offering, the nine-storey New Asia Hotel was Shanghai's first large-scale hotel to be financed, designed, constructed, and managed entirely by Chinese people. Established in 1934, New Asia hotel is located north slightly outside the city center. There is no subway station immediately on hand, but the hotel is still only a ten or fifteen walk from the the Bund and Nanjing Lu. New Asia Hotel's service may feel indifferent sometimes, and the rooms, while generally clean, can be hit or miss. Be sure that you see a few rooms before deciding on one, as the quality and degree of renovation can vary around the hotel. While it is not too far from Shanghai's hot spots, there are certainly other options with better service and more convenient locations. The hotel's lower prices make it a desirable destination.

Y.M.C.A Hotel

(jǐnjiāng qīngniánhuì bīnguǎn, 锦江青年会宾馆)

Located at 123 Xizang Nanlu,near the People's Square and across from the Shanghai Concert Hall; to get there take the subway to the People's Square Station; telephone: 021-63261040; fax: 021-63201957; website: www.ymcahotel.com

Rates: 380 RMB for a discounted single room, and 420 RMB for a standard double.

The Y.M.C.A. can be summed up in five words: great location and cheap rooms. Rooms are very clean, though rather minimalist as far as amenities and other facilities go. Expect an older television, and hard beds. You will be surprised to find decent internet prices, a reasonably priced cafe in the lobby, and mini-bar that does not charge an arm and a leg. The hotel also has a gym, massage, and even a karaoke room if you

are into that kind of thing. Located in a great part of town with access to the Bund and Chenghuang Miao the Y.M.C.A is a reasonable place to stay if you are on a tight budget. There are dorm beds available too, for 100 RMB a night.

Astor House Hotel

(pǔjiāngfàndiàn,浦江饭店)

Located at 15 Huangpu Lu, north of the Bund; the closest subway station is Henan Zhonglu, which is about a twenty minute walk away; telephone: 021-63246388; fax: 021-63243179; website: www.pujianghotel.com

Rates: A standard double costs 660 RMB and an executive room runs 1,200 RMB. Ask about discounts before booking.

With a history stretching back to 1846, the Astor Hotel was originally established as Richard's Hotel, a striking Victorian structure right off of the Huangpu River. The hotel moved to its current location in 1857, and renamed the Astor House, before being rebuilt and expanded into today's English Neo-classical structure in 1907. Astor Hotel is famous for a number of firsts, including being the location of Shanghai's first phone call and the site of Shanghai's first post-liberation stock exchange in 1990. Rooms at the Astor are generally large and clean, with wooden floors instead of carpets. Bathrooms are beautiful, although there are occasionally problems with the water pressure in the shower. An upgrade to a deluxe or an executive suite is entirely worthwhile for the gigantic rooms, much better facilities, and free internet. The hotel has a wonderful historical feel to it, and although not very close to the subway, a quick walk south will take you right to the Bund. Be sure to look out for substantial discounts on the internet.

At such low prices, if you can stand the less-than-pleasant staff, than the Astor Hotel is a great place to stay.

Budget Hotels: 300 RMB and Less

Captain Hostel

(shànghǎi lǎochuánzhǎng jiǔdiàn, 上海老船长酒店)

Located at 37 Fuzhou Lu, near the intersection of Fuzhou Lu and the Bund; to get there, take subway line two to the Henan Zhonglu station, or you can take a taxi or bus to the Fuzhou Lu-Bund intersection. Telephone: 021-63235053; Email: Captain@CaptainHostel.com.cn

Rates: Special-Class 1,200 RMB, Business Cabin 450 RMB, First-Class 550 RMB, and Sailor Bunk 60 RMB.

Captain hostel is a member of Hostelling International and is conveniently close to the Bund. Inspired with nautical themes, the hostel interior is warm and friendly, and the sailor bunk dorm beds were specially designed for backpackers. There are not many rooms, but they nevertheless all have their own individual designs. This is a place with a lot of character.

168 Motel

(shànghǎi mòtài168,上海莫泰168)

Reservation/Room service number: 8008207168: Shanghai Reservation/Room Service number: 021-63168168 (if you book a room through 168 Motel's reservation center, they will give you a 10 RMB discount on your room.)

Rates: Specially Priced Room: 168 RMB, Standard Room: 208 RMB. All credit cards accepted.

This is the first of several Chinese hotel's bearing the"motel" name, and it was designed to meet international economy hotel standards. This hotel chain can be found all over Shanghai, and has all of the amenities that you would expect in a modern hotel, such as satellite TV, local and international telephone service etc... 168 Motel branches can be found in places such as Huoshan Lu, Zhoujiakou Lu, and Anyuan Lu, so feel free to choose one in a location that best suits your travel plans.

Shanghai 24K International Hotel

(shànghǎi 24Kguójì jiǔdiàn, 上海24K国际酒店)

Located at 155 Weihai Lu; to get here, take bus lines 18, 46, 925, and 46. Be sure to get off at the People's Square bus stop. Other branches can be found at WuZhonglu and Fuzhou Lu; telephone: 021-51096884

Rates: The price of a standard room ranges from 218 RMB to 280 RMB. Some

rooms do not have windows, so insist on seeing your room before deciding you want to stay here.

This is another chain hotel with branches in several strategic spots around the city. Rooms here tend to be a little small, but they have all of the amenities you need. Every single and double room has a computer with free internet access. Shanghai 24K also has a family room with one big and one small bed, specially designed for a family of three.

Shanghai Travellers' Youth Hostel

(shànghǎi lǚxíngzhě guójì qīngnián lǚshè, 上海旅行者国际青年旅舍)

Located in the Huangpu District at 450 Jiangxi Zhonglu; to get there take the subway number two line to the Henan Lu station; telephone: 021-63297889

Rates: Double Room: 160 RMB; single room: 100 RMB; Dorm room: 45 RMB (listed prices are Hostelling International member prices. Nonmembers should expect to pay between 5 to 20 RMB extra.)

Each room has a television and shower. Double rooms have air conditioning, and the small single rooms have an electric fan. Dorm rooms are frequently fully booked and reservations are not accepted.

This is another youth hostel right off of the Bund. Rooms here are small but comfortable. The hostel is frequently booked solid and it does not take reservations. Differences in price for members and nonmembers are small, but if you plan on staying for a few days, it is still worth buying a hostel international member card for the discounts.

Shanghai Easy Tour Hostel

(shànghǎi yìtú qīngnián lǚshè, 上海易途青年旅舍)

Located in the Huanpu District at 57 Jiangyin Lu; to get there, take the subway

to the People's Square; telephone: 021-63277766

Rates: Double rooms: 200 RMB; Single rooms: 180 RMB; Dorm rooms: 45 RMB.

Right off of People's Square, the hostel is located inside a traditional residential three-sided courtyard with its own open-air terrace. Easy Tour Hostel's location is ideal for visiting all of Shanghai's major attractions, many of which are just a few steps away.

All rooms include air conditioning, hot water showers, a television and other normal hotel amenities. The hostel was newly renovated in early 2006.

Renting Houses and Apartments

If you decide to stay in Shanghai for a month or longer, you may want to consider renting a privately owned house or even a luxury apartment. Many luxury apartment buildings calculate their rent in terms of US dollars and their prices vary according to their location and the quality of their facilities. Expect to pay anywhere from1000 to several thousand dollars per month. For up-todate information, you can consult English language expat web sites such as www.mlpsh.com; www.cityweekend.com.cn/en/shanghai; www.shanghaiist.com, and www.thatssh.com. That's Shanghai and City Weekend are locally produced English language publications that are available free of charge in cafes, bars, and hotels. Each has its own extensive real estate and apartment listings.

If you decide to opt for a much cheaper standard apartment, you should be able to find a centrally located double occupancy for 1,500 to 2,000 RMB a month. You will probably need to have a Shanghai resident help you make proper arrangements before you arrive because renting local apartments can be a draining and time-consuming process. You can also try to find a short term sublet on online classified web pages such as craigslist (shanghai.craigslist.org).

Of course, you may choose to enlist the help of a real-estate broker. Brokers tend to charge massive broker fees that can reach as high as an entire month's rent. Real estate brokers in China are not known for their honesty, so you had best explore other options first before finally running to a broker for help.

Food and Drink

Without a doubt, Shanghai is one of China's great gastronomical centers. If you do not experience Shanghai's cuisine to the fullest, then you are depriving yourself an essential part of Shanghai life. Chinese people have always placed top priority on food, and Shanghai is no exception. Shanghai has been developing its own distinctive local cuisine for over one hundred years. At the same time, this historical port city has tolerantly and appreciatively welcomed the best international cuisine from around the world. World famous international restaurants have been gradually making their way into Shanghai to set up shop. As a result, French, Japanese and Italian restaurants together make up eighty percent of Shanghai's high-end cuisine, many of which are on par with some of the best restaurants in the world. Shanghai locals are proud of

their city's fine eateries and have come to see them as one of the definitive trademarks of their home. Never tired of discussing the newest international restaurant in town, Shanghai locals are willing to spend top-dollar — sometimes huge chunks of their pay checks — for a new dining experience. Chinese newspapers and lifestyle magazines do not spare any ink reporting on the city's newly opened establishments. Do not be surprised to see streams of upper class Chinese people filing in and out of the ultra fancy restaurants in Three and in Eighteen on the Bund. You would be challenged to find another city in China that turns eating out into such an extravagant display.

Expensive cuisine is fine for an occasional splurge, but for the rest of the time take comfort in knowing that Shanghai abounds with mid-level working class eateries. Every flavor and every price range is accounted for on the Shanghai streets, and you can easily indulge in some fine cooking without doing too much damage to your wallet. Choices here are not limited to local Shanghaiese and regional Huaiyang cuisines. You can also find Sichuan, Cantonese, Hunan, and Guizhou style restaurants. Every once and a while you may even run across signs for restaurants serving Peking Duck.

Just a few years ago, restaurant-lined food streets were extremely popular in Shanghai. Huanghe Lu Food Street near the People's Square, the Zhapu Lu Food Street near the Qipu Lu Wholesale Clothing Market, and Yunnan Lu Food Street on Fuzhou Lu were once veritable bee hives of small restaurants and swarming customers. Aside, perhaps, from Huanghe Lu, most of these food streets have since fallen back down to Earth, and are no longer the bustling venues they once were. That being said, most of the restaurants there still operate and beacon to customers with advertisements bearing their signature dishes or a special style of food preparation.

It is not hard to find a restaurant in Shanghai. Like most large cities in China, each of Shanghai's large avenues has an almost limitless selection of eateries. Another fact about Shanghai that international visitors

may not be aware of is that most department stores and shopping malls have food courts on their top or basement floors. Usually packed with dozens of stands, these food courts serve small portions of precooked items, and there is usually so much variety that choosing what you want to eat can be a real challenge. Most food courts require that you first purchase an electronic card at the sales counter, which you can then use to buy food. When you have finished your meal, you can return your card to the sales counter and they will refund the money left on your card. Most food courts offer pretty reasonable prices. Expect to pay 40to 50 RMB per person — not a bad price for a decent dinner. If you want to go even cheaper, than stick to the traditional Shanghai snacks like "xiaolongbao steamed" buns, which can fill you up for about 20 RMB. In contrast, a dinner in a swanky upscale restaurant can set you back over 500 RMB.

If you want to avoid Chinese food, but still do not want to pay high restaurant bills, McDonalds and KFC are absolutely everywhere. Shanghai is one of China's most westernized cities, and you can also find some locally operated restaurants selling simple western fare such as pizza, pasta, and hamburgers. Their prices are cheap too, and you should be able to fill up for about 20 to 30 RMB.

Upscale Restaurants

Three on the Bund

(wàitān sānhào, 外滩3号)

Telephone: 021-63233355; website: www.threeonthebund.com

There is a collection of first class Chinese restaurants in the Bund's seven storey building number Three, including the Whampoa Club, Laris, and New Heights. Three on the Bund is also home to the worlds second Evion Spa, China's first Armani flagship store, and Three fashion store. The Third Degree Music Lounge and Shanghai Gallery of Art give this building an extra degree of cultural depth. Three on the Bund is located at 3 Zhongshan Dongyilu on the fourth floor of the Bund's building number three. (Near the Guangdong Lu intersection.)

Jean Georges

Fourth floor, telephone: 021-63217733

Jean Georges was opened by the innovative world-famous chef, Jean-Georges Vongerichten.

Recommended Dishes: Frogs legs and mustard greens fried in thyme and tender garlic, black sea bass with sweet and sour sauce (specialty dish), lobster tartine and lemon grass, and pea flour cakes with tomatoes.

The restaurant's wine cellar has private rooms with enough table space to fit 30 people.

Whampoa Club

(huángpǔhuì jùlèbù, 黄浦会俱乐部)

Fifth floor; telephone: 021-63213737; open from 11:30 am to 2:30 pm and 5:30 pm to 10 pm.

Fee: Expect to pay 600 RMB per person.

The Whampoa Club is set in an expansive 1,800 square meter interior designed by famed Hong Kong designer, Chen Youjian. Made with ornate and extravagant colors and building materials, the Whampoa Club exudes a enthusiastic charm and is considered a modern masterpiece of art deco design. Once ranked one of the twenty-five most expensive restaurants in the world, the food here is exquisite.

Recommended Dishes: Smoked fish, silver cod baked with onions, goose liver, drunken chicken, goose liver with glutinous rice and dates, mustard shrimp balls, and goose liver pate.

Laris *(lùwéixuān, 陆唯轩)*

Sixth floor; telephone 021-63219922; hours of operation 11:30 am to 2:30 pm and 6 pm to 11 pm.

Fee: Expect to pay 500 RMB to 800 RMB per person. Martini Night will cost you around 150 RMB.

Established by world-renowned Australian chef, David Laris. One of Laris's most eye-catching sights is the seafood bar, Fins, Claws & Wings, where patrons can sample elegant fresh seafood. Fins, Claws & Wings has a large seafood display where you can see mussels, clams, frogs, oysters, large lobsters, local and imported fois gras, and caviar resplendently on show. You can also choose to sit across from the chef and watch as your seafood selections get transformed into delectable entrees. At Laris, you can choose you order entrees off of the traditional menu or create your own personalized menu together with the chef. Not surprisingly, in 2005 Laris was rated one of the best restaurants in Shanghai.

Every Thurday, Laris holds Martini Night in its bar, the Vault. The event lasts from 9pm to 2am. Prices are not too expensive and it is definitely worth an evening of your time.

New Heights

(xīnshìjiǎo cāntīng jiǔláng, 新视角餐厅酒廊)

Seventh floor; telephone: 021-63210909; hours of operation: 11:30 am-3:30 pm and 6 pm to dawn.

Sitting on the top floor of Three on the Bund, New Heights has a full 180 degree panoramic view of Pudong and the Bund. The 1850 square meter restaurant can fit 100 people, and off to the side is a bar that seats 45. Glass walls completely draw the scenery into the restaurant making New Heights a feast for the eyes as well as the stomach. Recommended Dishes: The ever popular fried fish in hot sauce, Thai-style red curry pork, grill-fired tuna and fennel, and a delicious fish and chips.

Third Degree Music Lounge

Located on the building's highest floor, the salon is open from 7pm to 2am and is famous for its rare spirits, comfortable and extravagant surroundings, and elegant but diverse selection of music. But, the prize spot in the Third Degree is the open terrace under the stars. Treat yourself to a glass of cognac brandy or a nice glass of Champaign as you enjoy the splendorous panoramic view of the northern Bund showcases the glorious silhouettes of historical architecture. Third Degree Music Salon has prepared a selection of great food, like oysters and fois gras, all put together with unique colors and flavors.

The Cupola *(wàngjiānggé, 望江阁)*

Located on the top floor; telephone: 021-63233355 and 13817876975.

This was once the building's bell tower, commanding the highest point in all the Bund. Today it has been transformed into Shanghai's most exclusive and original dining room. The Cupola's first floor has only eight seats and the second floor has only two. The second floor is a most extraordinary dining room with an eight meter tall vaulted ceiling that radiates neoclassical warmth. The room has a 360 degree view of the surrounding skyline and only has one table and one two-person sofa. This is certainly one of the most romantic spots in China. Naturally, the Cupola requires that you reserve a table in advance. Not a full restaurant on its own, the Cupola will have you choose from set menus offered by Laris, Jean Georges, or the Whampoa Club.

M on the Bund

(mǐshì xīcāntīng, 米氏西餐厅)

Located in the Huangpu District at 20 Guangdong Lu, on the seventh floor of the Nissin Shipping Building. There are a number of buses you can take to get here including lines 20, 22, 37, 55, 71, 135and 921. Guangdong Lu is also the final stop on bus line 42 and the Tunnel Line number Nine; telephone: 021-63509988.

Fee: Expect to pay between 300 and 800 RMB per person

Some people say that the view from this restaurant's terrace out onto the Huangpu River and the Bund is Shanghai's most beautiful and most picturesque sight. As the London's Sunday Daily once said, at M on the Bund "nothing is more satisfying than a stroll on the terrace with a full glass of Champaign or chardonnay." Once selected as one of Shanghai's best spots for a wedding proposal, M on the Bund is considered one of the Pacific region's most fashionable and expensive restaurants.

Recommended Dishes: The soufflés, roasted leg of lamb, and all kinds of desserts.

Sens & Bund

(yădéxī cāntīng, 雅德西餐厅)

Located at 18 Shandong Yilu, on the sixth floor of Eighteen on the Bund (at the intersection of Nanjin Donlu); telephone: 021-63239898.

Fee: Expect to pay 250 RMB to 400 RMB per person for lunch (mainly set meals); dinner runs round 300 to 800 RMB per person.

Opened by the fabulous French brothers, chefs Jacques and Laurent Pourcel, Sens & Bund selects seasonings and ingredients according to season. The Pourcels are extremely particular about the ingredients they use, and frequently mix local and imported items. Their goose liver, beef and some special vegetables are imported from France. Fish and seafood are bought locally.

Recommended Dishes: Duck breast and lobster terrine with wild herbs and vanilla flavored oil, classic roasted pigeon with

western celery and bitter cocoa sauce, and French style flaky bitter chocolate cake.

Xintiandi's Fine Cuisine

Xintiandi (新天地) is a great place to dine. Passing by the Starbucks will take you to Shanghai's most fashionable restaurant, La Villa Rouge, where Shanghai's neuveau riche and young upstarts come to splurge. For more information about Xintiandi please visit this book's chapter on Xintiandi and Shikumen.

La Villa Rouge *(xiǎo hónglóu, 小红楼)*

Located at 811 Hengshan Lu (inside Xujiahui Park); to get there take the subway number one line to the Xujiahui Station; telephone: 021-64316639; hours of operation: 11 am to 2 am.

Fee: Expect to pay 200 RMB per person for lunch and 550 per person for dinner. After 9 pm, the action at La Villa Rouge's bar picks up and you can enjoy live music performances. La Villa Rouge has a wide selection of spirits and cocktails. Drinks run 50 RMB and up.

La Villa Rouge seems to have thought of everything with both buffet and menu dining options. Their dishes show a lot of innovation, and their Japanese chef puts together quite daring creations.

Recommended Dishes: Some of the best options on the menu are the Italian meat and potato wrap, mutton, and cod which are all cooked to perfection and the fish dishes seem to just melt in your mouth. A few people have noted that the food here can be quite salty.

Sasha's *(sàshā cāntīng, 萨莎餐厅)*

Located at 11 Dongping Lu (at the corner of Hengshan Lu); telephone: 021-64746628; happy hour is held from Monday to Friday, 5:30 pm to 7 pm. Happy hour drinks are half price. Wednesday and Thursday have live music in the evening, and dart competitions are held on Tuesday.

Fee: Expect to pay between 150 to 300 RMB per person.

Sasha's is split into three levels. English-

style bar can be found on Sasha's first floor; the second floor has a western restaurant serving excellent French entrees and Swiss fondue; a tidy Havana cigar and spirits bar is on the third floor and is loaded with 120 different European wines. This building was once home to Song Ziwen of the powerful Song family and its exterior has been featured in many films. Sasha's frequently attracts celebrities and VIP guests such as tennis star Andre Agassi, fashion and make-up designer Anna Sui, Zhang Zhi, and Gu Juji.

Recommended Dishes: Fried Shrimp with Mango, Papaya and Shasha (a warm roasted Pacific salad prawn), rack of lamb, and desserts and cakes.

Paulaner Brauhaus

(bǎoláinà cāntīng, 宝莱纳餐厅)

Both Ambrosia and Paulaner Brauhaus are located at 150 Fenyang Lu. Too get there take bus line 42 or 96 and get off at the Fenyang Lu. You can also take the subway to the Hengshan Lu station and walk over. Telephone: 021-64745700; Hours of Operation: 11 am to 2 am.

Fee: Expect to pay about 200 RMB per person including drinks. Paulaner Brauhaus offers three types of buffets: the Bavarian buffet, European-style buffet, and European-Asian buffet. All three buffets include two drinks (Paulaner Brauhaus's own beer, soft drinks, fruit juice, coffee, and tea.) An extra 70 RMB will get you three hours of free refills.

One of Paulaner Brauhaus's main attractions is its beer, freshly brewed on location. The brew master adheres to the strict German brewing methods set down in 1516. Paulaner Brauhaus's beer comes in three types: the Paulaner Lager, Paulaner Weissbier, and the Munich Dark. A half liter will set you back 68 RMB and a full liter 105 RMB.

Recommended Dishes: Pig elbow, a basket of assorted Bavarian dishes (both entrees are served with mashed potatoes and sauerkraut); and a beef and vegetable stew made with lots of beef and served with crackers and bread.

Ambrosia

(xiānzhìxuān, 仙炙轩)

Hours of Operation: 11:30 am to 2:30 pm, and 5:30pm to midnight.

Fee: Expect to pay between 128 RMB to 500 RMB per person.

Set inside a French style villa commonly referred to as "Shanghai's Little White House", Ambrosia is the place to come to for some serious Japanese barbeque. The restaurant is split into three levels, the first and second floors serve items on the set menus, and the third floor serves a la carte

items from the regular restaurant menu. Barbequed meat is Ambrosia's calling card. While serving excellent renditions of the usual barbequed beef, chicken and fish options, at Ambrosia you can roast pretty much anything else you can imagine. Try the conch which is prepared by slicing the snail meat, marinating it in a soup of dried cod and ginger, and cooking it for three minutes on the grill. The conch comes out with a distinct but delicious flavor. Ambrosia's set meals give you a lot of bang for your buck, but, be warned, the set meals are portioned for not one, but two people. With 128 RMB, 188 RMB, and 200 RMB varieties, the set meals serve up plenty of meat, all cooked on an iron skillet. The 188 and 200 RMB varieties include thin slices of Australian beef, and the 200 RMB versions also have dried scallops and shrimp. For most people, the 128 RMB set meal is more than enough to satisfy. It comes with mushroom soup, bread, vegetable salad, tennbura, rice, fish, chicken, and iron skillet items such as beef and fish. Considering the size of the portions, the price is not bad at all. If you come alone, we recommend ordering a la carte off the menu.

Recommend Dishes: Roasted thin slices of salmon. It tastes great even without any seasonings. The tempura is served fresh, and is delightfully crisp on the inside.

Aside from its saki, Ambrosia also serves Paulaner Brauhaus beer off the tap. If you order off the menu, expect to pay between 200 and 500 RMB.

The Yongfoo Elite
(yōngfúhuì, 雍福会)

Located at 200 Yongfu Lu. You can get there on bus lines 328, 506, and 548. Be sure to get off the bus at the Fuxing Xilu stop; telephone: 021-54662727; hours of operation: lunch: 11:30 am to 2 pm; afternoon tea from 2 pm to 5:30 pm; dinner from 6 pm to 10 pm. The bar is open from 6 pm to midnight.

Fee: Expect to pay 300 RMB per person for lunch, 180 RMB for afternoon tea, and 500 RMB for dinner. Women must pay a three year membership fee of 10,000 RMB and men pay 20,000 RMB for a three year gold card. Members must also pay an additional 2,400 RMB annual membership fee. Non-members are required to pay a 15% service fee when dining at the restaurant.

This mysterious but romantic early-twentieth century villa on Yongfu Lu, is drenched in neo-classical luxury. According to the Asian Wall Street Journal, Yongoo Elite "gives you a true understanding of the luxury experienced by the powerful Chinese families of the 1920's and 1930's". Its remarkable design earned it Wallpaper's runner-up award for Best Club of

2004. The Yongfoo Elite house was built in the 1930's, and was turned into the British Consulate in 1980. Because of the building's advanced state of dilapidation, it was eventually abandoned by the consulate members. It took over two and a half years of renovation to restore the building to its original majesty and turn it into the sumptuous and exclusive club of today. The list of Yongfoo Elite's distinguished guests include: French first lady, Burnadette Chirac, Luxemburg Prime Minister, Jean-Claude Junker, Vice Chairman of the European Commission, Loyola de Palacio, Microsoft China CEO, Chen Yongzheng, golf master, Gary Player, French maestro, William Chrisite, and NBA basketball star, Yao Ming. Yongfoo Elite is also a favorite haunt of celebrity watchers as it has hosted such stars as The English Patient male lead, Ralf Fiennes, mega star, Tom Hanks, action hero, Jackie Chan, legendary Hong Kong actress Maggie Cheung and many others.

Ding Yongqiang, Yongfoo Elite's head chef, is a pupil of master chef, Chen Borong, and specializes in local Shanghai delicacies. Cantonese flavors and innovative cuisines often show up on the menu as well.

Recommend Dishes: The house specialty made with chicken and shrimp cooked in brown sauce, scallops, and gingko nuts. The menu also features meat cakes, Fenggang duck, cold vegetables with raw fish, scallops in white sauce, crab roe with bean curd pan-browned with scallions and garlic, shrimp roe with water-oat shoots, smoked fish, Xueyu fish stir fried in sauce and water, a pig's feet and soybean soup, cookies with date paste, and mango pudding.

Grand Hall

(dà gōngguǎn, 大公馆)

Located in the Xujiahui District at 7 Donghu Lu (near Xiangyang Park); you can get here on the subway number one line, or bus lines: 926, 911, 920, 02, and 42; telephone:

021-64157777 and 64156666.

Fee: Expect to pay over 200 RMB per person for lunch or dinner and 68 RMB per person for afternoon tea. This is a nice place to sit and let the time fly.

Jewish businessman, Ray Joseph, hired architects Davis & Brooke to build the Grand Hall in 1921. The construction is an old Shanghai-style French manor, and after its completion, it became the center of Ray Joseph's trade and cultural activities in Shanghai. For a while, the manor became a hot spot for gossip and social affairs. In the 1930's the Grand Hall was purchased for a large fee and given as a gift to Shanghai bigwig, Du Yuesheng. The manor was passed along yet again in 1946 to Du Li, a secret agent for one of China's warlords. Du Li, liked to play fast and loose with his money, and almost immediately transferred the property to one of his contemporaries, a popular celebrity, and the manor eventually became a gathering point for Kuomintang personnel and famous Chinese and international guests. When World War Two ended, the Chinese governor leased the manor to the occupying American military, and in the 1950's it was converted into the Consulate of the Soviet Union. Shanghai's first post-war mayer, Chen Yi, frequently used the Grand Hall to entertain important guests.

The Grand Hall's first floor has a cigar bar where famous jazz bands perform live music Monday through Friday, and a restaurant on the second floor serves local Shanghai cuisine. This is a hot spot for celebrities who you can occasionally see here mingling with other important Shanghai figures.

Recommended dishes: Pork braised in soy sauce, braised Chinese mitten crab, roast fish, and goose liver. Some of the other options on the menu still leave plenty of room for improvement.

Local Shanghai Fare

Shanghaiese cuisine is often referred to in Chinese as Shanghai's "ben bang cai" *(běnbāngcài, 本帮菜)* or "local dishes". Because this local cuisine really encapsulates both the Shanghai temperament and regional characteristics, when you come to Shanghai, sampling "ben ban cai" is a must. Shanghai cuisine employs a variety of cooking and food preparation methods including: braising wth soy sauce, frying and broiling, stir frying, steaming, cooking over charcaol, and pickling. To most people, the main characteristics of "ben bang cai" can be roughly boiled down to heavy oils and red sauces. Shanghai cuisine indeed frequently employs thick juices, heavy flavors, lots of oil and sugar, and bright colors. It may be more accurate to generalize Shanghai cooking as a type of soy sauce braising. Still, "ben bang cai" is not the be all end all of Shanghai cuisine. Some people clearly differentiate "ben bang cai" and "hai pai cai" — "the Shanghai school of cooking". At the end of the Qing Dynasty and the beginning of the Republic, there were a total of 16 different styles of cooking that coexisted in Shanghai, called "shiliu bang" or "the sixteen groups" of which the "ben bang" was considered the most local. Today restaurants serving "ben bang cai" advertise that they serve the most original and authentic of Shanghai flavors. In reality, "ben bang cai" shows significant culinary influences from Suzhou andYuxi. "Hai pai cai" is considered the new wave of Shanghai cuisine, and has incorporated cooking methods from Cantonese, Sichuan, Nanjing, Yangzhou, Suzhou, Yuxi, and even western styles of cooking. "Hai pai cai" focuses on retaining the best of traditional Shanghai cooking and improving it with the best aspects of other culinary schools.

Many of Shanghai cuisine's most famous

dishes trace back to humble peasant beginnings. Shredded pork and soybean soup has direct links with the popular old dish "meat and bean stew". The fermented earthen bowl is a dish that comes straight out of the suburban Shanghai farming houses. A recipe that has been around in one form or another for two hundred years, the fermented earthen bowl combines pig innards, pig feet, fresh soup, and fermented glutinous rice and barley gravy into an earthen jar, which is then steamed. The dish has a clear refreshing broth and carries the fresh fragrance of spirits. Over the last one hundred years, ingredients and cooking methods used in the earthen bowl have continued to improve, and the earthen bowl has been replaced with a ceramic one.

Fermented gravies and dishes marinated in fermented gravy are unique to Shanghai cooking. Cold dishes included chicken, pig's feet, bean pods, winter bamboo shoots and tripe marinated in a gravy of fermented barley and rice. Hot dishes also use marinated items such as deep fried mackeral marinated in fermented sauce *(tǔnzāo qīngyú, 汆糟青鱼)* and shredded pork and soy bean soup *(ròusī huángdòu tāng, 肉丝黄豆汤)*.

Traditional cooking methods aside, some famous contemporary chefs have increased the scope of Shanghai cuisine with some innovative new dishes such as mackerel liver *(qīngyútūfèi, 青鱼秃肺)*, small shrimp with sea cucumber *(xiāzǐ dàwūcān, 虾子大乌参)*, crabs cooked in butter *(chǎoxièhuángyóu, 炒蟹黄油)*, and eight treasures in hot sauce *(bābǎolàjiàng, 八宝辣酱)*. The following restaurants are well known for serving up some great local Shanghai cuisine. Included in the list are several chain restaurants.

Ye Olde Station Restaurant
(shànghǎi lǎozhàn, 上海老站)

Located at 201 Caoxi Beilu. To get there, take bus lines 926, 920, 02, 42 or subway line number one to the Xujiahui station. Ye Olde Station Restaurant is right by the subway exit; telephone: 021-64272233. Hours of Operation: 11 am to 2 pm and 5:30 pm to 10 pm. The restaurant stops taking orders at 10 pm. Reservations are necessary for dinner.

Fee: 100 RMB and 150 RMB per person is enough to eat quite well.

The Ye Olde Station Restaurant occupies what was once a monetary connected to the

Xujiahui Catholic Church. Fully enveloped in its Shanghai hai pai style, Ye Olde Station brings old Shanghai to life. Serving up 1920's and 1930's era Shanghai cuisine, Ye Olde Station avoids heavy oils and dense colors. The chefs here also cook without MSG, to preserve the fresh flavors of their ingredients. Try to get a table near the window to enjoy views of the garden.

Recommendations: Celery and bean curd rolls, special vegetarian chicken, tofu and crab meat, stir-fried shelled river shrimp, minced crabmeat and tofu, spiced duck with lotus leaves, yellow croaker chowder with shepherd's-purse, stir-fried stewed eel's pudding, fried and braised clover, date paste cookies, and a shiitake mushroom vegetable wrap.

Xi's Garden

(xíjiā huāyuán jiǔjiā, 席家花园酒家)

Located at 1 Dongping Lu, right next to Sasha's; telephone: 021-64747052 and 64729041. This is a popular restaurant so it would be best to call and make reservations before you go.

Fee: Expect to pay 60 RMB to 100 RMB per person.

Xi's garden was originally the residence of Xi Dexian, president of the Kuomintang government's Central Bank of China. Built in 1913, this Spanish style house was the centerpiece of the Xi family's five garden residences. People say that when the restaurant was opened, Xi Dexian's three daughters made a special trip Shanghai to visit the Xi's Garden. Serving classical Shanghai dishes, we recommend Xi Garden's mashed green soybeans, roasted pigeon, crystal shrimp, and quick-boiled crab.

Peace Mansion

(hépíngguāndǐ, 和平官邸)

Located at 158 Fenyang Lu; to get there the take the 42 and 96 bus lines to the Fenyang Lu stop; telephone: 021-57575777; hours of operation: 11am-11pm.

Fee: Private rooms require a minimum expenditure of 500 RMB; tea runs at 35 RMB per pot; if you do not want to reserve a private dining room, expect to pay about 100 RMB per person.

This old house was once the official residence of Kuomintang intelligence chief, Dai Li. After the Chinese civil war, the house was taken over by Lin Liguo. After the Peace Mansion moved in, this manor immediately became a prime location for sampling traditional Shanghai fare. Each of the restaurant's rooms is named after a different Nobel Peace Prize Winner (thus the name of the restaurant). Peace Mansion's kitchen turns out Shanghai, Cantonese, Sichuan, and old style stewing cuisines, and each cooking style is under the control of a different chef.

Recommendations: Goose liver, which runs 178 RMB for about sixteen slices; other house specialties include: snow vegetables and roasted cod, Grandma's Soy Braised Pork, egg yolk with crispy beans, small white shrimp in fermented sauce (38 RMB), and steamed green crab.

Victorian Home

(lǎoyángfáng huāyuán fàndiàn, 老洋房花园饭店)

Located in the Luwan District at 27 Shanxing Lu (between Shaanxi Nanlu and Rui Jin Erlu); to get there, take the subway to the Shaanxi Nanlu Station, and then follow Maoming Lu to Shaoxing Lu; telephone: 021-64333506.

Fee: Expect to pay 100 RMB to 150 RMB per person.

Du Yuesheng was one of early twentieth century Shanghai's most legendary figures. Originally a vagrant, Du Yuesheng managed to grab a foothold on this "paradise of foreigner travelers" and eventually become the leader of Shanghai's organized crime syndicates. He became involved in a number of local industries such as entertainment, culture, education, finance, and news. This two storey garden residence was Du Yuesheng's gift to his fourth wife, though it has since been converted into an upscale Chinese restaurant. Serving Shang-

hai manor-style cuisine, the food here has both the comforting feeling of home and old Shanghai style care and craftsmanship. The flavors are very authentic.

Recommendations: The potato salad and mashed taro has a very good reputation around town. Made with a lot of butter, the mashed taro is tastes very sweet. Victorian Home's high grade beef is a little expensive at 68 RMB; it is fresh and tender, but the portion is a bit small. The cheese baked silver cod is a bit more reasonable, and the chef has added the citrus flavors of orange to offset the fish's richness. The traditional smoked fish is sweet. The eight treasures chili paste New Years cake is 48 RMB per serving. It is small but tender, made with fruits, shrimp, and bamboo shoots. It is worth a try, as does the fried baozi (stuffed buns), a common recipe to which the Victorian Home adds its own flair.

Old Shanghai Moon

(lǎoyèshànghǎi, 老夜上海)

Located at 59 Maoming Nanlu. To get there, take the subway number one line and get off at the Shaanxi Nanlu station. This restaurant has a number of branches around Shanghai, and serves authentic modern Shanghai cuisine, Shanghai night snacks, quality stir fried dishes, specially prepared slow-cooked noodles, and local dim sum. Expect to pay 100 RMB per person.

Home's

Located at 791 Julu Lu, right off of Fumin Lu; to get there you can take subway line one to the Shaanxi Nanlu station or bus lines 911, 02, 104, 24, 94, 128, 41 to the Julu Lu stop; telephone: 021-54030010 and 54030060.

Converted from a three storey old western-style residence, Home's elegant Shanghai cuisine will make you feel as if you are a guest in a traditional Shanghai home.

Recommendations: the house soy braised pork (32 RMB); an innovative cold dish: duck tongue and fruit salad; special hand torn salty chicken; and smoked butterfish. Try some of the small dim sum as well, such as the mango pudding, polished glutinous rice with red dates, fermented glutinous rice soup and rice flour dumplings, and deep fried glutinous rice cake. Expect to pay 100 RMB per person.

Le Ting *(lètíng, 乐庭)*

Located at 878 Julu Lu (near Shu Lu); to get there, you can take subway line one to the Shaanxi Nanlu station or bus lines 911, 02, 104, 24, 94, 128, 41 to the Julu Lu stop; telephone: 021-62475557.

Fee: Expect to pay 150 RMB per person.

Established inside a 1920's era French house, all of Le Ting's service staff wears 1930's long gowns and mandarin shirts.

The restaurant only seats 30 people. Le Ting specializes in imperial cuisine, and they never use spices or MSG. Everything you reserved here is cooked in its own original juices and flavors.

Recommendations: Taibai drunken chicken, sweet dates stuffed with lotus seeds, smoked ocean eel cubes, frozen cured pork, oil fried river shrimp, small shrimp with bamboo shoot slices; twice flavored mandarin fish, kungpao shrimp, black pepper beef, Jiangnan crispy duck, and a mixed vegetable dish made with tomato, beans, and yangkaihua squash.

Wang Bao He
(wángbǎohé jiǔjiā, 王保和酒家)

Located at 603 Fuzhou Lu; telephone: 021-633223673.

Shanghai locals love crab, and Shanghai's most famous and expensive crab feast was created at Wang Bao He, otherwise known as "the Crab King". Expect to pay between 200 and 500 RMB for the Wang Bao He's crab dinner. Wang Bao He serves other dishes as well, but they are all pretty mediocre. Crab is what people come for, and Wang Bao He is prepared with specialized crab eating utensils. Wang Bao He will open your eyes to crab dishes you never knew existed.

Shanghai Snacks

In the eyes of Chinese northerners, Shanghai snacks are sweet and bland. This is partially true, but the sweet flavors you find in Shanghai snacks are not sickeningly sweet like candy. They have a sweetness uniquely tinged with a bit of salt, creating a flavor that you will not become easily tired or bored of. This salty sweetness is found in many traditional Shanghai sauces and gravies, such as those found in t s traveled more modest quarters of the city.

Lübolang
(lǜbōláng, 绿波廊)

Found in the following locations: 1) Inside the Huangpu District at 115 Yu Yuan Lu (near Chenghuang Miao's Bridge of Nine Turnings); telephone: 021-63280602; 2) Inside the Huangpu District at 10 Wenchang Lu (near Jiuxiaochang Lu); 3) In the Pudong New District at 838 Zhangyang Lu, on the second floor of the Shanghai Huadu Building (near Laoshandong Lu), telephone: 021-58201279.

Lübolang is one of Shanghai's most respected "ben bang cai" (local cuisine) restaurants. Expect to pay 50 RMB per person for afternoon tea and a set meal. There are a great variety of snacks to choose from.

Huxin Ting
(húxīntíng, 湖心亭)

Located in the Huangpu District at 257 Yu

Yuan Lu (on the Lotus Flower Pool in the Bridge of Nine Turnings area); telephone: 021-63736950. Huxin Ting is mainly a tea house, but there is also a small selection of snacks on the menu. While their snacks are not the best, it is still a nice place to relax with a cup of tea and watch tourists walk through the garden. Onion noodles and small zongzi *(zòngzǐ, 粽子)* — glutinous dumplings wrapped in tea leaves — are the specialties here.

Wang Jia Sha Snack Shop

(wángjiāshā diǎnxīndiàn, 王家沙点心店)

Found in the following locations: 1) 805 Nanjing Xilu (near Shimen Lu); 2) in the Jingan District at 673 Wanhangdu Lu (Cao Jiadu); 3) 1533 Beijing Xilu (at the Changde Lu intersection).

This old standby serves classic Shanghai snacks. Their crab meat treats, tangbao, and spring rolls are all pretty good.

Qiao Jia Zha

(qiáojiāzhà, 乔家栅)

Found in the following locations: 1) 289 Xizang Lu (near Shouning Lu), telephone: 021-63282948; 2) in the Xujiahui District at 313 Xiangyang Nanlu (near Yongjia Lu), telephone: 021-64374174 or 64711956; in the Huangpu District at 33 Shanxi Nanlu (near the Hanko Lu intersection); 3) in the Xujiahui District at 196 Xinle Lu (near Donghu Lu), telephone: 021-54044255; 4) in the Huangpu District on Guangxi Beilu (near Fuzhou Lu); 5) in the Xujiahui District at 361 Wulumuqi Zhonglu (near Fuxing Xilu), telephone: 021-54044255; 6) in the Hongkou District at 335 Linping Beilu (near Tianbao Lu).

This old Shanghai favorite sells Shanghai snacks. There are many branches throughout the city, each with its own specialty item. Classic items include rice cake logs, green grass rice cakes, ribs with New Years cake, pot stickers, steamed dumplings served with minced meat, and stuffed steamed dumplings.

Da Fu Gui Restaurant

(dàfùguì jiǔlóu, 大富贵酒楼)

Located at 1409 Zhonghua Lu (near Fuxing Donglu).

This traditional old restaurant is full of old Shanghai character. The snacks served on the first floor are made according to strict traditional standards, and are a real bargain. Be sure to try their excellent wontons.

Types of Snacks

Fried stuffed buns and small steamed stuffed buns

(shēngjiān bāo生煎包, xiǎolóng bāo小笼包)

The kings of the Shanghai snack world, Shanghai locals have an uncommon affection for "shengjian bao", fried stuffed buns. Anywhere you find "shengjian bao", you will usually find long cues of people lining up to get their hands on these snacks. A conservative estimate still places hundreds of "shengjian bao" stalls around Shanghai. Made with a skin of partially rising dough, the buns are stuffed with a mixture of minced pork, soy sauce, chopped ginger and scallions, and ground wild pepper. The filling is flavored with sesame oil. The fried buns are cooked in oil on a flat pan and sprayed intermittently with water until they are finished.

Steamed buns, "xiaolong bao", are also extremely popular. Stuffed bun stalls and shops can be found all over the city. They are also frequently sold in Shanghai restaurants.

Steamed and fried stuffed buns are usually filled with lots broth. Be careful when you eat them that you do not drip juice on your clothes or burn your tongue with scalding juice. Take note that Shanghai locals sometimes call stuffed buns, "mantou".

Xiaoyang Shengjian

(xiǎoyáng shēngjiān, 小杨生煎)

Locations: 1)54 and 60 Wujiang Lu (near Nanjing Xilu), to get there, get off the subway at Jingan Si; telephone: 021-62676025; 2)678 Shaanxi Beilu (at the Wuding Lu intersection); telephone: 021-62721581.

Feilong Shengjian

(fēilóng shēngjiān, 飞龙生煎)

Locations: 1)Nanjing Lu Promenade, near Zhidi Plaza; 2)2002 Sichuan Beilu on the first floor of the Dongtai Xiuxian Plaza (near Liyang Lu); telephone: 021-65877822 or 65877833.

Cai Jisheng's Old Shengjian Shop

(càijì shēngjiān lǎodiàn, 蔡记生煎老店)

Locations: 1) 142 Yunnan Zhonglu (between Fuzhou Lu and Guandong Lu); tel-

ephone: 021-63611917; 2) in the Huangpu District at 530 Sichuan Zhonglu (near the intersection of Beijing Donglu).

Fengyu Shengjian
(fēngyù shēngjiān, 丰裕生煎)

Located at 303 Xuanchuan Lu near Yanchang Xilu.

Guyi Yuan Garden Restaurant
(gǔyīyuán cāntīng, 古猗园餐厅)

Located in the Nanxiang Zhen town, at 218 Huxuan Gonglu near the Guyi Yuan Garden's southern gate. This restaurant once served the most authentic "xiaolong bao" found in Shanghai, although the quality has dropped off in recent years; telephone: 021-59121335.

Nanxiang Mantou Dian
(nánxiáng mántóudiàn, 南翔馒头店)

Located at 85 Yu Yuan Lu (near Bridge of Nine Turnings), telephone: 021-63554206 or 63265265.

Jiajia Tangbao
(jiājiā tāngbāo, 佳家汤包)

Locations: 1) 90 Huanghe Lu (near Fengyang Lu); telephone: 021-63276878; 2) In the Huangpu District at 638 Henan Nanlu (near the Wenmiao Lu intersection).

Fuchun Xiaolong Dian
(fùchūn xiǎolóng diàn, 富春小笼店)

Located at 650 Yu Yuan Lu (at the Zhenning Lu intersection); telephone: 021-62525117.

Ribs with New Years Cake
(páigǔ niángāo, 排骨年糕)

Slivers of New Years Cake are placed on top of pork ribs, which are first cooked in oil and then boiled. Xiandelai Snack Shop makes the most authentic variation in Shanghai.

Xiandelai *(xiāndélái, 鲜得来)*

Locations: 1) In the Huangpu District at 69 Yunnan Nanlu (near Ninghai Donglu), telephone: 021-63366108; 2) In the Luwan District at 15 Yandang Lu (near Huaihai Zhonglu), telephone: 021-63868377; 3) In the Pudong New District at 180 Mo Lu (near Zhaoyuan Lu, next to the Shanghai East Hospital); telephone: 021-58769716.

Yellow Croaker and Slow-cooked Noodles *(huángyú wēimiàn, 黄鱼煨面)*

This is a noodle soup made with chewy noodles, fresh, tender, boneless croaker, and a seafood broth made with shellfish.

Langui Fang *(lánguìfāng, 兰桂坊)*

Locations: 1) 417 Loushan Guanlu (near the Xianxia intersection); telephone: 021-62740084; 2) 88 Zunyi Nanlu on the first floor of the Xietai Center (near Xianxia Lu); telephone: 021-62199177.

Xia Noodle Shop *(xiàmiànguǎn, 夏面馆)*

Located at 1266 Nanjing Xilu on the fifth floor of the Plaza 66 (near the intersection of Shaanxi Beilu).

A Niang Noodle Shop *(ā niáng miànguǎn, 阿娘面馆)*

Located in the Luwan District at 19 Sinan Lu (near Huaihai Lu).

"Foot Binding Cloth" *(bāojiǎobù, 包脚布)*

An egg and flour pancake wrapped around a fried donut, this snack can be frequently seen on the streets of Shanghai. In recent days it has been turned into a type of breakfast on the go. Despite its terrible name, a Foot Binding Cloth still tastes great. Many people add sweet sauce or hot sauce and sprinkle it with pickled mustard tuber and cilantro.

Fried Tofu and Glass Noodle Soup *(yóudòufǔ fěnsītāng, 油豆腐粉丝汤)*

A soup made with fried tofu and bean starch vermicelli, fried tofu and glass noodle soup is usually topped with cilantro and scallions. Shanghai locals like to pair this soup with "shengjian bao" — fried stuffed buns.

Bei Wan Xin *(běiwànxīn, 北万新)*

Locations: 1) 434 Rui Jin Erlu (near Zhaojiabang Lu), telephone: 021-64733638; 2) 243 Julu Lu (near Rui Jin Yilu and Yan'an Lu) telephone: 021-53834498 and 63279493.

This store also sells buns, stuffed steamed dumplings, and shredded radish cakes.

Fried Tofu and Glass Noodle Soup Restaurant *(油豆腐粉丝汤)*

Located at Huangpi Nanlu (near the Yongnian Lu intersection).

Little Shaoxing Chicken Porridge *(xiǎo shàoxīng jīzhōu, 小绍兴鸡粥)*

This rice porridge was named after the chef who created it, a man from Shaoxing. It is made with gluttonous white rice, chicken meat, crispy skin, aromatic chicken bones, and cooked with chicken broth. The chicken meat is white, tender, and delicious, and the porridge has a strong lasting flavor.

Xiao Shaoxing Ji Porridge Shop *(xiǎo shàoxīng jīzhōu diàn, 小绍兴鸡粥店)*

Located at 69 Yunnan Nanlu (near Ninghai Donglu), telephone: 021-63260845; This is a well-known porridge shop. Other locations: 1) in the Hongkou District at 461 Liangcheng Lu (between Guangling Silu and Wenshui Donglu), telephone: 021-65929797; 2) in the Pudong New District at 125 Dong Dadao (near Jimo Lu), telephone: 021-58828334 .

The Crab Shell *(xièkéhuáng, 蟹壳黄)*

This treat is made by first forming a dough of oil and yeasty flour, and then shaping it into an oblate form. A layer of sesame seeds is then added, and it is baked on top of a hot oven. The hard yellow crust that forms resembles a crab shell, thus the name. The Xiekehuang is often filled with scallion oil, fresh meat, sugar, or red bean paste.

Wuyuan Bread Shop *(wúyuàn bǐngjiā, 吴苑饼家)*

Located in the Jingan District at 255 Yanping Lu (near Kangding Lu), telephone: 021-62565556, this shop produces a ton of different Shanghai snacks including the Xiekehuang.

Xigong Snacks *(xīgōng xiǎochī, 西宫小吃)*

Located at 520 Caoyang Lu (Behind the Huxi Worker's Cultural Palace). This shop makes Shanghai snacks for the masses, and is very popular with locals.

Classic Shanghai Favorites

Shanghai Classical Hotel *(shànghǎi lǎo fàndiàn, 上海老饭店)*

Located at 242 Fuyou Road, you can get here on bus lines 930, 920, and 11. Get off at the Henan Zhonglu stop and walk along the Bund until you arrive at the Shanghai Classical Hotel; telephone: 021-63552275 and 63282782. Hours of operation: 10 am to 10 pm; website: www.laofandian.com

Established in 1875, the Shanghai Classical Hotel was originally named Rongshun Guan. It was, and still is, a prosperous vendor of Shanghai cuisine, and is well known for its meticulous selection of ingredients and authentic flavors.

Recommendations: oil fried river shrimp; eight treasures duck; the three delicacies of

ham, bamboo shoots, and chicken breast; eight treasures hot sauce, spiced salt ribs, blast fried croaker fish, and bamboo shoots with stewed eel pudding. Expect to pay about 100 RMB per person.

Lao Zheng Xing Restaurant

(lǎozhèngxīng càiguǎn, 老正兴菜馆)

Located at 556 Fuzhou Lu; to get there, take the subway and get off at the People's Square or Henan Zhonglu stations; telephone: 021-63222624; website: www.laozhengxing-sh.com

Founded in 1862, Lao Zheng Xing serves traditional Shanghai fare.

Recommendations: oil fried river shrimp, spiced salt spare ribs, yellow croaker braised in soy sauce, sturgeon braised in soy sauce, stir fried eel, phoenix tail steamed dumplings, and scallion pancakes. Expect to pay 100 RMB per person.

Mei Long Zhen Jiujia

(méilóngzhèn jiǔjiā, 梅陇镇酒家)

Located at lane 1081, 22 Nanjing Xilu (near Jiangning Lu); telephone: 021-62566688 and 62535353; hours of operation:11am-2pm and 5pm-10pm.

Mei Long Zhen was established in 1938 and serves traditional Shanghai and Huaiyang cuisine. From the food to the decor, older Shanghai residents claim that this restaurant has remained unchanged since the 1930's.

Recommendations: stir-fried shelled prawns, prawns with pepper sauce, Yangzhou-style shredded bean curd, crystal prawns, stewed pork meatballs, pancakes and twice cooked pork. Expect to pay 100 RMB per person.

Laobanzhai Restaurant

(lǎobànzhāi jiǔlóu, 老半斋酒楼)

Located at 600 Fuzhou Lu (near Zhejiang Zhonglu); to get there take the subway to the People's Square station; telephone: 021-85654123; 6am-2pm (Laobanzhai will not take orders past 2pm), and 5pm to 8:30 pm (no orders past 8:30).

This restaurant serves Huaiyang cuisine. Established in 1905, this is Shanghais first Huaiyang style restaurant. The cooking here is simple, but the chefs are particular about

selecting ingredients, and their slicing, carving, and chopping skills are unparalleled, and carefully control the cooking temperature. Laobanzhai's food is famously authentic with moderately sweet and salty flavors.

Recommendations: crystal salt cured pork, banzhai salt-cured chicken, stewed crab meat balls, winter vegetables and slow-cooked noodles, fried fish strips and cooked in chicken sauce, and special black rice cake. Expect to pay 20 RMB to 50 RMB per person.

Vegetarian Cuisine

There are a handful of vegetarian restaurants in Shanghai. Temples such as the Jade Buddha Temple, Jing'an Si Temple, and Long Hua Temple all have their own vegetarian restaurants and Chengxiang Ge near the City God Temple has a vegetarian restaurant called Songyue Lou. Aside from these temple affiliated establishments, you can also find vegetarian food in other parts of town. We have listed some of the more notable establishments below.

Gongdelin Vegetarian Restaurant

(gōngdélín shūshíchù, 功德林蔬食处)

Located at 445 Nanjing Xilu; to get there, take the subway to the People's Square station; telephone: 021-63270218; hours of operation: 6:30am to 9:30 am and 11 am to 10 pm.

Established in 1922, this is China's oldest Buddhist Vegetarian Restaurant. The restaurant's founder, Zhao Yunshao, was the pupil of Master Gao Weijun, one of the main Buddhist monks at Hangzhou Chenghuang Shan Mountian's Changji Si Temple.

Recommendations: Gongde Sausage, vegetarian duck, vegetable steamed buns, five flavors wheat gluten, buttered minced crab meat, jadeite fish slices, shredded eel with sesame oil, olive seeds with chicken slices and mixed vegetables, shiitake mushroom and vegetable steamed buns. All of these dishes are made of vegetables or bean products such as tofu. Be warned that some dishes incorporate real eggs.

Zao Zi Shu

(zǎozi shù, 枣子树)

Locations: 1) 77 Songshan Lu; telephone: 021-63848000; 2) Located in the Gubei District at 848 Huang Jian Cheng Dao; telephone: 021-62751798; Expect to pay 40 to 60 RMB per person.

This is a strict vegetarian restaurant that allows no smoking or alcohol, and uses no MSG, eggs, or dairy products. Zaozishu serves organics teas, fruit plates, vegeta-

ble and mushroom dishes, and of course, meat dishes simulated with bean and wheat products.

Jue Lin Vegetarian Restaurant

(juélín sùcài chù, 觉林素菜处)

Located at 250 Jinling Donglu (Henan Nanlu); telephone: 021-63260115; hours of operation: 6:30am to 7:30pm.

Jue Lin serves vegetarian fare made with no eggs, dairy products or MSG. This is a smoke free liquor free establishment. Expect to pay 30 RMB to 50 RMB per person.

The Tiffin Vegetarian Cafe

(rénwén měixué sùshí kāfēi, 人文美学素食咖啡)

Locations: 111 Huaihai Zhonglu on the third floor of the Shanghai Times Square; telephone: 021-63910639; hours of operation: 11:30am to 9:30pm.

You will find strict vegetarian fare at The Tiffin Vegetarian Cafe. As with most vegetarian restaurants, you will find no eggs, meat, MSG, alcohol, or cigarettes here. Tiffin Vegetarian Cafe does carry good food, coffee, and a relaxing atmosphere. Expect to pay about 50 RMB per person.

L' Arbre de Provence

(pǔluówàngsī de shù, 普罗旺斯的树)

Located in the Xujiahui District at 1111 Zhaojiabang Lu in the Metro City; to get there take the subway number one line to the Xujiahui Station; telephone: 021-64267698; hours of operation: 10am to 10:30pm.

With European decor and a mix of Chinese and Western cuisines, inspiration for this restaurant comes from southern France. Still, the food here is all vegetarian with no eggs, meat, cigarettes, alcohol, or MSG. L'Arbre de Provence uses only purified water and serves vegetable and fruit dishes from all over the world. From Monday to Friday you can enjoy an economical set lunch for 19 RMB per person. There is also a Chinese-Western buffet for 39 RMB per person.

New Age Veggie

(xīn sùdài cāntīng, 新素代餐厅)

Located in the Pudong District at 168 Lujiazui Xilu on the fifth floor of the Super Brand Mall; to get there, take the subway line number two to the Lujiazui Station; telephone 021-50471880; hours of operation: 10am to 10pm; tea time is from 2pm to 5pm.

Recommendations: five color Chinese yam, racked abalone, roasted vegetarian ribs, and lucky raw vegetable stuffed buns. New Age Veggie also has plenty of spicy options on the menu. As usual, there are no eggs, alcohol, or dairy, and no smoking allowed. Only organic vegetables are used. Expect to pay 50 RMB to 70 RMB per person.

Miaoxiangyuan Of Long Hua Hotel *(lónghuáyíng bīnguǎn miào xiāngyuǎn, 龙华迎宾馆妙香苑)*

Located at 2787 Longhua Lu; you can get here on bus lines 44, 864, 933, 41, 104, 73, 733, 732, and 871; hours of operation: 11am to 2 pm and 5pm to 8:30pm; telephone: 021-64570570-1133.

Recommendations: Longhua vegetarian duck, sausage, vegetarian stuffed buns, peony crab, and other imitation meat dishes. No meat or fish is served, but some dishes use egg.

Deling Fang Vegetarian Restaurant *(délínfāng sùshí cāntīng, 德林坊素食餐厅)*

Located at 259 Baolin Lu; you can get here on bus lines 531B, 116, 90, 848, 849, 53, 541, the Wusong Warf special line, 813, 53, and 728; hours of operation 6am-8pm; telephone: 021-56106029.

DelingFang sticks to the strict vegetarian and health standards — no eggs, alcohol, cigarettes, or MSG. Breakfast is served daily, and there is a small shop selling Shenzhen's Qishan series of food items as well as their own home made vegetable stuffed buns and cakes.

King Guo Pure Vegetarian Restaurant

(guō dàwáng jìng sùfāng, 郭大王净素坊)

Located at 151 Haimen Lu (near Tangshan Lu); you can get here on bus lines 19, 13, 22, and 922; telephone: 021-65371763; hours of operation: 6am to 8 pm.

King Guo serves a soup-pot series of vegetarian cuisine and observes the usual taboos against eggs, alcohol, and cigarettes. King Guo also does not cook with onions or garlic. Fast food runs about 6 RMB per person, and if you order five portions or more, they can deliver. Breakfast begins at 6 am.

Natural Healthy Vegetable Restaurant *(tiānrán jiànkāng shūshíguǎn, 天然健康蔬食馆)*

Located at 390 Shaanxi Nanlu (at the intersection of Fuxing Lu); telephone: 021-64370632; hours of operation: 6am to 10pm.

Recommendations: the vegetable wrapped (fake) meats, deep fried strong-smelling tofu, three cup monarch mushrooms, and herbal medicine hot pot. No eggs, meat or alcohol. Expect to pay 20 RMB to 40 RMB per person.

Entertainment

Nightlife

When the Communist Party liberated China in 1949, the all-night party that characterized Shanghai in the 1930's was shut down in the blink of the eye. The "City that Never Sleeps" was finally put to bed and covered with a large red flag. Shanghai remained this way for 40 years until Deng Xiaoping opened the city to economic reform, and the world let out a loud sigh of relief. The nightclub scene began its slow comeback in 1992, and in the fourteen years between then and now, Shanghai has come a long way in returning to its former greatness. Travelers now have a variety of entertainment options when they are in town. If you come with an open mind and an adventurous spirit, you will discover that Shanghai is a fun place to visit.

Unlike most small cities in China, the Shanghai nights are far from quiet and still. Shanghai is a city with two faces. In the daytime, it is a whirlwind of suits, brief-

cases, people and vehicles. As night falls, Shanghai comes ablaze with street lamps and neon lights. Everyday the city undergoes a new makeover, with flashy new watering holes popping up and closing down every day. Shanghai now has more bars than you can swing a dead cat at, providing the traveler with a great variety of options and an equally great variety of prices. A recent government clampdown on nightclubs open later than 2am took the edge off of the scene for a while, but the bars are back up and running again, and going strong. Club nightlife is closely connected to the bars, which are usually found in the same areas. Shanghai has different clubs to suit different tastes, with music ranging from salsa and hip-hop, to trance and Chinese-techno, to gay venues.

For those looking for other more culturally related forms of entertainment, Shanghai is more than willing to please. Travelers will be able to take on some Broadway shows, see gravity-defying acrobatics at a nearby circus, or enjoy a symphony at the Shanghai Grand Theater. And then at the end of the day, finish it all off by heading to a masseuse, and letting your worries get rubbed away.

Bars and Nightclubs

If you are looking for evening on the town, Shanghai has a number places to go to. Upscale establishments center on the Bund, and more personalized choices can be found at Fuxing Park and Jingan Si. Maoming Nanlu, Hengshan Lu, and Huaihai Zhonglu are all known as blue collar spots for the average Joe, where you will not have to break the bank to party til dawn.

Cloud Nine and the Sky Lounge

(jiǔchóngtiān, 九重天)

Located at 88 Shiji Dadao,inside the Jin Mao Tower; to get there, take the subway to Lujiazui, telephone: 021-50491234, ext. 8098 .

You need to make three separate elevator trips to get from the ground floor to the bar. The first will take you to the Grand Hyatt lobby on the 54th floor. Take the second elevator from the lobby to the 85th floor and the final elevator up to the 87th floor. Note that the bar requires a minimum purchase of 88 RMB per person, and the minimum jumps up to 120 RMB on Saturdays with an additional 15% service fee. Try out one of the bubbling cocktails. There is one called the "cloud nine" that runs for 87 RMB. A beer will cost you around 50 RMB. Hours of operation: 5pm to 1am.

Peace Hotel Old Jazz bar

(hépíngfàndiàn juéshìjiǔbā, 和平饭店爵士酒吧)

Located at 20 Nanjing Lu inside the Peace Hotel; telephone: 021-63216888 ext. 6210.

If you are willing to pay a steep cover charge for the privilege of buying drinks and listening to some corny jazz, than this is the place for you. Hours of operation: 8pm to 2am. You need 50 RMB to get in the door.

CJW

Locations: 1) 222 Yan'an Donglu on the 50th floor of the Bund Center near Jiangxi Zhonglu; telephone: 021-63391777 and 63392777; 2) 123 Lane 2 Xingye Lu on the bottom floor; telephone: 021-63856677; hours of operation: 6am to 2am. Happy hour runs from 5pm to 7pm.

If the stratospherically priced drinks and cigars do not dissuade you, then come out for the some great live jazz playing from 9pm to midnight.

Mint Club

Located at 333 Tongren Lu; to get there; take the subway to the Jingan Si station; telephone: 021-62479666; hours of operation: 11am to 2am, open from 11 am to 4am on Friday and Saturday.

This is the site of the illustrious Green House. The Green House was Hungarian architect, Laszlo Hudec's last building on the Bund. Finished in 1938, the English-language China Daily commented in 1939 that the Green House was "the premier luxury house in the far east". Its original owner, Wu Tongwen —"the pigment king" — was a wealthy Shanghai figure. The building was outfitted with what were then the most cutting edge facilities in the world, including spring floorboards on the second floor and the world's most modern elevator. All of the house's furniture was custom made by famous American furniture makers on Nanjing Xilu. On the day the Green House was completed, Hudec turned to Wu Tongwen and said, "I can guarantee that in fifty years time, this house will not lose its modern feel. In one hundred years, this house will still be in style. It is simply a classic". To preserve his Green House's individuality, Wu Tongwen bought out all of the building's blueprints and designs and locked them away in a safe. On Christmas eve in 1948, a foreign

diplomat offered to trade a ten thousand ton ship and 500 thousand dollars for the right to turn the house into a foreign consulate. Wu Tongwen refused the offer. He said, "When I die, I want to die inside the Green House." As fate would have it, in August 1966, Wu Tongwen's wish came true when he and his mistress consumed a large number of sleeping pills with their coffee and turned on the home's natural gas. They both died inside the Green House.

The Mint Club is the main attraction of the Bund's late night scene. Decorated with red and black tones, the garden is a composition of colored waterfalls. Popular music from around the world pipes in from all directions, adding contemporary textures to an atmosphere that contrasts old and new. 11 pm is when the action really begins at the Mint Club. Ladies night is Wednesday between 9 and 11 pm, welcoming women with free drinks, hot dogs, and popcorn. You can pick up peppermint candy as you walk in the door. Other than the wait staff, on Wednesday night, the entire bar is filled with women. Salsa dance parties are held on Thursday; drinks average to about 50 RMB each.

Yanyangtian is restaurant on the building's bottom floor that serves mostly mild Cantonese cuisine. Recommended dishes include papaya and silver cod, Longjing shrimp, veal with golden garlic, and spiced salt gold needle mushrooms. Expect to pay about 150 RMB per person.

If you come during the day time, you can sit in the garden and enjoy the soft wind as you listen to the sound of rustling leaves, and soak up the warm sun. Smell the fresh grass, look onto Tongren Lu, and you will understand why its owner was so enchanted with the Green House.

Malone's American Cafe

Located at 255 Tongren Lu; to get there, take the subway and get off at the Jingan Si station; telephone: 021-62472400; hours of

operation: 11am to 2am.

This is American-style bar serves huge portions of classic American and Tex-Mex fare, such as terrific hamburgers and burritos. You can take comfort in the usual bar pastimes of darts and billiards, of plop down in front of their many TVs and take in a baseball game. Live music on Monday.

Manhattan

Located at 88 Tongren Lu; telephone: 13501647257; hours of operation: All hours.

The doors are always open at this noisy bar. With an old Shanghai feel and shaking tunes, this is a great place to let yourself go. The bar gets packed between three and four am. Billiard tables are on the second floor.

Blue Frog *(lánwājùlèbù tóngrénlùdiàn, 蓝蛙俱乐部铜仁路店)*

Location 86 Tongren Lu.

With its cool color decor the Blue Frog's bar counter on the first floor has been completely taken over by the international set. Flickering candles and a warm homey atmosphere make the second floor much more suitable a laid back evening with a small group of friends. Drinks run 30 to 50 RMB, and there are free peanuts.

Blue Frog *(lánwājùlèbù lúwāndiàn, 蓝蛙俱乐部卢湾店)*

Located at 207-6 Maoming Lu (near Fuxing Zhonglu), telephone: 021-64456634; hours of operation: 11am to midnight.

Blue Frog offers one of the best deals in town. Just stepping in the door will get you five free drinks, and their menu has several hundred to choose from. After downing your five samples, you will probably want to stick around. This is a nice place to sit, drink, and chat. Crowds here are light.

Long Bar

Located at 1376 Nanjing Xilu on the second floor of the Shanghai Center; to get there, take the subway to the Jingan Si station; telephone: 021-62798268; hours of operation: 11 am to 3am; happy hour is from 5 to 8pm.

Long bar features live jazz Tuesday nights and Sunday afternoons with a live "Five Guys On A Train" act that cannot be missed. A drink here will set you back. Do not be surprised when they tack on a 15% service fee.

Park 97

Located on the side of Huaihai Zhonglu inside Fuxing Park; you can get there by taking subway line one and getting off at the Huangpi Nanlu station. Walk over to Huaihai Zhonglu from Yandang Lu. Traveling by bus, you can take lines 02, 17,

24, tunnel line eight, 304, or 932 and get off at the Huangpi Nanlu stop. Telephone: 021-53832328.

Established inside one of Shanghai's oldest parks, Park 97 has been at the forefront of Shanghai fashion since its first conception. Officially called the California Club, most people come here for Park 97's provocative warm colors. Geometrical in design, the bar is flooded with mist, cold pink light that shines off of the mirrors, and huge freehand oil paintings of the human body. International music groups perform in the evenings, and there is outdoor seating in the summer where you can enjoy the fresh air. Expect to pay 100 RMB or so.

Langui Fang on Park 97's first floor, has also proven to be an extremely popular bar. Sharing a front entrance with Park 97, Baci Italian Restaurant serves excellent Italian food in a rich Italian atmosphere. Baci offers two set lunches: a 97 RMB two-course lunch and a 119 RMB three course lunch. Other menu options include Italians soups, the rabbit with salad, tomato and cheese pizza, and fried salmon.

Guandi Bar *(guāndǐ jiǔbā, 官邸酒吧)*

Located inside Fuxing Park near Park 97. Telephone: 021-33080726.

Well-known Taiwanese artist, Wu Dawei, is one of Guandi Bar's shareholders, and celebrities such as Xu Ruyun, Lin Xinru, Su Youpeng, Zhang Shi, and Xie Hui were all in attendance at the bar's opening. Luminary singers such as Liu Jialing, Chen Xiaochun, Mo Wenwei, Meng Guangmei, and Faye Wang have all staged performances here. In the blink of and eye, Guandi has become the most popular gathering place in Shanghai, and complaints about Guandi's sky-high prices have not stopped the crowds from coming in. Here you will find Shanghai's most complete collection of champagne as well as well-regarded wines, many types of whisky, special cocktails, and handmade Cuban cigars. Members are presented with a Guandi electronic door card. Swipe the door card over the sensor and the door will open for you. You do not need to ring the door bell.

Cotton Club

(miánhuā jùlèbù, 棉花俱乐部)

Located at 1428 Huaihai Zhonglu (at the intersection of Fuxing Lu). You can get here by taking the subway to the Hengshan Station. Telephone: 021-64377110.

One of the best live music places in town

completely composed of local clientele with a pretty good atmosphere — a must see. Expect to pay about 65 RMB per person.

West Side

237 Hengshan Lu (near Gaoan Lu) Telephone: 021-64724327.

If you are after a little peace and quiet, than West Side is the place for you. Although West Side's cocktails have received mixed reviews, most agree that it is a good place to sit back with a drink, talk with friends, and listen to music. The house singers are always open to requests.

Mural Bar & Restaurant

Located at 697 Yongjia Lu (near Hengshan Lu); telephone: 021-64335023 and 64339671.

Shanghai pub dwellers love this basement-level establishment. When you are heading in this direction, keep your eyes peeled because Mural's sign is not exactly eye-catching. As you come down the steps, you will discover that Mural is a different world. Usually Mural has an entry free of 50 RMB; however, 100 RMB will not only get you in the door but give you all you can drink on Fridays. Once you pay for a ticket, you will get a stamp on your hand. The bar is usually so busy that the bartenders are in a constant state of motion. Mural's four walls are covered in ancient writing and Buddhist relief sculptures. It feels just like walking through a Buddhist stone grotto. Mural's boss is a handsome young Frenchman and he has arranged the pub with couches and beds, making it popular with people who want to indulge their laziness. Eclectic performances are common and attract a crowd of international students.

O'Malley's Irish Pub

Located at 42 Taojiang Lu, (one street over from Hengshan Lu); to get there take the subway to the Changshu Lu station; telephone: 021-64370667 and 021-64744533.

A typical Irish pub with a beer garden and live music Irish music that gets cranking at 8:30 every night except Sunday. Hours of operation: 11:30am to 2am.

Amber

Located at 184 Maoming Nanlu (near Yongjia Lu); telephone: 021-64665224.

This is a nice place to come and talk with friends. According to legend, in the old days China's Shanghai-based foreign correspondents used to gather here. There is a movie projection room on the bottom floor and people occasionally come here to see films. You probably cannot find any reporters here any more, but there are still plenty of internationals who flock here in droves.

1931 Pub

Located at 112 Maoming Nanlu (near Nanchang Lu); telephone: 021-64725264.

Old style gramophones, old Shanghai

movie star posters, an old style telephone on the wall, dusky lighting, and service women in black cheongsams, this pub will transport you straight back to old Shanghai. While you are here, you should try a glass of their salt soda water and have an assortment of Shanghai-style snacks (fried wontons, spring rolls, lobster slices). You can skip the main dishes here, which are somewhat mediocre. Try not to let the service staff's less-than-professional attitude get to you. Just sit back and enjoy the ambiance. Expect to pay 100 RMB per person.

Yelaixiang *(yèláixiāng, 夜来香)*

Located at 58 Maoming Lu on the third floor of the Okura Garden Hotel; telephone: 021-64151111 ext. 5217.

Yelaixiang is the prince of Maoming Lu and is rich with European ambiance. Nightfall is the most ideal time to come, when you can sit outside and gaze upon blooming flowers in the French garden. Prices here are on the expensive side.

Wynn Win Club

Located at 1266 Nanjing Xilu (near the Shaan Xilu intersection) on the fifth floor of the Plaza 66; telephone: 021-62886222; hours of operation: 8:30pm-4am.

A new establishment, the Wynn Win Club is full of 1980's style hippy extravagance. It has a somewhat retro-modern feel. An awesome DJ spins the tunes.

Glamour Bar *(mèilì jiǔbā, 魅力酒吧)*

Located on the seventh floor of the Bund's building number five (near Guangdong Lu); telephone: 021-64319390; hours of operation: 5:30pm-late.

Soft comfortable tones and a great bartender make Glamour Bar — the sister bar to M on the Bund — definitely worth a visit. Look out from Glamour Bar's glass windows to the beautiful night scenes outside. Music concerts and song and dance performances start at 5pm and last late into the night. Expect high prices.

Dance Clubs & Discos

Due to barflies' lazy nature it is a good thing bars and the dance clubs are clustered together in groups, and it is not necessary to have to walk very far to get to one. Shanghai clubs are part bar and part dance floor, so you can be get your drink and groove on all in one place. Many clubs now are inviting a lot of on foreign DJ's which adds variety and spice to the Shanghai nightlife .So, sharpen up your moves and go join the locals on the dance floor.

Judy's Too

Located at 176 Maoming Nanlu; telephone: 021-64731417; hours of operation: 8pm-late.

Once located right beneath a police hall, Judy's Too has been in operation 11 years, and was one of the first foreign-owned bars in the city. With a look that is clearly nostalgic for 1980's music and culture, Judy's Too serves German beer and frequently attracts both internationals and people from China's literary and art circles. It can sometimes be a tight squeeze because space here is limited. This is especially true on the dance floor. Red is clearly the bar's overlying tone and the entire structure is designed around the red door, and the old Shanghai storefront. Old Shanghai streetlights can be found shining in the corners, and revelers dance on top of the round Judy's Too's symbol painted on the middle of the dance floor. A beer will set you back 20 RMB during happy hour and 40 RMB on the weekend.

M-FACTORY

Located at 170 Maoming Lu (near Fuxing Zhonglu); telephone: 021-64151088; hours of operation: 8pm-6am.

Long and narrow, this warehouse style bar has only a slim strip for a dance floor, but this does nothing to damper its popularity. Do not feel too bad if you step on someone's foot when you are dancing, because when you consider the space, it is almost unavoidable. The strange thing is that live bands also squeeze onto the narrow dance floor, sharing space with the dancers and making for a tight fit and a rather chaotic scene. When you begin to feel too claustrophobic, you can escape to the half courtyard-half patio outside where you can look out upon the city lights. Expect to pay 50 RMB per person.

Pegasus Club

Located at 98 Huaihai Zhonglu, on the second floor of the Golden Bell Plaza; to get there takes the subway to the Huangpi Nanlu station; telephone: 021-53858189.

One of Shanghai's most popular clubs known for bringing in DJ's from around the world. Hours of operation: 6pm to early morning.

100 Degrees CLUB

Located in the Xujiahui District at 10 Hengshan Lu just underneath the Zhenai Lou.

Split into the performing arts bar and the disco, the 100 Degrees Club plays some rockin' heavy metal and throws in a little hip-hop for good measure. There are a total of eight DJs at the club who switch in and out to keep the music fast and fresh. Expect to pay 70 RMB per person.

New York New York Disco

Located at 146 Huqiu Lu; telephone: 021-63216097.

Come see what a Chinese club is all about as young locals shake it while just standing still. You have to see it.

Bourbon Street

Located at 191 Hengshan Lu; telephone: 021-64737911; hours of operation: 7pm-2am.

Brimming with American-style enthusiasm, this three-storey wooden structure cannot help but attract crowds of disco-loving young people. Bourbon Street has American-style food and drinks, American music, and American-style service. Lively dance performances are the norm. As its reputation among tourists grows, however, Bourbon Streets reputation among locals falls. Expect to pay 80 RMB per person.

ROJAM Disco

Located in the Luwan District at 283 Huaihai Zhonglu on the fourth floor of the Hong Kong Plaza. To get there, take subway line one to the Huangpi Nanlu station; telephone: 021-63907181.

Personally created by the Japanese godfather of music, Komuro Tetsuya Rojam is at the vanguard of Shanghai's disco scene. Inside you will find two completely different dance floors, a variety of differently-styled bars, and over a dozen different karaoke rooms. You can enjoy a buffet with beverage for 38 RMB Monday through Friday and 60 RMB on weekends. Lady's night falls on the first day of every month. Women enjoy free entry that day. Rojam's Birthday Night is on the last Saturday of the month, and anyone celebrating a birthday that day is allowed free entry and receives a small gift.

Shanghai Tempest SOS Disco

Located in the Xujiahui District at 1111 Zhaojiabang Lu on floors five through seven of Metro City; telephone: 021-64268333.

Tempest SOS is Shanghai's largest disco with a total area of 2,100 square meters and a capacity to hold 2,000 people. Come for the eccentric parties on the weekend.

KK Super Disco

Located at 558 Kaixuan Lu; telephone: 021-62127318; hours of Operation: 8pm-3am.

Located on the north west side somewhat outside town, KK is a nice place to go if you live in the area. Here you will find the latest western and Chinese techno. Cover charge: RMB 30 on weekdays, RMB 40 on weekends.

Hit House

Locations: 1) in the Wujiaochang district at 2069 Siping Lu (near the Guoding Lu intersection). 2) Near Jingan Si at 384 Yu Yuan Lu.

Cheap drinks, fine atmosphere, and dancing. This place really gets going after midnight.

Theaters and shows

To DVD or not to DVD?

One problem that has persistently plagued China's movie industry is that movie theaters are expensive, and cheap pirated DVDs are too big a temptation to refuse. Illegally copied DVDs can usually be found circulating on the Shanghai streets within hours (and even sometimes before) a film's world premiere. Indeed, most people prefer seeing a movie in the theater, but how could anybody possibly turn down the chance of owning a movie for ten times less than the cost of a movie theater ticket?

Another factor that tends to feed the problem is that China imposes strict limits on the number of foreign films released to Chinese viewers. Most of the time, pirated DVD stores are the only realistic option for viewing fine cinema. Until somebody finds a way to bridge the gap between movie theater ticket prices and dirt-cheap pirated

DVD's, movie theaters in China will continue to be a net-loss venture.

For travelers who still want to catch a movie in the movie theater but hesitate because you do not understand Chinese, you are in luck. In the past, most foreign language films shown in Chinese theaters were dubbed into Chinese, but recently, more and more foreign language films are shown in their original language. Original language versions of foreign films can be found in such places as the Paradise Theatre, Yong Le Gong, and the UME International Cineplex. So, if virtue wins you over, and you want to skip the DVD store to see the summer blockbuster as it was meant to be seen, in a crowded movie theater with a bottle of soda and a bag of sweet popcorn, then check out one of the movie theaters listed below and enjoy a show.

For more information about ticket purchases, check out the "Around Shanghai" section of the China Daily, or read the "What's on" section of Shanghai Talk. Otherwise ask or a friend or CITS representative to help you check the listings in the local paper.

Cinemas

Paradise Theatre *(yǒnglègōng, 永乐宫)*

Located at 308 Anfu Lu; to get there take the subway to the Xujiahui station; telephone: 021-64312961 and 64742606. Enjoy a small selection of movies in English with Chinese subtitles.

Daguangming Movie Theater *(dàguāngmíng diànyǐngyuàn, 大光明电影院)*

Located at 216 Nanjing Xilu; to get there take subway lines one or two to the People's Square station; telephone: 021-63274260.

Daguangming is Shanghai's most representative movie theater, and one of the oldest movie theaters in China. Laszlo Hudec carried out the theater design and renovation infusing it with an imposing, almost arrogant, style. Decades later, theater visitors are still moved by the theater's grandness and luxury. In June 1931, the newspaper Shen Bao ran several days of full page advertisements announcing the theater's opening with the bold slogan, "The Greatest Theater in the Far East." But the ticket prices at Daguangming really took people's notice.

When the theater opened in the 1930's, the cost of a movie theater ticket in Shanghai was only half a Jiao (10Jiao make up 1Yuan or1 RMB), but a matinee ticket Daguangming's main hall would cost movie goers six Jiao, a balcony seat would cost one Yuan, and a box in the balcony would cost a full Yuan and a half. An evening show would push the price up yet another half Yuan. Between 1933 and 1942, Daguangming projected only one Chinese film. Everything else screened here were mostly American Hollywood productions. In or-

der to accommodate the Chinese viewers of American films, in 1939 Daguangming added a specially produced American-designed interpretation earpiece. The Chinese audience could pay 1Jiao for the earpiece. One of the theater personnel would narrate the different scenes and interpret dialogue. Watching a film at Daguangming became quite a status symbol, and high class internationals could always be seen coming and going from the movie entrance. Daguangming was packed every Saturday, and hundreds of cars could be seen parked along the streets near the theater. Today, both Chinese and Western films are played at the theater.

Studio City

(huányìdiànyǐngchéng, 环艺电影城)

Located at Nanjing Xilu 1038 on the 10th Floor of the Westgate Mall; to get there take the subway to the Shimen Yi Lu station; telephone: 021-62182173.

Enjoy a movie in one of Shanghai's top multiplex theaters with six big screens in Dolby surround-sound.

Ticket Prices: Prices depend on the film: 60 RMB to 70 RMB.

Cathay Theater

(guótàidiànyǐngyuàn, 国泰电影院)

Located in the Luwan District at 870 Huaihai Zhonglu; to get there, take the subway to the Shanxi Nanlu station; telephone: 021- 4040415 and 54042095.

Designed by Laszlo Hudec in 1930, the Cathay Theater is a French style construction with garnet red Taishan brick, vertical white inlays, and stair-step towers rising up from the top of the corner facade. Although not on the same level as the Daguangming Theater, the Cathay was still lavishly decorated and had over 1,000 seats. It utilized the most advanced projection equipment of its day. The second and third floors were used as entertainment and billiard rooms.

Finishing construction in January 1931, advertisements in Shen Bao declared: "The beautiful imposing Cathay theater is the king of Shanghai cinemas. It is a comfortable exquisite modern city of science". Originally located in the French Concession, the theater's American ownership hung English signs outside and hired British citizens to manage the theater. Most of the movie

theater's audience was made up of foreigners and so-called "high-class Chinese". Like the Daguangming Theater, in its early days the Cathay played mostly American films. Today you can enjoy both Chinese and foreign cinema.

Ticket Prices: Matinee features: 20 RMB to 25 RMB Evening features are 50 RMB.

Shanghai Film Art Center

(shànghǎi yǐngchéng, 上海影城)

Located at 160 Xinhua Lu; telephone: 021-62806088, Catch Hollywood releases on the big screen.

Ticket Prices: Prices vary according to the time of the show: 20 RMB to 60 RMB.

UME International Cineplex

(xīntiāndì guójì diànyǐng chéng, 新天地国际电影城)

Located at Lane 123, 6 Xingye Lu; to get there take the subway to the Huangpi Nanlu station; telephone: 021-63733333.

A theater with fully modern screens. For travelers who just can not forget about home, here you can enjoy Hollywood movies in English.

Ticket Prices: Regular Admission 60 RMB and 70 RMB.

Tickets are half price Tuesday before 7:30pm and Saturday and Sunday morning.

Kodak Cinema World

(kēdá diànyǐng shìjiè, 柯达电影世界)

Located at 1111 Zhaojiabang Lu on the fifth floor of the Metro City; telephone: 021-64268181. For more information, please visit the theater's website at: www.cinemaworld.kodak.com

This is the first Asian movie theater built to the "authorized standards of Kodak film projection" the results are extraordinary. A high-tech and imaginative facility, Kodak Cinema World has attracted waves of Shanghai youth. The newest films from all over the world are played here.

Ticket Prices: 60 RMB to 70 RMB.

The Performing Arts

For those of who want to put on nice suites and appreciate the lighter more uplifting side of culture, Shanghai offers western and eastern classical music, acrobatics, opera, and other forms of entertainment.

The Shanghai Symphony Orchestra was once one of the earliest assembled orchestras in Asia. Originally known as the Shanghai Public Band, it developed into a full orchestra in 1907, and was renamed the Shanghai Municipal Council Symphony Orchestra in 1922. Through the early leadership of Italian conductor, Mario Paci, the Municipal Council Symphony Orchestra laid the foundation for China's symphonic music tradition by both promoting western music and training young Chinese talent. The Shanghai Symphony Orchestra has been slowly gaining more recognition in music circles, especially since the release of its Oscar and Grammy winning sound track for the movie, Crouching Tiger, Hidden Dragon. The orchestra usually performs at the Shanghai Concert Hall.

Visitors and ex-pats do not have to travel back home anymore to enjoy shows like "Cats", the Three Tenors, and "Les Misérables" in new-state-in-the art theaters and auditoriums. In the realm of popular music, in recent times Shanghai has had trouble attracting anyone other than Mando-pop or Canto-pop stars to entertain its young Chinese music fans. But now, western rock, rap, and pop performers are beating down the doors, anxious to bring their music and their acts to Shanghai's shores.

If are looking to be thrilled and amazed by gravity-defying stunts, or feats of juggling, chair-stacking, and plate-spinning, then perhaps you should head out to see circus. One group worth mentioning is the internationally-renowned Shanghai Acrobatic Troupe, which now performs at its new home in the Shanghai Circus World. Performances are held Wednesday, Friday, and Saturday at 7:30pm. Check with your hotel for current schedules and tickets.

Farces *(huájīxì, 滑稽戏)*

Appearing in the 1920's, these acts are usually one-person shows. Performers speak in Shanghai or Zhejiang Provincial dialects and utilize exaggerated movements. If you are interested in Shanghai culture, you definitely want to catch one of these performances. Even if you do not fully understand what the actors are saying, you can still enjoy the dexterity of their movements and the audience's good cheer. Shanghai-style farces can be seen at the Lyceum Theater and Majestic Theater. Ticket prices usually run between 10 RMB and 30 RMB.

Tickets

Tickets for all arts performances can be purchased at the individual venues, or at the Shanghai Cultural Information and Booking Centre. Located at 272 Fengxian Lu, northeast of the Shanghai Centre, the Shanghai Cultural Information and Booking Centre can be reached at 021-62172426.

Tickets for the Grand Theatre can be purchased directly at its box office at 200 Renmin Dadao. (telephone: 021-63728701). Movie tickets can be bought right at the cinemas. If you do not have the energy to do it yourself, you should be able to get your hotel to help you purchase tickets for you. Expect to be charged a small fee.

Shanghai Concert Hall
(shànghǎi yīnyuè tīng, 上海音乐厅)

Located at 523 Yan'an Donglu; to get here, take the subway to the People's Square subway station; telephone: 021-64604699 and 021-63869153.

Come here for performances of western classical music.

Shanghai Grand Theatre
(shànghǎi dà jùyuàn, 上海大剧院)

Located at 300 Renmin Dadao; to get there take the subway to the People's Square station; telephone: 021-63728701 and 021-63728702.

This gigantic theater seats nearly 2,000 people. This is where the big names come to perform. Tickets range from the 50 RMB to the thousands for the superstars.

Shanghai Grand Stage
(shànghǎi dà wǔtái, 上海大舞台)

Located at 1111Caoxi Beilu, inside the Shanghai Stadium; take the subway to the Shanghai Stadium station;telephone: 021-64385200 and 021-64384952, ext. 2567. If you are looking to enjoy catching a rock and pop concert then this is the place for you.

Majestic Theater

(měiqídà xìyuàn, 美琪大戏院)

Located at 66 Jiangning Lu; to get there take the subway to the Shimen Yi Lu station; telephone: 021-62174409 and 021-62172813.

Catch Chinese Opera performances in this ornate old theatre. Tickets are bit pricey, ranging from 80 RMB to 580 RMB.

Lyceum Theater

(lánxīndàxìyuàn, 兰心大戏院)

Located at 57 Maoming Nanlu; to get there take the subway number one line to the Shaanxi Nanlu station; telephone: 021-62178530 ext. 210, 021-62564738 and 021-62172426.

Lyceum Theater was originally home to the British Amateur Dramatic Club, or ABC. ABC held mainly English language plays for Shanghai's British citizens, but there were also occasional performances of local plays, music, European dance, and traditional opera. Occasional movie screenings were also held here. Renowned Chinese musician, Mei Baiqi, and Peking Opera legend, Mei Lanfang both performed here. Today, you can enjoy music performances, the symphony, Peking Opera, and Shanghai farce performances at the Lyceum Theater. Ticket prices change depending on the performance. Some of the less expensive performances usually average 50 RMB per ticket. Suzhou storytelling and ballad singing usually only cost ten to 30 RMB.

Heluting Concert Hall

(hèlǜtīng yīnyuètīng, 贺渌汀音乐厅)

Located at 20 Fenyang Lu; to get there take the subway to Shanxi Nanlu; telephone: 021-62130162.

Located inside the Shanghai Music Conservatory, the Heluting's design refers to the Vienna Golden Music Hall for its auditory effect. There are music performances held daily and ticket prices range from 20 RMB to 120 RMB depending on the performance. There are music stores nearby selling mostly pianos.

Yifu Theatre

(yìfū wǔtái, 逸夫舞台)

Located at 701 Fuzhou Lu; to get there take the subay to the Henan Zhonglu station; telephone: 021-63514668 and 021-63225294. Come for the Chinese Opera performances. Tickets run 10 RMB to 500 RMB.

Shanghai Circus World

(shànghǎi mǎxìchéng, 上海马戏城)

Located at 2266 Gonghe Xin Lu; telephone: 021-56656622 ext. 2027. A must visit for those that want to see the Shanghai Acrobatic Troupe. Performances are usually held Wednesday, Friday, and Saturday at 7:30pm. Call for information on current scheduling and tickets. Tickets run 80 RMB to 580 RMB.

Go-cart Tracks

Feel the need for speed? Try out the go-karts at the following tracks.

Disc Kart Indoor Karting

(díshìkǎ sàichēguǎn, 迪士卡赛车馆)

Located at 809 Zaoyang Lu (Changfeng Park); telephone: 021-62222880 and 62857778; hours of operation: 2pm to 2am. A one-person cart costs 50 RMB per eight minutes. A two-person cart runs 70 RMB per eight minutes. At the moment, single person go-karts enjoy a "buy five rides get one free promotion".

Quyoung IB Racing Club

(IB qǔyáng kǎdīngchē jùlèbù, IB曲阳卡丁车俱乐部)

Located in the Hongkou District at 880 Zhongshan Beiyi Lu; telephone: 021-65316800; hours of operation: Monday through Thursday ten am to 6pm; Friday through Sunday 9am through 6pm.(Summer hours are slightly extended). Go-carts run from Monday to Thursday ten am to 6pm and cost fifty RMB for sixteen minutes of driving. Karts use Little Rabbit and FK9 designs.

East Asian Racing Club

(dōngyà sàichē jùlèbù, 东亚赛车俱乐部)

Located at 2100 Gonghexin Lu inside the Zhabei Stadium; telephone: 021-66527194; hours of operation: 12 pm to 6pm carts run 20 RMB per eight minutes; from 6pm to midnight carts run 30 RMB per eight minutes.

Baolu Karts

(bǎolù kǎdīngchēguǎn, 宝路卡丁车馆)

Located at 480 Yongqing Lu inside the Baoshan Stadium; telephone: 021-56117101; this is the only cart track in the China to use genuine imported German karts; hours of operation: from 2pm to 6pm karts run 20 RMB per eight minutes; from 6pm to ten pm karts run 30 RMB per eight minutes.

Jiangcheng Racing Entertainment Center *(jiāngchéng sàichē yúlè zhōngxīn, 江城赛车娱乐中心)*

Located at 3055 Zhoujiazui Lu; telephone: 021-65435182 and 021-65192503; hours of operation: Monday through Sunday from 6am to 10pm. This is Shanghai largest outdoor racing track. Prices are calculated per lap around the track. Four laps around costs 50 RMB; ten laps costs 100 RMB and one lap costs 15 RMB.

Massage

Massage parlors are a ubiquitous sight in every corner of every Chinese city. In a middle of working class residential areas, massages run from 30 RMB to 60 RMB per hour for a foot or full body massage. High class massage parlors in swankier parts of town charge 100 RMB to 180 RMB per hour. Hospitals offer massage therapy as at bargain rates (15 RMB to 30 RMB per massage), but you will need a physician to write you a prescription before you can receive treatment. If you suffer from pain in your waist or your back, or have any external injuries, do not visit a non-therapeutic massage parlor. Your best option is to visit the external medicine or massage ward at a Chinese hospital of Chinese medicine where you can receive profession care and attention.

For the Children

Shanghai Wild Animal Park

(shànghǎi yěshēng dòngwùyuán, 上海野生动物园)

Located at 178 Nanfang Gonglu; to get there take the Tourist Number two bus line from Shanghai Stadium to the Wildlife Park (yesheng dongwu yuan); telephone: 021-58036000.

Here you can take part in a Safari Shanghai style! Located 35 km from downtown Shanghai, kids can enjoy seeing wild life animals in a simulated natural habitat. Over 200 animal species such as: giraffes, lions, tigers, which can be viewed from the safety of a bus touring through the park. Admission: adults 100 RMB; children under 1.2m 50 RMB.

Dino Beach

(rèdài fēngbào, 热带风暴)

78 Xin Zhen Lu; telephone: 021-64783333

Who can resist a day at the beach? So grab your bathing suit, and head for the sand and the surf. Daily 9am-9pm. Entrance prices vary depending on the time you go.

Jinjiang Amusement Park

(jǐnjiāng lèyuán, 锦江乐园)

Located at 201 Hongmei Lu; to get there take the subway line one to the Jinjiang Amusement Park station; telephone: 021-6436495; hours of operation: 8:30am to 5pm.

This is one of Shanghai's largest amusement parks and has such attractions as a "huge skyscraping ferris wheel", "happy world", canyon rapids, "high-altitude space shuttle", a "two storey merry-go-round", and "spinning pulleys". Expect to pay 60 RMB for six rides. Tickets for single rides cost 10 RMB to 20 RMB.

Hawaii Water Park

(xiàwēiyí shuǐshàng lèyuán, 夏威夷水上乐园)

Located in the Chongming District at Huangsha Island's Dongbang Cun Village; telephone: 021-56890556.

This is a water-themed amusement park with indoor and outdoor attractions, and a natural spring. Hawaii Water Park has several water slides, and a Hawaii-themed show in the evening.

American Dream Park

(měiguó mènghuàn lèyuán, 美国梦幻乐园)

Located in the Jiading District's Huangdu Zhen town. American Dream Park is 20 kilometers outside the city center, right by 312 National Road. It is also two kilometers from the Huning railway's Huangdu Station, and three kilometers from the Huning Expressway's Jiasong entrance.

The amusement park has over fifty automated games, over 20 shows, and over 20 restaurants and gift shops.

Tom's World

(tāngmǔxióng huānlè shìjiè, 汤姆熊欢乐世界)

Located at 673 Nanjing Donglu on the basement floor of Baodaxiang Shopping Center; telephone: 021-63522813; hours of operation: 9am to 10 pm. This is one of Shanghai's early video arcades. 20 RMB will get you 40 tokens.

New York Fair

(niǔyuē jiāniánhuá, 纽约嘉年华)

Located at 1 Hongqiao Lu on the fifth floor of the Grand Gateway; to get there, take the subway line one to the Xujiahui station; telephone: 021-64079456.

The fair has a game center with nine activities including a duck pond, skatterball, Slam Dunk, basketball games, and gun ball. A combo ticket costs 25 RMB and lets you play each game once.

Sega World

(shìjiā yóuyì tiāndì, 世嘉游艺天地)

Located at 2-88 Nanjing Xilu on the eighth and ninth floors of the New World Mall. Sega World has over 100 arcade games of every size and shape including some old favorites like, Virtual Cop, Virtual Fighter Three, Street Fighter, flight simulators, and Time Crisis. Bring lots of money, because the games in this arcade run on a Western pricing scale.

alain manoukian
CHOW TAI FOOK
周大福

Shopping

Shopping

Shanghai has been hailed before as the "Shoppers Paradise" and "Oriental Paris" It is an ideal destination for those who love shopping. Shanghai has long been famous for its clothing and fashions. Its local fashion and garment industry has been China's trendsetter for decades. So, if you come to Shanghai for the historical and cultural sites, do not casually dismiss a local shopping excursion as mere consumerist trifle. From ancient Chinese artifacts to trendy western wear, Shanghai has everything that you could possibly want! Western-style shopping malls, huge department stores, small street stalls, and colorful open-air markets can be found all over Shanghai. Most shops

are open daily from10am-10pm, and also on weekends. Sunday is definitely China's busiest and craziest day to shop. Great shopping has become an indispensable part of Shanghai's tourism industry. So, take advantage of it, even if you are reluctant to do so, because it makes for a much more rewarding experience.

Shanghai is divided into a few main shopping areas. The most famous stop is Nanjing Lu, considered to be the number one commercial street in China. Nanjing Lu is lined with modern shopping malls and department stores, as well as smaller individually owned shops. The promenade on Nanjing Donglu is popular with tourists, while Huaihai Zhonglu is known for its elegance and for selling designer goods from around the world, including such brand names as Armani and Versace. For visitors more interested in crafts and wares, Hengshan Le, Shanghai's Chenghuang Miao, and the Dontai Lu curio market are three good places to go for antiques and local arts and crafts. Be sure to also take a look at Shanghai Lao Jie and Cangbao Lou, where you should be able to find ceramics, hand-made embroidery, teapots, painted fans, handbags, carpets, coins, painted snuff bottles, and peasant paintings.

Shanghai is also known for its wide range of low-priced Chinese silks. You should be able to find fabrics such as cotton, wool, and silk sold in markets or on the streets for decent prices. Shanghai is also an ideal stop for jade, gold, silver, and freshwater pearls. However, you have to be especially vigilant when shopping for jewelry, and just like in any other Asian city, bargaining is a must. Please do not mistake Shanghai with Hong Kong, as you will find no deals on electronics or high-tech goods in Shanghai. In fact they are often more expensive here than at home. But, if you need anything replaced, whether it is for your camera or your cellular phone, you should be able to find what you need. You should definitely try making a point of not focusing on the big malls, and try out the thousands of privately owned little stores that make up Shanghai. Just wander around and see where the wind takes you. Shanghai is full of great little shops just waiting for you to discover them.

Special Note

1. Bargaining

Bargaining is a skill that is necessary not only in Shanghai, but all over China. This is especially true in open air markets and places where small goods peddlers congregate. Aside from a few rare exceptions, Chinese store owners treat everyone equally. The price that they give you is just as high as the price they give their Chinese customers. In touristy markets, sometimes prices are inflated up to five or six times their actual worth. Do not feel shy or embarrassed when you bargain the price down. Most shop owners are happy to bargain with you for their goods. Please note that you can not bargain for goods in supermarkets, licensed boutiques (like an Armani or Nike store), and many state-owned enterprises.

2. Spale As the Local Saying Goes

"Everything is fake, only the fake things are real." Keep this phrase close to heart, especially in open-air markets and at kiosks near the entrances to major tourist sites. This is where many of the fake goods are usually found.

Best Places to Shop

Nanjing Lu *(nánjīng lù,南京路)*

Location: Nanjing Lu is connected directly to the Bund. To get here take subway lines 1 or 2 to the People's Square or Henan Zhonglu stations. You can also take bus lines 20, 37, 15, 18, 21, 49, 315, 330, 451, 921 to the People's Square or Fuzhou Lu stops.

At the beginning of the twentieth century, Nanjing Lu, the "paradise of foreign travelers", was one of Shanghai's representative symbols with its grand race track and famous shops.

In the 1990's Nanjing Xilu (the western end of Nanjing Lu) gradually transformed from a residential area to a commercial one, with the "golden triangle" of shopping malls, Plaza 66, Westgate Mall, and CITIC Plaza becoming established. Plaza 66 is modernist tower-style work of architecture with sky-scraping glass walls and shining main building. Designed by the American architectural firm, KPF, Plaza 66 has stores selling just about every international name brand and several of their Chinese flagship stores. In comparison, the Westgate Mall, ISTEAN, and CITIC are more down to earth, carrying middle class and upper-middle class brand names. This is where regular Shanghai people like to shop.

Wings Department Store

(hóngxiáng bǎihuò, 鸿翔百货)

869 Nanjing Xilu; telephone: 021-64870000.

A large department store with western clothes, shoes, cosmetics, and some children's clothes.

New World Department Store

(xīnshìjiè shānghcǎng, 新世界商场)

2 Nanjing Xilu;Local department store with a good selection of children's shoes, toys and kitchen tools.

The Landmark

(zhìdì guǎngchǎng, 置地广场)

409 Nanjing Donglu; telephone: 021-63513828; Dealing mostly in fashionable clothes for trendy young shoppers. Styles range from casual to business casual.

Shanghai NO.1 Department Store

(shànghǎi dìyī bǎihuòshāngchǎng, 上海第一百货商场)

830 Nanjing Donglu.

CITIC *(zhōngxìn tàikāng guǎngchǎng, 中信泰富广场)*

1168 Nanjing Xilu telephone: 021-62180180.

Plaza 66

(hénglóng guǎngchǎng, 恒隆广场)

1266 Nan Jing Xilu.

Westgate Mall

(méilóngzhèn yīshìdān, 梅陇镇伊势丹)

1038 Nanjing Xilu; telephone: 021-62187878 and 62721111.

Huaihai Zhong Lu

(huáihǎi lù, 淮海中路)

To get there, take subway line 1 to the Huangpi Nanlu, Shaanxi Nanlu, or Chanshu Lu stations.

Huaihai Zhong Lu is well-known for its great shopping malls and boutique stores selling the latest in high fashion. One such high class mall, Maison Mode, was opened in Shanghai by Hong Kong's Lane Crawford. Shanghai locals consider shopping at Maison Mode to be the ultimate in social prestige, a place where you can find clothes that are up to date with the latest fashions emerging on the streets of Europe. Beginning at the head of Xizang Nanlu there are several shopping malls that are popular with Shanghai yuppies, such as the Lansheng Dasha and Liu Lin Tower. Continuing west you will find, Shanghai Times Square, Golden Bell Plaza, Shanghai Square, Huaihai Shangdu, Lippo Plaza, Hong Kong Plaza, and Pacific Place. There is also the ISTEAN, Shanghai NO.2 Department Store, Parkson, and Printemps.

Be sure to also check out Maoming Lu, Taikang Lu, and Changle Lu area for excellent clothing shops and trendy stores. All three roads run right off of Huaihai Lu.

Pacific Place

(tàipíngyáng bǎihuò, 太平洋百货)

333 Huaihai Zhonglu, telephone: 021-53068888; Carrying top names in coswetics.

Shanghai Times Square

(dàshànghǎi shídài guǎngchǎng, 大上海时代广场)

99 Huaihai Zhonglu; telephone: 021-63910691.

ISTEAN *(yīshìdān, 伊士丹)*

527 Huaihai Zhonglu and 1038 Nanjing Xilu; Western clothes, athletic accessories and bed dressings from this Japanese-operated enterprise.

Parkson *(bĕishèng, 百盛)*

918 Huaihai Zhonglu.

Maison Mode

(měiměi bǎihuò, 美美百货)

1312 Huaihai Zhonglu, telephone: 8621-64711194.

Printemps

(bālíchūntiān bǎihuò, 巴黎春天百货)

9393 Huaihai Zhonglu.

Shanghai NO.2 Department Store

(shànghǎi dìèr bǎihuòshāngchǎng, 上海第二百货商场)

887 Huaihai Zhonglu.

Jin Jiang Dickson Shopping Store

(jǐnjiāng díshēng shāngshà, 锦江迪生商厦)

400 Changle Lu; telephone: 021-64726888.

Hong Kong Plaza

(xiānggǎng guǎngchǎng, 香港广场)

Located at 283 Huaihai Zhonglu; telephone: 021-63907181.

Lippo Plaza *(lìbǎo guǎngchǎng, 力宝广场)*

Located at 222 Huaihai Lu; telephone: 021-53965572.

Xujiahui Commercial Center

(xújāhuì shāngquān, 徐家汇商圈)

To get there, take subway line one to the Xujiahui Station, or you can take bus lines 42, 43, 15, 931, 548, 830, 824, 93, 44, 50, 02, 72, 50, 847, 572, and 926 to the Xujiahui bus stop.

Shanghai locals become nostalgic when they think Xujiahui's oldest department store, Shanghai Liubai. When it first opened, Liubai offered little more than sewing goods, bicycles, clothing, shoes, hats, and daily goods. Today, the shopping center of choice among young women is the Pacific Department Store. Other places of interest include the Grand Gateway, Metro City, Sunrise Department Store, and Huilian Store. Metro City definitely offers a captivating shopping experience. Metro City, is not just the province of the wealthy and fashionable; it is also a nice selection of goods for practical people and deal finders. Metro City's second floor sells cell phones. Computers and stereos can be found on the third floor, and the fourth floor has Scholar Book Store. Kodak Cinema World is locat-

ed on the sixth. If you want to buy gold or computers there are several stores to choose from such as Lao Fengxiang jewelry store, Buy Now computer store, Pacific Computers and Withub.

Shanghai Orient Shopping Center

(shànghǎi dōngfāngshāngshà, 上海东方商厦)

8 Cao Xilu; telephone: 8621-64070000.

Pacific Department Store

(tàipíngyáng bǎihuò, 太平洋百货)

932 Hengshan Lu.

Sunrise Department Store

(zhōngxīng bǎihuò, 中兴百货)

718 Caobao Beilu; Great place for home shopping.

Other Locations Worth Considering

Times Square

(shídài guǎngchǎng, 时代广场)

500 Zhangyang Lu, Pudong.

This modern department store in Pudong has seven floors, all very well arranged. It has everything from clothing, appliances, and toys to a food court including McDonalds. They stock good merchandise at fair prices. Just opposite to Yaohan.

Metro

(màidélóng shāngchǎng, 麦德龙商场)

Locations: 1) 1s425 Zhenbei Lu; telephone: 8621-62658888; 2) 418 Guangyue Lu in the Hongkou District; telephone: 021-65268888; 3) 80 Gudai Lu; telephone: 021-64808888; 4) 1425 Zhenbei Lu; telephone: 021-52504888.

A membership oriented wholesale warehouse. Very similar to Sam's Wholesale Club.

IKEA

(yíjiā shāngchǎng, 宜家商场)

585 Longhua Xilu; Swedish home out-

fitter well known for its affordable stylish furniture.

Friendship Shopping Centre in Hong Qiao *(hóngqiáo yǒuyí shāngdiàn, 虹桥友谊商店)*

Located on the corner of Zunyi Lu and Hongqiao Lu; carries a wide range of high-priced gift items. A western supermarket can also be found inside.

Friendship Shopping Centre On The Bund

(wàitān yǒuyí shāngdiàn, 外滩友谊商店)

40 Beijing Dong Lu. A nice place to stop for antiques and crafts.

Markets

When shopping in Shanghai's open air and wholesale markets, only one rule applies — anything goes. Shopping in street markets and alley bazaars will provide you with some interesting experiences. In these markets you can buy anything from crafts, antiques, coins to jewelry, but whether or not you come up with a good bargain depends on your bargaining skills. So, pull up your pants and roll up your sleeves, and get to it!

South Bund Cloth Market

(nánwàitān miànliàoshìchǎng, 南外滩面料市场)

Located at 399 Lujiabang Lu; to get there, you can take bus lines 65, 305, 324, 801, 868, 910 or 928.

The South Bund Cloth Market operates in wholesale fabrics selling silk, wool, tweed, cotton etc.. If you want to have a suit made, come prepared with an idea of what kind of style you want and possibly images to show and help guide the tailor. While the prices are cheap, you have to be assertive about what you want. There is no point in buying at all if you turn up with something you are embarrassed wearing. Expect a suit to take over a week. Open Monday through Sunday. Do not come on Monday, because that is the day the shop owners leave to bring in new shipments of goods.

Yuyuan Shopping City

(yùyuán shāngchéng, 豫园商城)

Located at 218 Anren Street. Come here for Chinese goods and local crafts.

Qipu Lu Wholesale Clothing Market *(qīpǔlù fúzhuāng pīfāshìchǎng, 七浦路服装批发市场)*

Qipu Lu is located at the intersection of Sichuan Beilu and Haining Lu. To get there take bus line 15 and get off at the Qipu Lu stop. You can also take lines 17, 55, 61, 100, 123, 147, and 307 to the Haining Lu stop and walk toward Qipu Lu.

The Wholesale Market is the prize of Qipu Lu. 200 RMB can get you a shirt on Shaanxi Nanlu, but it can buy you a full outfit at the Qipu Lu clothing market. The clothes that they make are of excellent quality and they

regularly receive orders from famous brand-name clothing outlets abroad. The businesses at Qipu Lu sell retail as well as wholesale. You can bargain with them too, but they will only budge 3 RMB to 5 RMB.

Dongtai Lu Antiques Market

(dōngtáilù gǔwánshìchǎng, 东台路古玩市场)

Located near the Huangpi Nanlu subway station.

Come before five pm or you will not make it before the shops clothes. Dongtai Lu is one of China's most famous curio markets. (For more information about Dongtai Lu, please turn to Dongtai Lu section right after Wenmiao and the Second Hand Book Market.)

Cangbao Lou Antiques Market

(cángbǎolóu, 藏宝楼)

Located at the eastern entrance of Shanghai Lao Jie.

More ceramics, coins, snuff boxes, and bronzes than you can imagine, this is one of the largest curio markets in China, with buyers and sellers from all over the country. Step out of the way and look on as the expert buyers go to work, appraising, examining, debating, and bargaining. If you can get up in the wee hours of the morning, come in for the ghost market, and try your hand at bargaining for that porcelain donkey that catches you out of the corner of your eye — the perfect gift for mom! (For more information regarding Cangbao Lu, please turn to the section right after Shanghai Lao Jie.)

Special note

The goods sold at the Dongtai Lu curio market and Cangbao Lou are almost all fakes. Do not be fooled.

Dimei Shopping Mall and Hong Kong Branded Street

(díměi & xiānggǎngmíngdiànjiē, 迪美与香港名店街)

Take subway line number 1 or 2 to the People's Square station. The subway station has a path leading to the store street. Just follow the signs. You can also take bus lines 18, 49, 71, 202, 127, 46, and 505 or tunnel line number six to the People's Square stop; hours of operation: 9am to 5pm.

If you long for the vigor of youth, freedom, and the avant-garde, you do not want to miss Dimei Shopping Mall and Hong Kong

上海寰球畫片公司
新記
UNIVERSAL SING KEE PICTURE CO.
TELEPHONE 99551
SHANGHAI CHINA
357 FOOCHOW ROAD
風景油畫及美術團扇承接各種印刷
本公司精出美女畫片四季屏條日曆
地址四馬路畫錦里口
電話九三五五一

Branded Street, Shanghai's two famous underground shopping centers. This is truly a new age Shanghai amusement park where you can buy inexpensive perfume, good quality nail polish, trendy, avant-garde and unique items. Everything here is fresh and out of the ordinary. Dimei and Hong Kong Branded Street are connected together and known collectively as "*xiǎo yāo dè jiē*" — Little Demon Street.

Jingan Xiaoting Market

(jìngānxiǎotíng, 静安小亭)

Located next to the Jingan Si Temple, to get here, take the subway to the Jingan Si Station.

You can find just about anything you want in this swarming market. Fashionable designs, meticulous craftsmanship, and great prices make this a prime shopping location. No wonder the locals often say, "When I get off work, if I'm not at Jingan Xiaoting, than I am on the way there!" Before you go, you had better polish your bargaining skills. Otherwise, you may become what the locals call "an onion" — a sucker.

Taikang Lu Art Stores

(tàikānglùyìshùdiàn, 泰康路艺术店)

To get there, you can take bus lines 17, 24, 96, 43, 786, 864, 869, 931, 984, and 986, the airport line number three, or tunnel line number eight. You can also take subway line number one to the Shaanxi Nanlu station.

Taikang Lu is full of art studios and young fresh designers. They are all independent artists who create original and distinctive works. All of the art work is open for public viewing. You can choose to buy or reserve a work, or simply come by to look. This street is pretty bleak in the morning. The best times to come by are between 2pm and 6pm.

Changle Lu *(chánglè lù, 长乐路)*

To get there take the subway number one line to the Shaanxi Nanlu station. When you come out of the exit, walk over from Maoming Lu.

People come to Changle Lu to buy Chinese cheongsam dresses and ceremonial outfits. This street has so many cheongsam tailors that it may be difficult for you to get your bearings at first. From materials to tailoring, to the elderly women watching the store, these stores all have a very local feel. Many young couples stop by here to check out cheongsams to wear for weddings. Other stores on Changle Lu sell blue prints, art work, and country style furniture. Bars can be seen here and there up and down the street, and little tasteful boutiques can be found nearby. There is also a rather large concentration of stores selling antiques.

Books

Go book shopping on Fuzhou Lu, right off of the Bund, or the Wenmiao Weekend book market held every Sunday at the Wenmiao Confucian Temple. If you cannot find any English language materials to satisfy you here, you can check out small book shops in the larger hotels, or branches of the widespread Xinhua Book Store, which tend to carry a selection of American bestsellers and Victorian Age novels.

Cameras & Film

As far a camera and camera accessories are concerned, anything you need you will definitely be able to find. Be warned that prices on photography equipment are similar to those in the west, so do not come to Shanghai expecting to find deals. Here you will be able to find Kodak and Fuji stores carrying brand name film, as well as Chinese store selling both local and foreign brands of film. For those needing their quick fix of pictures, 1-hour developing stores are very easy to find, especially in areas catering to tourists. For minor repairs, enquire at your hotel's front desk about the nearest location of a local camera and lens technician.

Downtown

Around The Bund

(wàitān, 外滩)

People traditionally used rivers to orient themselves in the regions that make up today's Shanghai. Upstream areas were designated as li or "inner" and the downstream was wai or "outer." Waitan, the outer shoal, is a strip of muddy land between the Xinkai and Wusong Rivers. Originally, the waitan referred to an even larger strip of land on the Huangpu River's western bank, running between the old Shanghai town and the southern bank of Suzhou River, and dividing the land into inner Huangpu shoal and outer Huangpu shoal.

At the beginning of the nineteenth century, the waitan was open countryside with bountiful traversing rivers. At that time, it became a popular spot for foreign residents to spend the weekend. They would travel in by boat, hunt birds, and have cook outs with wild game. In 1845, after a short period of negotiation, the waitan was ceded to the British, becoming part of the British Concession. Soon after, a British Consulate and a number of foreign firms began spilling into the area, building houses and towers on the Hunagpu River. That same year, the construction of the Huangputan Road came to a completion. The foreign residents called it "the Bund". The meaning of "The Bund" slowly evolved over time, referring in a more general sense to Western colonies in the Far East.

At the beginning of the twentieth century, Shanghai had already evolved into China's financial center, and large bank syndicates began large-scale construction on the Bund, putting up large luxurious mansions and buildings. What had once been a narrow stamped dirt path for boat crewman and coolies had become a forest of tall buildings, the heavily trafficked "Wall Street

Transportation

1. (Via Subway)Take the number two line to Hennan Zhonglu. Exit from the station and follow Nanjing Donglu. Traveling on foot, you can reach the Bund in a few minutes.

2. (Puxi) (By Bus) Take the tourist line number 8 or lines 20, 71, 55, 65, 37, 42, 26, 123, 135, 145, 251, 305, 311, 316, 317, 320, 330, 503, 576, 868, 926, 921, 934, or 940. Get off at one of the stations along the Bund. You can also take lines 17, 64, 801, 61, 21, 220, 939, and tunnel line number nine. You can get off at one of the many stops near the Bund and walk the rest of the way.

3. (Pudong) (By Bus) (浦东) Take the following lines to the ferry crossing at Dongchang Lu: 81, 86, 313, 338, 339, 630, 797, 818, 977, 978, switch over to the Dongjin line (traveling from Dongchang to Jinling Donglu). The ferry will arrive at the Bund.

4. (Via Subway) Take the one or two line to the People's Square or Fuzhou Lu stations.

5. (By Bus) You can take the following lines to the People's Square or Fuzhou Lu 20, 37, 15, 18, 21, 49, 315, 330, 451, 921.

6. Huangpu River Tour Boat:Short one-hour day trip. One ticket from Zhongshan Dong Er Lu to the Yangpu Bridge is 40 RMB; the two o'clock three hour boat trip to the mouth of the Wusong is 70 RMB for a lower cabin and 120 for an upper cabin (including drinks and snacks); the short evening trip, runs 35 RMB per person on a small (100 person) boat and 50RMB per person on a larger (800 person) boat. The service does not run in the winter. Operating hours: 9:30am-21:30pm

of the Far East." With its blending of the classical and the modern, today "Bund" is still an economic hub, and Shanghai's finest restaurants, bars, and clothing boutiques are almost concealed within the Bund's grand classical architecture.

Two of Shanghai's most influential streets Nanjing Road and Fuzhou Road (heretofore mentioned as Nanjing Lu and Fuzhou Lu) developed in step with the Bund. Nanjing Lu is the more boisterous of the two, typically packed with tourists year round, while Fuzhou Lu is relatively quiet. On the other side of the Bund is the Huangpu River. This heavily trafficked "golden waterway" is not only a key gateway for China's foreign trade and an important link between Shanghai's New Pudong District and the Pacific; it has also become an important venue for sightseeing. Every day, tour boats take off from "The Glory of Pudong", heading to places where Huangpu River and the Yangtze, the world's third great river, converge and meet the sea. This point, known as the "three merged waters", is located just outside the mouth of the Wusong River.

If you stand at the edge of the Huangpu River, you can peer across at the famous skyline of Lujiazui that includes the world famous "Oriental Pearl" Television Tower, the Jin Mao Tower, and the Shanghai International Convention Center.

Architecture on the Bund

The glory and refinement of Shanghai is concentrated on this stretch of the Huangpu River extending from Yan'an Donglu to the Waibaidu Bridge. This 1.5 kilometer avenue is called Zhongshan Dong Yi Lu. In the days before the Oriental Pearl Tower caised into the clouds on the other side of river, passersby would stop and gaze upon the Bund's tall buildings as they stretched out like a painted Chinese scroll. To stand before their massive ashy grey stone columns is to let your heart and mind fill with wonder. The buildings are all numbered, and we have listed them in sequential order beginning with the Asia Building at 1 Zhongshan Dong Yi Lu, and moving north along Yan'an Lu. Aside from the Peace Hotel and the main lobbies of the bank buildings, many of the buildings here do not allow visits or tours, and are strict about not allowing photography inside.

The Asia Building-originally the McBain Building

(yàxìyà dàlóu, 亚细亚大楼)

Year of Construction: 1906

Background: This imposing and refined structure is called "this premier building on the Bund" not only because it holds the most coveted address at number one, but also because when this building was originally constructed, at eight stories tall it was easily the largest and most magnificent building in Shanghai. As Shanghai developed from a township into a city, the building, originally under the ownership of the British H. Fogg & Co., transferred possession to an American company, Samuel Russell & Co. In 1891 Samuel Russell & Co. closed down, and the building fell into the hands of the Shanghai Navigation Company. What came afterwards was a revolving door of ownership which ended with building's demolition in 1913 and the construction of a newer larger building with investment from the McBain Company. The mighty British Asiatic Oil Company bought the McBain

Travel Plan

The best way to explore Nanjing Lu, Fuzhou Lu, and the Bund is to go the point where they intersect and start walking. If you want to fully immerse yourself in Shanghai's history and architecture, and also want to take some time out to go shopping and book hunting, than you will probably need to set aside a full day to explore this area. Otherwise, half a day should suffice. For those who are serious about photography, afternoon and evening is a great time to visit this area. Late scenes from the Bund have seduced many a photographer over the years, and the restaurants atop the Bund's many tall buildings are perfect spots for some high-rise photography. We suggest taking a few aerial shot from the Panorama *(hǎiwān dàshà, 海湾大厦)* near the Waibaidu Bridge.

Tourists can also be found congregating and snapping photos daily at the plaza in front of the Huangpu Park *(huángpǔjiāng gōngyuán, 黄浦江公园)*. Dusk is a great time to come if you want to avoid the crowds.

Food and Drink

Lavish upscale restaurants can be found on the Bund in buildings 3, 6 and 18. Do not expect to find any culinary bargains here. A quick detour onto Nanjing Lu or Fuzhou Lu, however, will lead you to a number of more economical eateries.

That being said, sit-down restaurants on Nanjing Lu still tend to be on the expensive side; however, cheap snack shops abound. Why not try some of the steamed buns stuffed with mustard greens *(méicài bāozi, 梅菜包子)* and roast pork tenderloin *(chāshāobāo, 叉烧包)*, or a plate of boiled Daniang Dumplings *(dàniáng shuǐjiǎo, 大娘水饺)?* You should be able to fill yourself up for 10 RMB or less.

building in 1917. At one time, Asiatic Oil Company provided China with one quarter of the nation's total oil needs. During the Pacific War, the McBain building was taken over by the Japanese, and its British staff escaped to the inland city of Chongqing. Normal business did not resume until after the end of the war. During the Bund's building exchange in 1996, the Asia Building became the headquarters of the China Pacific Insurance Company. The building stands today as an imposing and magnificent piece of architecture that remains luxurious in its simplicity. Its outer appearance is eclectic in style with a grand baroque facade. The main entrance is framed by two massive iconic columns, which at one time were hugged by two bronze placards. Afterwards, the placards were taken down and brought to the company's Yuanmingyuan office area. As historical artifacts, they are now part of the collection at the Shanghai History Museum.

"Japanese London" — the Dongfeng Hotel

(dōngfēng fàndiàn, 东风饭店)

Year of Construction: 1901

Background: Built in the Renaissance architectural style, this building's exterior is a study in British Classicism. Clear influences from the Japanese Imperial Hotel can be seen in its structure, which explains how the building received its name, "Japanese London." In its early years, this was home to Shanghai's most extravagant club, The Shanghai Club, which boasted the longest bar in the East at 34 meters. The walls of the interior in some places are decorated in the style of the British Royal Palace, and the billiard room is adorned with Elizabeth I-style fixtures. The Shanghai Club bar was frequently referred to as the "royal club" due to its King James I-era decor. "Japanese London" is also home to a triangle-shaped elevator, built over 80 years ago by Siemens. Hong Kong director, Wang Kar Wai, chose the Dongfeng Hotel to be the exterior setting of room 2046 in his film, 2046.

The Dongfeng Hotel's history does not begin and end with sumptuous colonial lifestyles and art house film, though. The building's second floor is also home to China's first KFC, the American fast food chain whose restaurants surged into China in the 1980's.

For reservations at the Dongfeng Hotel, call 021-63280018.

Mercantile Bank of India — "The Union Building"

(yǒulì , 有利大楼)

Year of construction: 1916

Background: In 1860, the British Adamson & Company constructed a three-storey wood and brick building on this spot. Though good times did not last, and in 1914 Adamson & Company went bankrupt and their office building was leased out to a consortium of Chinese insurance companies including Baoan and Baojia, who changed the building's name to Lianhe Dalou (Union Building). The structure was demolished in 1916, and a new building designed by the British Company, Palmer & Turner Architects and Surveyors, and built by the construction firm, Yuchangtai, was put in its place. At six stories tall, the new building was Shanghai's first structure to incorporate a steel framework. The steel frame was produced in the famous German Krefeld factory. In 1936 the British bank, Chartered Mercantile Bank of India, London, and China, bought part of the building's property rights for 80 thousand pounds. The Mercantile Bank of India was headquartered in London, and it's first Shanghai branch was opened in 1854.

Food and Drink

Beautifully Fragrant Roast Meat Stand

(měizhēnxiāng kǎoròupù, 美珍香烤肉脯)

Located at entrance of a food shop on 720 Nanjing Donglu (near the intersection with Guizhou Lu), Shanghai's most well-known roast meat stand serves sweet-flavored meats. Prices here tend to run a little high though. A grab-bag of samples can reach 20 RMB to 30 RMB.

Emerald Pavilion *(cuìtíng, 翠亭)*

This is a nice place to go for cheap local specialties. The Emerald Pavilion is located on Shanxi Nanlu, close to the intersection with Nanjing Donglu. Expect to pay about 30 RMB per person. Look out for their narrow staircase.

Taikang Tangbaoguan

(tàikāngtāng bāoguǎn, 泰康汤包馆)

Located at 766 Nanjing Donglu on the second floor of Taikang Food Store, Tangbao makes some great tangbao *(汤包)*, steamed dumplings filled with minced meat. Here you will be able to find authentic minced crabmeat tangbao, "xiaolongbao" *(小笼包)* — small steamed buns stuffed with crab and fresh meats, and meat and vegetable or shrimp-filled wontons. 20 RMB to 30 RMB should provide enough to satisfy your appetite.

Raffles City on the side of Nanjing Lu is the place to go for Chinese-style fast food. Here you will be able to find all kinds of cuisine including the Ajisen Ramen *(wèiqiān lāmiàn, 味千拉面)* stretched noodle restaurant among others.

Running near Nanjing Lu, Fuzhou Lu was famous in old Shanghai for its restaurants. The storied Xinghua Restaurant *(xìnghuālóu jiǔjiā, 杏花楼酒家)*, located at 343 Fuzhou Lu, was built in 1851 as a Cantonese restaurant. It moved in 1928 to the intersection of

It was one of the first foreign banks to enter Shanghai. At the end of the Second World War, the Bank reopened and relocated from its original location at Renji Street (today's Dianchi Lu) to the Bund. After the move, the building's name was changed to Mercantile Bank of India.

In August 2002, the Union Building's new owner, Singapore's Jiatong Personal Investment Company, Ltd. thoroughly remodeled the building. Armani recently opened a flagship store on the building's first floor, and the fashion master, Georgio Armani, himself has graced this place with his presence.

Nishin Navigation Company Building *(rìqīng dàlóu, 日清大楼)*

Date of Construction: 1925

Background: Also called the *Hǎiyùn Dàlóu* or Maritime Shipping Building, the Nishin Navigation Company Building was originally planned for construction by the Japanese Nishin Navigation Company. The building's design came from Lester,Johnson & Morriss. When Nishin's funding ran short, they decided to bring an outside Jewish investor into the venture. The Japanese and Jewish parties were each responsible for three of the building's six floors, and the resulting architecture was termed by contemporaries as "Japanese-Jewish" in style. The Japanese built the three bottom floors and the basement level, with exterior styling that can best be described as reserved. The Jewish group built the top three floors and paid careful attention to its ornamentation. During the Cultural Revolution the

building changed its name to Shanghai Shipping Company, and in the 1980 an extra floor was built in the east wing to house the Ocean Shipping Bureau's transmission house. A branch of Huaxia Bank occupies the building's bottom floor.

China Merchants Bank Building

(zhōngguó tōngshāng yínháng dàlóu, 中国通商银行大楼)

Date of construction: 1897

Architectural Style: In May 1897, China funded the opening of its first bank — China Merchants Bank. The original building was a three-level East Indian-style wood and brick structure, but it was knocked down in favor of a new structure in 1906 in order to keep up with the bank's rapid growth. The British company Morrison & Gratton designed the new building, and F. M. Gratton was in charge of the main design work.

Food and Drink

the Four Horse Road (today's Fuzhou Lu) and Shandong Lu. Local private houses were demolished to make way for this four-storey structure that is as wide as seven shop fronts. This establishment once hosted important figures such as government officials, celebrities, and international consuls. Xinghua still serves classic Cantonese cuisine. Their moon cakes are especially famous, and you can see long lines of people waiting to buy them during China's Mid-Autumn Festival.

Laobanzhai Restaurant

(lǎo bànzhāi jiǔlóu, 老半斋酒楼)

Located at the intersection of Fuzhou Lu and Zhejiang Zhonglu, this establishment serves Huaiyang-style cuisine. Once famed as the favorite haunt of the Shanghai literati, celebrated literary figures such as Lu Xun and Liu Yazi all came here to feast on culinary treats. In addition to its more traditional sit-down menu, Laobanzhai currently also serves Yangzhou-style. snacks such as wontons and steeped rice. Retaining its fresh authentic flavors, the fast food is a great value; you should be able to fill up on only a few RMB.

Wangbaohe Restaurant

(wángbǎohé jiǔjiā, 王保和酒家)

This well-known upscale crab house is located at 603 Fuzhou Lu, right across the street from Laobanzhai. Known as the "Crab King", the expensive and renowned crab feast was founded here. Bring a stack of cash, because you will pay between 200 and 500 RMB per person for the honor of dining here. When you are ordering, it is recommended that you stick to the restaurant's famous crab dishes. The other features on the menu are bit mediocre.

English-Gothic in style, the building exterior has many of the hallmark characteristics of European religious architecture, and Catholic styling such as crucifixes adorning the top. In 1956, work done at China Merchants Bank was allocated to the People's Bank, and the building was given to the Shanghai Changjiang Navigation Company. Today, the building is occupied by the Hong Kong Qiaofu International Enterprise Company, Ltd.

Telegraph Building *(dàběidiànbào gōngsī dàlóu, 大北电报公司大楼)*

Year of construction: 1908

Background: The Telegraph building is an outstanding example of Renaissance style architecture. Each floor is adorned with classical pillars, supports, or ornamentation, but the most striking aspect of this architecture is the multi-shaped windows on each of the building's-four sides. It is also worth pointing out the roof of the building which is designed with two Rococo-style black vaulted structures. With a history that spans one hundred years, the building has seen many different owners over its lifetime. Originally belonging to Samuel Russell & Co. enterprise, it was eventually bought out by the Shanghai Navigation Company before coming under the jurisdiction of Great Northern Telegraph Company. After World War Two, China Merchants Bank bought the building and changed its name to the New Merchants Bank Building. The building changed hands again after the Chinese civil war, and the building was taken over by the Shanghai Changjiang Navigation Company. After a property exchange in the 1990's, the building's rights of use were given to Bangkok Bank Public Co. Ltd.. The Kingdom of Thailand's Consulate General of Shanghai is located on the building's third floor.

China Shipping Merchant Company Building

(zhāoshāngjú dàlóu, 招商局大楼)

Date of Construction: 1901

Background: The China Merchant Steamship Navigation Company headquarters building is 105 years old and has a history that Chinese people can be proud of. In 1901, the first modern Chinese-managed steamship enterprise — the Merchants Navigation Company was established here. The China Merchant Steamship Navigation Company was founded by Li Hongzhang in 1887. He used 22 million 50-gram silver pieces to buy the plot of land here at the Bund number 9, and had the building designed by the British Atkinson & Dallas Architects and Civil Engineers Ltd. A three-storey wood and brick structure, two tall and spacious French windows can be found on both sides of the front entrance, and the outer wall uses a granite lining. Af-

ter two years of renovation, China Shipping Merchant Company Building is one of the few fully restored buildings found on the Bund, and it is a sterling example of turn of the century Bund architecture.

Pudong Development Bank Building-originally the Shanghai Municipal People's Government, and Hong Kong & Shanghai Banking Corporation Building *(pǔdōngfāzhǎn yínháng dàlóu, 浦东发展银行大楼)*

Date of Construction: 1923

Background: Originally a branch of the American-owned Hong Kong and Shanghai Banking Corporation, the building's owners once boasted that a more exquisite building could not be found anywhere from the Suez Canal to the Far Eastern Bering Strait. During construction, two large eye-catching copper lions were placed at the front entrance. Story has it that the copper molds used to cast the lions were destroyed in order to ensure that the lions would remain original one-of-a-kind works. The lions currently reside at the Shanghai History Museum. The main attraction here is the colorful mosaics inlaid into the ceiling of the building's octagonal entrance hall. Made of several hundred thousand tiles measuring only a few square centimeters each, each mosaic depicts scenes from eight early twentieth-century cities, Shanghai, Hong Kong, Paris, London, New York, Jakarta, Tokyo and Bangkok. Another huge mythic mural also adorns the ceiling, displaying the forms of 24 mythical animals. Feel free to step in and enjoy the Pudong Development Bank Building's magnificent lobby. The rest of the office building is, unfortunately, off limits.

Shanghai Customs House

(shànghǎi hǎiguāndàlóu, 上海海关大楼)

Date of Construction: 1927

Background: The Hong Kong Shanghai Banking Corporation's sister building, the Shanghai Customs House, has a ten-storey tower meant to be a reproduction of the clock tower found in the United States Congress Building. Construction of the clock tower was first completed in the United States and later shipped to Shanghai for installation. This, the biggest clock tower in Asia, was said to have cost a total of two thousand 50 gram silver pieces. It is one of the biggest clocks in the world.

Bank of Communications Building

(jiāotōng yínháng dàlóu, 交通银行大楼)

Date of Construction: 1940

Background: The Bank of Communications was founded in 1906, and a Shanghai branch was established that same year. In 1880 a consortium of German banks bought the property at the Bund number 14 from Dent & Co, and set up German Asiatic Bank. When the first World War broke out, the German Asiatic Bank was taken over by the Bank of Communications, and their operation was moved into the building. In 1946, the old building was torn down and a new one was constructed on the original site. This became the last building to be built on the Bund before liberation. Today it operates under the Shanghai Council of Trade Unions.

Russo-Asiatic Bank Building

(huá é dàoshèng yínháng dàlóu, 华俄道胜银行大楼)

Time of Construction: 1920's

Background: Including shareholders from Russia, China, and France, the Russo-Asiatic Bank was the first Chinese-foreign joint venture bank to be established during the Qing Dynasty. In 1896 the bank set up a branch in Shanghai, and in 1910 purchased the property at the Bund number 15. Reconstruction began immediately, and the resulting French classical architecture was complete with the heads of mythical figures sculpted onto the upper portions of the columns. The two pillars on each side of the main entrance were once decorated with exquisite statues of human figures, but they were later destroyed during the Cultural Revolution. Due to a failure in stock trades in 1926, the bank was forced to sell. It was bought out by the bank Central Bank of China (a bank personally founded by Chinese leader Sun Yat-sen), which then moved into the building. A succession of different businesses and organizations later came to occupy the building, including the Kuomintang Central Bank, Shanghai Aerospace Department, and the China Foreign Exchange Trade Center. Its final and current occupant, the China Foreign Exchange Trade Center, moved in on April fourth, 1994.

AIA Building-Originally the Guilin Building and North China Daily News Building

(yǒubāngdàlóu, 友邦大厦)

Year of Construction: 1924

Architectural Style: This was originally the home of the largest foreign news publication agency in Shanghai — the North China Daily News. Created in August 1850, North China Daily News was the earliest English language newspaper in Shanghai, and moved into the Bund in 1901. A general ban on foreign-run news reportage and the gradual disappearance of the expatriate

community, led to the end of the paper's publication in March 1951, and the building was taken over by the Inland River Shipping Bureau and the Shanghai branch of the China Silk Company. In 1996, after an exchange of properties, American International Assurance Company took over the building. The building's name later changed to the AIA Building.

Bank of Taiwan Building
(táiwān yínhángdàlóu, 台湾银行大楼)

Year of Construction: 1924

Background: Designed by the Lester, Johnson & Morriss Company and employing modern Western architectural styles, the Bank of Taiwan building was originally founded by Japanese businessmen. It widely adopted the strong points of many different architectural styles, combining them into an eclectic organic whole. Stylistically, the building was very similar to some of its contemporaries in Osaka and Yokohama. After liberation, the building was taken over by the Arts and Crafts Import & Export Corporation, and it is currently home to the Shanghai Branch of the China Merchants Bank.

Peace Hote *(hépíng fàndià, 和平饭店)*

Year of Construction: Southern building 1906; Northern Building 1926

Background: Originally called the Palace Hotel, the Peace Hotel's South building is one of Shanghai's first hotels. The International Opium Conference was held here in 1909, and in 1996 the Peace Hotel convened the Expert Meeting on Amphetamine-type Stimulants held by United Nations International Drug Control Programme. A sign was

placed to commemorate the old International Opium Conference during this meeting in 1996. The Palace Hotel is probably most famous for holding Sun Yat-sen's welcoming reception, convened by the China Alliance in 1911, as Sun left Shanghai for Nanjing to assume the office of the provisional presidency of the Republic of China.

The sumptuous and imposing North Building, originally the Cathay Hotel, finished construction and opened for business in 1929. Built by Victor Sassoon, a Sephardic Jew and a British national, the Sassoon Building at the time was the tallest building on the Bund. The Hotel interior had suites ranging in eight styles from English, American, Indian, German, and French, to Japanese, Spanish, and Chinese. On March 9, 1936 famed comedic master, Charlie Chaplin, stayed in the hotel's luxurious 5A special suite (today's room 568), as did his Modern Times female lead, Chaplain's wife and colleague, Paulette Goddard. Playwright Noel Coward wrote his most famous play, Private Lives, in the Cathay Hotel, and George Bernard Shaw stayed here in 1933. Other distinguished guests included US General AC Wedemeyer, General Marshall, Leighton Stuart, and famous Indian poet Rabindranath Tagore. Indeed, famed socialites, important Shanghai figures, and government VIPs from all over the world, have all left their footprints in this famous hotel. With over thirty movies filmed on the premises, and the recent addition of the 100 year museum, the Peace Hotel has become the silent storybook of this "shiliyangchang" — the paradise of foreign travelers.

Bank of China Building

(zhuōngguó yínháng dàlóu, 中国银行大楼)

Year of Construction: 1923

Background: The Shanghai branch of the Bank of China was founded in 1912 at 50 Hankou Lu, the former location of the Da Qing Bank. In 1923, Bank of China moved onto the Bund at the address then known as Huangpu Tan's 22 Renji Road. It is one of the few examples of Bund architecture with Chinese features.

Jardine Matheson Building

(yíhéyángháng dàlóu, 怡和洋行大楼)

Year of Construction: 1943

Background: With the opening of Shanghai's ports in 1843, foreign businessmen began opening a succession of businesses in town. Jardine Matheson & Company was one of the first companies to arrive, and it quickly became involved in a huge number of trade activities. Built in typical Renaissance style, the Jardine Matheson Building's architecture is rich in classical Western European features, which can be seen in the main entrance's two semi-circular stone arches and the twin window frames. A relief sculpture of a sheep's head sits over the building's entry way and the Corinthian columnar-like supports on the third through fifth floors, give the Jardine Matheson Building an imposing classical quality.

Meteorological Tower-Bund Observatory

(wàitān qìxiàngtǎ, 外滩气象信号塔)

Year of Construction: 1879

Background: An unexpected bombardment from a typhoon at the end of the nineteenth century led to serious losses among shipping vessels on the Huangpu River, and both foreign enterprises and steamboat companies became anxious to receive accurate local weather forecasts. On May 27, 1883, the Chinese customs funded the building of a meteorological signal tower on the Bund. The signal tower that they built was a simple wooden structure using a wooden rod as the main part of the construction. An anemoscope and wind speed meter was installed at the top of the rod, and a ball sat under the wind speed meter in order to announce the correct time.

Nanjing Lu
(Nánjīng Lù, 南京路)

Nanjing Lu, a so-called "metropolis of foreign adventurers" and a microcosm of Shanghai's 100 years of development, has once again become one of the great symbols of Shanghai. Beginning in the east at the Bund, Nanjing Lu stretches as far west as Jingan Si. While its eastern section has been separated off and dressed-up into a promenade, the rest of Nanjing Lu remains undivided in its original natural state.

150 years ago, a horse racing track was established near the area occupied by the Lihua Department Store, and a small road was built to link up the track with the Bund. This humble precursor to Nanjing Lu — officially named Park Lane — was called "horse road" by the local Chinese residents because of the westerners on horseback they would frequently see riding up and down the road. In those days, Park Road only ran between the Bund and today's Henan Lu, but because of its proximity to the race track, the street attracted network of service and entertainment businesses. In 1862, the foreign concession's governing body extended the road west across the border of the concession (today's *Xīzàng Zhōnglù*) to Jingan Si in order to help the foreign troops conveniently reach the frontlines of the Taiping Army. This new section of road was named Bubbling Well Road after the famous fountain in front of the Jingan Si Temple. Later, the road's name changed to Jinan Si Road.

As the road continued its expansion westward, at the end of 1865, the western colonials formally renamed it Nanjing Lu. Shops and small businesses rapidly sprouted up along both sides of the road, creating a flourishing strip of land across this develop-

ing city. Nanjing Lu gradually established itself as the birthplace of modern commerce in Shanghai. When you hear local people speak of the Big Horse Road or the prosperous and commercial Nanjing Lu, they are generally referring to the eastern section of Nanjing Lu.

By the 1930's, word of this "metropolis of foreign adventurers" became well known in China and abroad. Four of China's largest and most modern early twentieth century markets, Xianshi (a garment company), Yongan (today's *Huálián* Commercial Building), Xinxin (a food company), and Daxin (Zhongbai Yidian) all located on Nanjing Lu, were able to continue their thriving operations well after the Chinese civil war. To this day you can still find a number of traditional 100 year-old stores on Nanjing Lu — Pengjie Fashions, Pei Luomeng Western Clothing, Wang Kai Photography, Guan Long Photographic Equipment, Shao Wansheng Southern Chinese Goods Store, Zhang Xiaoquan Knife and Scissor store, Wu Liangcai Glasses, Duoyun Xuan, and Heng Deli Watchmaker, to name a few. Here you can also find such venerable yet striking buildings as the old Fuli Company Building (today's Jeanswest Store), Yongan Department Store, and the Peace Hotel.

Nanjing Donglu's popular bustling promenade might be worth a quick look, but you probably do not want to spend too much time there. Aside from the large crowds of tourists and shimmering Shanghai-style neon lights, the promenade has little of real interest, and there is probably little here that you could not find in any other city. On the other hand, the charming small alleys lining both sides of the promenade are definitely worth exploring. The more traditional atmosphere along these lanes is enough to make one nostalgic for Shanghai's past. Historic residential architecture on the stretch of land between Nanjing Lu and Sichuan Zhonglu such as the Jialing Building, Meilun Building, and Buneimen Building are all over one hundred years old.

Special Note

The Nanjing Lu Promenade stretches from Xizang Lu to Henan Zhonglu. The Shanghai NO.1 Department Store, Hualian Commercial building, the New World Mall, Yongan Department Store, and Shanghai Landmark Plaza can all be found on this street. Walking down to the street's eastern end will take you to the Peace Hotel and the Bund. Most of the stores on the promenade sell casual clothing suitable for young shoppers. If you can make it here during the between-season sales, you should be able to find some great deals.

The promenade also has a tourist tram that runs between 8 am and 10:30 pm. Tickets cost only 2 RMB a piece, but all in all, it is probably more convenient for you to walk.

Upscale malls on the opposite end of Nanjing Xilu include Westgate Mall, CITIC Square, and Plaza 66, which sell high-end name brand goods. You get here by taking the subway's number two line to the Henan Zhonglu or People's Square Stations or on bus lines 20 and 37.

Fuzhou Lu

(Fúzhōu Lù, 福州路)

Steeped in the history of China's literary giants, Fuzhou Lu is marked with the brands of its era and civilization. This 1.5 kilometer road is a landmark of Shanghai culture.

The tale of Fuzhou Lu, traces back to the beginnings of urban Shanghai. Before the opening of Shanghai's ports, Fuzhou Lu was nothing more than a collection of four dirt paths (called the "Four Horse Roads" by locals) leading to the Bund. By the 1850's, these four dirt paths came to be called "Evangelical Road" because Walter Medhurst, a director at the Municipal Council and a missionary with the London Missionary Society, did missionary work nearby. After the ports opened, Fuzhou Lu was scheduled for construction after Xuandao Road (later called two horse road and today's Jiujiang Road) and together with Yingda Malu (Nanjing Donglu).

Today's sleepy Fuzhou Lu, palled and plain, was once a fountainhead of Shanghai culture and literature. The fluent Chinese-speaking British evangelical missionary and sinologist, Walter Henry Medhurst, founded China's first publishing organization, The London Missionary Society Press, on a ring of land around Shandong Lu. This area eventually came to be called the Mai Fam-

ily Circle after Medhurst's Chinese name, Mai Dusi. To facilitate the propagation of western learning throughout China, Medhurst hired a group of down and out writers as his "gunners". Called the binghua bishi or Master China Writers, these highly educated writers had a strong foundation in Chinese civilization and Western culture. In the years to come, these men would become the originators of a new Shanghai culture and literature. Many of the Master Writers remained on Fuzhou Lu, establishing a large succession of the newspaper offices, book stores, and printing houses.

On April 30, 1872 British businessman, Ernest Major, founded modern China's oldest Chinese language newspaper, Shenjiang Xinbao (*Shēnbào*), on the stretch along Fuzhou Lu, Wangping Street, and Three Horse Road. The editors in chief at the time blended concepts of Eastern and Western media and formed a media company with its own Shanghai style. Chinese newspaper writers from all over the country flocked into the area, and before long, this 1453 meter stretch of the Four Horse Roads became a surprisingly boisterous collection of over 100 book and newspaper organizations. With publishing houses both big and small, the Four Horse Roads were at the veritable forefront of Shanghai publishing. The 1872 creation of Shenbao was followed in 1893 by Xinwenbao, and soon, over ten different newspapers were packed onto this small strip. Newspaper dealers would swarm the area twice a day, at dawn and in the afternoon, selling papers and creating a general hubbub.

Over a century later, Fuzhou Lu is still a publication center. The Shanghai Technology Book Company (上海科技图书公司), the Distribution Office for Business Book Printing (商务印书馆发行所), Shanghai Foreign Language Book Company (上海外文图书公司), the Shanghai Book Mall (上海书城), and the Huangpu District Library (黄浦区图书馆), can all be found here as well as a hefty collection of independent book stores and libraries.

Not surprisingly, this is a great place to come book shopping. If you do not understand Chinese, you may have to look hard to find something to interest you here. Perhaps you may stumble across a hidden gem in one of the foreign language bookstores.

Raffles City

(lǎifúshìguǎngchǎng, 来福士广场)

Located at the corner of Fuzhou Lu and Xinjiang Lu, this was once the location of Hui Le Li, known by the locals as "Prostitute's Den" due to the 151 brothels opened in the 28 stone warehouse buildings along this lane. The brothels were all shut down by 1948.

Raffles City currently occupies this former address of ill repute. This market carries everything you could expect to find in a store of its size.

Yifu Theater *(yìfūwǔtái, 逸夫舞台)*

Another of Fuzhou Lu's famous spots is the Yifu Theater (also called the Tianchan Theater), located on the corner of Fuzhou Zhonglu and Yunnan Lu. This, at one time, was the largest theater in Shanghai. In 1921, wealthy Shanghai merchant and author Li Zhiwu leased a huge tract of land along Fuzhou Lu stretching from Xizang Zhonglu to Yunnan Nanlu. He paid the English property holder a huge amount of money for a 25 year long lease, and then hired a British designer to design the theater. Construction was completed in 1925, and for a short while, it became the largest Chinese Opera Theater in Shanghai, and attracted famous artists such a Lü Mudan (Huang Yulin), Qi Lintong (Zhou Xinfang), and Gai Jiaotian to perform on stage. Famed Peking opera artists from Beijing, Mei Lanfang, Li Wanchun, and Jiang Miaoxiang also journeyed south to Shanghai to perform on the theater's new stage. The "sold out" sign became a daily fixture hanging from top of the theater entrance. Tickets for the new theater were priced at 50 pieces of gold.

In 1957 the newly formed Beijing Peking Opera Company, which included such notable performers Ma Lianliang, Zhang Junqiu, and Qiu Shengrong, performed to full houses at the Yifu Theater for two straight months beginning in April 14 and lasting until June 6. Wealthy industrialist and patriot, Shao Yifu, donated money in 1994 to reconstruct Tianchan Theater. In honor of his contribution, the theater's name was formerly changed to the Tianchan Peking Opera Center's Yifu Theater, known today simply as the Yifu Theater.

Aside from Peking Opera, the theater also holds performances of Shaoxing Opera, Shanghai Opera and others. Please visit their English language website for up-to-date information about current and future performances.

Website: www.tianchan.com/e/index.htm

Special Note

Fuzhou Lu is lined with old buildings and attractive architecture. The most famous of which can be found at intersection of Fuzhou Lu and Jiang Xilu. Built in the 1930's, these three buildings are built of equal height and similar appearance. The Hamilton House (today's Fuzhou Building) is located at the southeastern corner of the road. To the Northeast is the Metropole Hotel, and the Development Building is in the Southwest. These three structures, which fan into a U shape around the street corner, were the skyscrapers of their day. A British style bar is located on the bottom floor of the Hamilton House.

Lovers Wall

(qíngrén qiáng, 情人墙)

Nothing but painstaking effort and the indomitable Shanghai spirit could have created the lush forest on the infertile strip of land along the Huangpu River floodwall. Spanning the Huangpu River from Huangpu Park to Xinkaihe, the wall has long been the province of lovers drifting along the trees on midsummer nights. In a time when there were few places in town for young lovers to be alone, the tree lined floodwall was a natural sanctuary where young people could rendezvous. Over the course of time, the wall developed into a tourist attraction, and the government erected a sightseeing terrace for the convenience of increasing visitors. As the numbers of tourists have increased, the number of young couples along the wall has dwindled. Twilight views across the Huangpu River from the sightseeing terrace do much to compensate for the lost romance.

Huangpu Park

(Huángpǔ gōngyuán, 黄浦公园)

Built in 1886, Shanghai's earliest European-style garden bore witness to one hundred years of history on the Bund. The park which infamously hung the sign "Chinese and Dogs Not allowed" at its entrance, was at one time a humiliating symbol of European colonialism in China. But with the Monument to the People's Heroes; the large inspiring Pujiang Chao, a bronze sculpture of a worker-hero battling an ocean swell; and One Hundred Years of Shanghai Wind and Clouds — a granite relief sculpture of Shanghai's revolutionary history — things are looking a lot more positive these days in Huangpu Park.

Hours of Operation
Open from 6 am to 12 am.

Bund Sightseeing Tunnel and the Shanghai Wing of the Chinese Museum of Sex Culture *(wàitān suìdào & zhōnghuá xìng wénhuàbówù guǎn, 外滩隧道与中华性文化博物馆)*

If you are on the Bund and need to get to Pudong (Lujiazui) in a hurry, take the Bund tunnel. It will take from two to five minutes to walk through the 646.7 meter walkway, which passes under the Huangpu River and deposits you on the opposite bank at the foot of the Oriental Pearl Tower. This is also the place to come to find the Chinese Museum of Sex Culture. Located in the Lujiazui's underground exhibition hall, the Museum of Sex Culture's visitor's entrance can be found right inside the Bund tunnel. Please note that to reach the museum, you must first buy two tickets: one for the tunnel and the other for the Museum of Sex Culture.

The Museum of Sex Culture was first constructed in 1999 on the Nanjing Lu promenade. But, it attracted little interest from the Shanghai public, and was forced to move when its expenditures exceeded its income. The collections currently on exhibit include 500 works of sexually themed art by Liu Dalin, and exhibits about sex in primitive society, women and marriage, sex in daily life, and special topics in sexuality. Here you can also learn about the worship of sexuality in ancient antiquity; marriage, families, and their relation to female oppression; and religious and foreign sexual cultures.

Tickets

Tunnel Entrance Fee: 20 RMB

Tunnel Fee Plus Museum Entrance: 55 RMB

Around People's Square

(rénmín guăngchăn, 人民广场)

People's Square occupies the most central space in Shanghai. Here you will find a continuous stream of people coming and going from when the sun comes up in the morning to when the sky darkens in the evening. They are off to visit the Shanghai Museum, listen to an evening of opera at the Shanghai Opera house, or shop at one of Shanghai's hundreds of shopping centers. In this square of velvet grass and luxuriant flowers, everyone is on the move, thousands of people heading to thousands of different destinations

People's Square and the People's Park have a combined area of 140 thousand square meters, including 320 square meters of circular fountains and 80,000 square meters of green space.

Before liberation, the People's Square was ironically the location of the famous (or infamous) horse track. In 1861, director of the Shanghai horse racing society colluded with the British Consul to demand a piece of land from the Shanghai magistrate for horse racing. 31.1 hectares of land were conscripted at the lowest possible price, forcing countless numbers of farmers off their land, and building what was claimed to be the premier racing hall of the Far East.

All traces of the horse track have long since disappeared, and a new crop of structures have sprung up to take its place, beginning with the City Government Building, the new section of the Shanghai Museum, the Shanghai Grand Theater, Shanghai Art Museum, the underground mall, and Asia's largest underground electronic transformer substation. Naturally these structures have breathed new life and vitality into the Peoples' Square.

Mu En Methodist Church

(Mù ēn táng, 沐恩堂)

Mu En is arguably the most beautiful church in Shanghai. Its rhombus flower windows give it a sense of elegance and respect not usually found in many other Shanghai churches. A visit to Mu En (whose name means "bathed in grace" in Chinese) should allow you a few moments of peace

Transportation

The People's Square is located in the center of Shanghai, and connects to Nanjing Lu's promenade and the western part of Xizang Zhonglu. Transportation to and from here is extremely convenient. By Subway: Take subway lines one or two and get off at the People's Square Station. By Bus: You can reach Peoples' Square on the following lines: 123, 503, 925, 925B, 952, 952B, 112, 46, 916, the Tunnel Number Six Line, 574, 581, 201, 203, 531, 145, 934, the Tunnel Number Three Line, and Tourist Line Number Ten.

Be sure to get off at Xizang Zhonglu; you can also take bus lines 71, 127, 202, 775, 789, 831, 935, 936, and the Tunnel Number four and five lines to Yan'an Lu; or take lines 23 or 109 and get off at Huangpi Beilu; if you take lines 17 or 864, get off at the Fuzhou Lu stop.

Travel Plan

The following three attractions include museum-like exhibitions. The Shanghai Museum and the Shanghai Art Museum have year round exhibits and are especially worth visiting during special exhibitions. If you want to see Mu En Church, the best plan of action is to visit over the weekend. Mu En Church does not frequently open on weekdays.

Food and Drink

If you are looking for something to eat, you will not find a lot of choices on the Peoples' Square proper, but if you are willing to explore the immediate surrounding area you should be able to find something. Your best bet for finding a decent restaurant is probably along Fuzhou Lu and Nanjing Lu's promenade.

and serenity before you return to the Shanghai streets.

Originally, named Moore Church, the church was established as a managing hall in 1887, by C.F. Reid, a missionary with the American Methodist Episcopal Church. In 1900, the managing hall was named Moore in memory of the assistance that Arthur J. Moore provided the organization.

Originally built at the intersection of Hankou Road Yunnan Road, the rapid spread of Christianity in Shanghai lead to a dramatic explosion of church membership in 1920. The church was simply too small to accommodate such a large influx of new followers, and in 1929, a new larger church began construction at 316 Xizang Zhong Road. Finishing construction in 1931, the church showed off a new modern style of architecture, glistening with the spirit of the age.

Because of Shanghai's special topographical considerations, many churches here do not face north and south, and Mu En is no exception. Mu En's orientation is arranged so that the front of the Church faces West, making it a daily witness to the Shanghai sunset. At 3138 square meters, the Church's size is significant. Designed by the famous Hungarian architect, Laszlo Hudec, the church's makes free use of its planes and its shape, filling it with a simple and Heavenly mystery. When Mu En's construction was completed in 1931, it was widely admired as a magnificent work of architecture and the considered first among China's churches.

In 1936 money was donated to place a motorized five meter neon crucifix at the top of the spire. When the motor at the bottom of the crucifix was turned on, the crucifix slowly rotated and could be seen far and wide. Still there today, the neon cross has greatly increased the church's visibility,

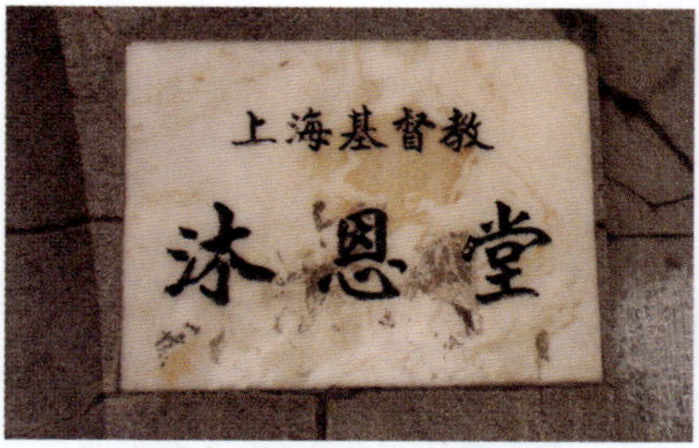

and helped spread its fame in and around Shanghai. Church services were halted during the Cultural Revolution, and for a time, the church was utilized as a subsidiary of Nanjing Middle School. Services resumed in 1979, allowing the sounds of prayer to once again reverberate throughout the Shanghai air.

Telephone

021-63225069

Hours of operation

Usually not open to the general public. Services are on Sunday mornings at 7am and 9pm, and in the afternoons at 2pm and 7pm.

Shanghai Museum
(shànghǎi bówùguǎn, 上海博物馆)

Right off the bustling din of the People's Square, the Shanghai Museum sits quietly, steeped in the profundity and dignity of history. You will notice that the round fountain in front of the museum no longer operates, and has become a temporary amusement park for frolicking children. Museum construction began in 1993 and was completed within three years. Some people claim that when viewed from a distance, the museum roof and the top of the arched door combine to form the image of a Chinese bronze urn. It can be pretty

Food and Drink

Maxims *(mǎkèxīmǔ xīcāntīng, 马克西姆西餐厅)*

Located on the Shanghai Grand Theater's eighth floor banquet hall, this restaurant serves decent French cuisine, but its main attraction is probably the incredible panoramic view of the People's Square off of the restaurant's terrace.

If you need a fix of mainstream caffeine, there is a Starbucks coffee house located diagonally across from the theater. It is a nice place to kick back with a cup of coffee and let your mind wander as you watch the late afternoon sun slowly droop toward the horizon.

Huanghe Road's Food Street
(huánghélù měishíjiē, 黄河路美食街)

Huanghe Lu's Food Street is no longer as popular as it was in its heyday, but it is still worth a visit at nightfall when the street is ablaze with lights. It does not matter if you are looking for Shanghai, Sichuan, or Cantonese Cuisine; you can find it all here for reasonable prices. There are a few western restaurants at the head of the street, the most noticeable of which is the Taco Bell Mexican Restaurant.

The restaurants along Huanghe Lu will not blow you away with their unimposing store fronts, but their many charms become apparent when you step inside. Most eateries here are built in multiple storied buildings, so if the bottom floor of your favorite establishment seems full, than you can always check for an open table on the second or third floor. One thing to look out for is the particularly annoying restaurant solicitors along the road. Usually young males, these hawkers tend to camp out near the Taisheng Yuan Restaurant *(苔圣园)* at the top of the street. When pedestrians pass by, the men will dart in, one from the right and one from the left, and try to convince you to come over to their places of business. If you are wandering through the area without a set destination, this can be a somewhat disorienting experience.

hard to see without a fruitful imagination. In reality it resembles something like a flat pan with ears.

Museum collections include 120 thousand priceless artifacts with a focus on ancient Chinese bronze ware, ceramics, and historical paintings and calligraphy. The bronze collections are made up of pieces from collectors in Southern China, and artifacts discovered after the 1930's. Objects of particular interest are the famous Dakeding urn and a collection of Hunyuan ritual vessels including an extremely intricate sacrificial wine vessel. Ceramics collections primarily include rare works from southern China, prehistoric carved ceramics from the ancient Liangzhu culture, and primitive celadon ware. Spanning Yuan, Ming and, Qing Dynasties, pottery from the famed Jingde Zhen Jiangxi pottery center has already been placed in its own independent collection. The painting and calligraphy collections also lay claim to a large number of priceless southern Chinese works. For coins, jade, and other antiques, the museum's new wing has a great preservation system.

To get the most out of your museum visit, it is essential that you take the museum's audio tour. Each showroom provides a small, lightweight, prerecorded listening device that explains the history and significance of the artifacts on display. All you have to do is punch in an artifact's identification number, and then you can listen to a detailed explanation. Listening devices are provided in English, Chinese, and a variety of other languages.

The Shanghai Museum is divided into five different levels, including four aboveground floors and one underground level. Its 12 different showrooms are divided by topic. Ancient Chinese bronze ware, sculpture, and the large exhibition hall can be found on the first floor. The second floor houses ancient ceramics and the Zandelou ceramic wing and exhibition hall. Historical calligraphy, paintings, and Chinese seals are found on floor three, while ancient jade, coins, Ming and Qing Dynasty furniture, and the minority crafts exhibit and exhibition hall are located on the fourth floor.

Address

201 Renmin Dadao

Hours of Operation

Every day from 9am to 5pm. (Ticket sales end at 4 pm. The museum stays open until 7pm on Sunday.)

Telephone

021-63723500

Tickets

20 RMB, children and student tickets are five RMB. Groups of over 20 people will receive a 10% discount. Seniors and military personnel are allowed free entry. You are also allowed entry with a Shanghai Culture Tour Pass and Shanghai Peoples' Square Tour Ticket. The former can be purchased for 50 RMB, and includes entry to the Shanghai Grand Theater, Shanghai Museum, and Shanghai Museum of Art. The later can be purchased for 60 RMB, and includes entry into the Shanghai Grand Theater, Shanghai Museum, and the Shanghai Urban Planning Centre.

Food and Drink

Chicken Hotpot *(Chóngqìng jīgōngbāo, 重庆鸡公煲) (84 Huanghe Lu)*

People come to this restaurant for their signature Jigongbao Chicken *(jīgōngbǎo, 鸡公煲)*. Cooked in a chaffing dish, you stew bits of chicken and vegetables yourself as you would with any hot pot. This is a place where you can get great value for your money.

Bandao Restaurant

(bàndǎo jiǔlóu, 半岛酒楼) (95 Huanghe Lu)

Bandao Jiulou is the busiest place on Huanghe Lu, and its easy to see why. This restaurant serves great local dishes at great prices. Some interesting entrees to try include the drunken shrimp, garlic ribs, crabs, and the cilantro with shredded snail meat.

Taisheng Yuan Restaurant

(táishèngyuán, 苔圣园) (50 Huanghe Lu)

This traditionally run restaurant serves local Shanghai fare. We suggest you try the steamed scallops in butter; and the beef ribs with black pepper.

Xiaonanguo Restaurant

(xiǎo nánguó, 小南国)

Located between214-216 Huanghe Road. Xiaonanguo is a chain restaurant found all over Shanghai. The original restaurant is located here on Huanghe Roda. Xiaonanguo serves authentic local cuisine. Try the crabmeat tofu , drunken chicken, and crabs. Prices here tend to run a bit high. Expect to pay 100 RMB per person.

Jiajia Tangbao *(jiājiā tāngbāo, 佳家汤包)*

This is a restaurant of the people that will never go out of style. Every night you can see a classic scene play itself out as card-playing customers lounge around waiting for their number to be called. The tangbao here come in with three different fillings, shrimp, pork and crab. We recommend you go for all three. Expect to fill up on about 10 RMB per person.

Shanghai Urban Planning Centre *(shànghǎi chéngshì guī huà zhǎnshìguǎn, 上海城市规划展示馆)*

Centered on the themes of city, people, environment, and development, this exhibition uses high-tech displays give you an understanding of Shanghai's huge post-liberation achievements in construction. It also provides a grand blueprint of Shanghai's century spanning development, giving you an introduction to the great destinations of the past, present, and future. The center's basement level has a 500th scale recreation of 1930's Huaihai Road. Though not large in size, the model still includes such details as trolley cars, rickshaws, and old stores.

Address

Huangpu District, 100 Renmin Dadao

Hours of operation

Wednesday through Sunday 9am- 4pm

Tickets

25RMB, free entry for children under 0.8 meters tall, Children accompanied by an adult are allowed free entry with the presentation of a valid student ID. Tickets run 20 RMB per person for groups of over 20 people.

Shanghai Art Museum *(shànghǎi měishù guǎn, 上海美术馆)*

Established in 1956, this grand hall is dripping with artistic ambiance. Once known as 325 Nanjing Xilu's Kangle Restaurant, Shanghai Mayor Chen Yi hosted the dedication and ribbon cutting ceremony when this building was converted into the Shanghai Art Museum. Eventually the museum's collections outgrew the museum's size and facilities, and it was rebuilt in 1986 at its original Nanjing Xilu location. The new museum preserved and expanded upon the original structure of this 1930's English-style building, keeping its red brick and iron railing. Not counting the old clock tower, the art museum's main building is four stories and 21 meters tall, and still retains a portion of its old basement level. Today, the museum's collections include over 4,000 pieces, and they are definitely worth exploring. With frequent activities and visiting exhibitions, there is also a nice variety of things to see in addition to the main collections. The Shanghai Biannual Art Expo is held at the Shanghai Art Museum every two years. For more information about upcoming events please check out the museum's web site at: www. cnarts.net/shanghaiart/.

The Shanghai Theater Art Gallery sits right next to the art museum. The Gallery holds frequent exhibitions, and many of the original works on display are for sale. If you have time, stop in for a look.

Address

325 Nanjing Xilu, located next to the Shanghai Theater.

Telephone

021-63272829

Hours of Operation

9am-5pm (Museum does not allow in new visitors after 4pm)

Tickets

Tickets are 20RMB each. Student tickets cost five RMB, and seniors over 70 years of age, military personnel, the disabled, and retired cadres with valid identification may enter the museum free of charge. Tickets for special exhibitions are sold separately.

Park Hotel
(guójì fàndiàn, 国际饭店)

During the fifty year span from the 1930's to the 1980's, the Park Hotel was one of Shanghai most identifiable buildings. The hotel's origins trace back to a four-bank savings society established in 1923 by Dalu Bank, Yanye Bank, Jincheng Bank, and Zhongnan Bank. The savings group attracted over five million Yuan in investment to build an imposing building near Huanghe Lu. Originally meant to be called "The Twenty-two Floor Shanghai Four Banks Savings Building", during preparations for the building's construction, one of the saving's society's charter members, Wu Dinghang, was told that he would make more money if he built not an office building, but a luxury hotel. Wu took the advice to heart and decided to build the Park Hotel instead. Daguangming Movie Theater designer, Laszlo Hudec, was hired to design the building, and construction of the building's foundation started in May 1931. The result was a study of American skyscraper architecture, utilizing its three-dimensional feel to great effect. The Park Hotel quickly became a popular destination for Chinese and international military officers, political VIPs, and celebrities.

The Park Hotel's significance is not limited to banking history and famous hotel guests; the building also played an important role in surveying Shanghai's geography. In November 1950, the Shanghai government's land administration bureau used the Park Hotel's flag pole as a zero center point for the first official survey of Shanghai's geography and in the establishment of Shanghai's first plane coordination system. During the Hotel's remodeling in October 1997, this fact was commemorated with placard in the hotel lobby directly under the flagpole with the designation "Shanghai's Zero Center Point" To learn more about the Park Hotel please visit their web page at: www. parkhotel. com. cn.

Address

170 Nanjing Xilu

Around Lujiazui

(Lùjiāzuǐ, 陆家嘴)

Huangpu River cuts through the middle of Shanghai, splitting it into two geographical and thematic halves. History is found in Puxi off the river's western bank; the future can be found in Pudong, a vast tract of land to the river's east. Lujiazui is one of the representatives of this future. This bright, brand-new, skyscraping place interacts coolly with the people who go there. For those revolving around its modernist orbit, it is often hard to locate Lujiazui's human touch.

But, what Lujiazui lacks in emotion, it makes up in bustle and impressive architecture. Shanghai's most avant-garde structure, the Oriental Pearl Tower, towers over the masses of Pudong residents emerging from and disappearing into the Huangpu River Tunnel. Here you will also find other major elements of the Pudong skyline such as the Shanghai International Convention Center and the imposing 88 storey Jin Mao Tower. Each is an ideal place to stop in and enjoy bird's eye view of Shanghai.

Oriental Pearl Television Tower *(dōngfāngmíngzhū guǎng bō diànshìtǎ, 东方明珠广播电视塔)*

From the Bund you can gaze out onto Oriental Pearl, this ball-shaped structure that reaches into the clouds. At 468 meters tall, the Pearl is the tallest tower in Asia and third tallest building in the world. The 50 person two-storey high speed elevator takes tourists up to the ball's 263 meter-high sightseeing level at a rapid 7 meters per second. On sunny days, you can take in the entirety of Shanghai's grand scenery with a mere tilt of the head. The Shanghai Municipal History Museum is located inside the tower's middle "pearl". Here you can learn about Shanghai's last one hundred years of development.

Address

1 Shiji Dadao

Telephone

021-5879188

Hours of Operation

8am-9:30 pm

Transportation

Take the Subway number two line and get off at the Lujiazui station. From the Bund you can arrive on foot by simply crossing the sightseeing tunnel under the Huangpu River. Bus lines to Lujiazui include, 583, 621, 623, 776, 778, 870, 872, the Shengao Line, and the Jiangyuan Tourist Line (get off at the final stop, Binjiang Dadao), 82, 85, 581B, 795, the Lujiazui Huanxian Loop Line (get off at the final stop, the Lujiazui subway station), 81, 797, 983, the Number 3 Tourist Line, and the Jinjiang Tourist Bus.

Travel Plan

Shanghai Ocean Aquarium and the Shanghai Natural Wild Insect Museum visitors aside, most people come to Pudong to gaze out onto the Bund's evening skyline. Of course, you should also make time to ascend to the top of the Jin Mao Tower or the Oriental Pearl Television Tower. The best time to do this is in the late afternoon or early evening right before the sun sets. At this time, you will witness the sky fill with the afterglow of the setting sun, and the Bund fade into an inky black at your feet. Wait for a minute or two, and in the twinkle of an eye, you will see the Bund's colorful lanterns magically light up together. Admirers of modern architecture will enjoy exploring Jin Mao Tower. You can choose to go to Cloud Nine Bar on Jin Mao's 87th floor or to the bar on level 56. Both bars have minimum expenditure requirements for those who are not guests at the hotel. Nevertheless, it is a real treat to relax in one of the two places with a beer or coffee and stare out onto the evening sky.

Shanghai International Convention Center

(shànghǎi guójì huìyìzhōngxīn, 上海国际会议中心)

Spanning 110 thousand square meters, the Shanghai International Conference Center building has over 30 conference rooms; each has a total capacity that ranges from 50 to 800 people. The last FORTUNE Global Forum of the twentieth century was held here in September 1999.

Address

2727 Binjiang Dadao

Telephone

021-50370000

Hours of Operation

8:30am- 4:30pm

Tickets

50 RMB; tour groups of over 20 people pay 45 RMB per person; seniors with valid ID and children under 1.2 meters tall pay only 25 RMB per ticket (Only tour groups are allowed to book in advance. Prior confirmation is required before visiting.)

Jin Mao's 88th floor Observation Deck

(jīnmào 88céng guānguāngtīng, 金茂88层观光厅)

Since becoming fully operational in 1999, the Jin Mao Tower with its 420.5 meter height and its blend of avant-garde and classical architectural styles has become one of Shanghai's most representative pieces of modern architecture. The proud work of the world-renowned architectural firm, Skidmore, Owings & Merrill, Jin Mao de-

Tickets

A 50 RMB ticket will take you to the 263 meter observation level in the first ball. You will need 85 RMB for entry into the Shanghai Municipal History Museum in the second ball. 100 RMB will take you to the third and highest ball.

rives its basic design elements from an ancient Chinese pagoda, and blends them with modern concepts. It is currently the fourth highest skyscraper in the world.

The Jin Mao Tower is made up of office buildings, the Shanghai Grand Hyatt Hotel, and observation decks, the highest of which is located on the 88th floor, 340.1 meters off the ground. It is the highest observation platform in China and its views of Puxi are spectacular. Glass walls in the deck provide the largest possible field of vision. Two high-speed elevators, traveling at 9.1 meters per second, will rocket you to 88th floor in 45 seconds.

Address

88 Pudongshiji Dadao

Telephone

021-50475101

Hours of Operation

8:30am-9:30pm

Tickets

Tickets for the 88th storey observation deck 50 RMB; children: 25 RMB; students with a valid student ID: 25 RMB

Food and Drink

There are fewer people in Lujiazui than on the Western bank of the Huangpu River, and, not surprisingly, there are fewer dining options as well.

Lujiazui Food Street

(Lùjiāzuǐ měishíchéng, 陆家嘴美食城)

Located in the heart of the Lujiazui financial district, there are over fifty eateries in this plaza serving a diverse array of cuisines. If you are in the mood for a dance or a stiff drink, you should be able to find bars and discos here as well.

There are also a number of restaurants to check out in the 88 storey Jin Mao Tower. Each establishment offers stunning panoramic views of city. Some of Jin Mao's more interesting choices include, **Cucina** *(yìlú, 意庐)*, an Italian restaurant with a wood-burning pizza oven, **Kobachi** *(rìzhēn, 日珍)*, a Japanese restaurant where fresh sushi and barbequed chicken are prepared right before your eyes, and **The Grill** *(shāokǎo cāntīng, 烧烤餐厅)* for great steaks and seafood.

Shanghai Ocean Aquarium

(shànghǎi hǎiyáng shuǐzúguǎn, 上海海洋水族馆)

"Traversing Five Continents with the World of Water" is the theme prominently on display at the Shanghai Marine Aquarium. The aquarium is divided into 28 separately themed exhibition areas, which are clustered within eight larger subject areas: Asia, South America (Amazon), Australia, Africa, cold water, the poles, sea water, and deep sea. Here you will find over 300 hundred different aquatic species from four oceans and five continents, as well as over 10,000 rare and endangered fish. Of particular interest are the poison arrow frogs, jellyfish, sunfish, leafy sea dragons, monarch penguins, and albino giant perchs. This is currently the largest scale modern marine aquarium in Asia.

The aquarium has four tunnels, totaling 168 meters in length, with 180 degree and 270 degree panoramic viewing windows.

Address

158 Yincheng Beilu, next to the Oriental Pearl Tower and the Jin Mao Tower.

Telephone

021-58779988

Hours of Operation

9am-9pm

Tickets

Adults 110 RMB, Children under 1.4 meters 70 RMB

Shanghai Natural Wild Insect Museum

(shànghǎi yěshēng kūnchóng guǎn, 上海野生昆虫馆)

If you like insects, you can not miss the Shanghai Natural Wild Insect Museum. The fact that a place like this exists on Lujiazui is truly something to rejoice. Displays here are divided into specific exhibitions: the insect corridor, butterfly valley, amphibian and reptile cave, interactive ecological zone, interactive water zone, tropical rain forest zone, insect salon, and science classroom. Not only can you view and interact with lifelike insects, you can also create your own insect specimens. Species of insects on display vary throughout the four seasons, and as a result, the insect museum presents you with different seasonal charms and attractions throughout the year.

Insect salons are held frequently in order to encourage interaction between Shanghai's amateur entomologists.

Address

1 Fenghe Lu, Pudong New District

Telephone

021-58405921

Hours of Operation

9am-5pm (open until 5:30pm on weekends.)

Tickets

Adults 35 RMB, Children 20 RMB

Around The City God Temple (Chénghuáng Miào, 城隍庙)

Most cities have places that seem to naturally invoke nostalgia and memory in the people who visit. In Shanghai, Chenghuang Miao is without a doubt, the place that most inspires a longing for the past.

Chenghuang Miao began its evolution from temple to marketplace during the reign of Qing Dynasty emperor, Qian Long. At that time, there was a period when the famous Yu Yuan Garden had been converted into Chenghuang Miao's "West Garden". In 1855, Yu Yuan's newly restored Huxin Ting Pavilion was converted into a tea house, and brought the first whiff of business into the West Garden-Chenghuang Miao area. From then on, business began to flow in, transforming this former gateway to the spirit world into a bustling market.

In the early days, Shanghai people residents loved coming to the Chenghuang Miao. Anything that anyone could possibly want to buy was sold right around the temple; there were tea houses, restaurants, stalls filled with goods, general merchandise, and snacks. Craftsmen would also collect along the entrances to the lanes and alleys nearby, fixing bowls and plates, fixing barrels, kneading dough boys, providing letter writing services, performing tricks, pulling teeth, and telling fortunes. These roadside merchants and craftsmen have long since disappeared into the tides of history, becoming nothing more than a part of our written and oral memory. They have been replaced with large stores and seemingly ubiquitous small souvenir shops. Today there are no traces of the Chenghuang Miao's famous curio market on Fuyou Lu, but you can now find the "treasure building", Cangbao Lou, which is widely influential in the curio world. The burgeoning Shanghai Lao Jie (the Shanghai "Old Street"), Fuyou Street Market, Fuyuan Mall, crystal-selling street, and other streets selling small merchandise, make up the fresh new face of today's Chenghuang Miao.

Transportation

Chenghuang Miao is located at 1 Yicheng Lu in the Huangpu District. You can get there by taking bus lines 932 and 569 to their final stops (the Fuyou Lu — Lishui Road intersection and the Henan Nan Road — Mingxing Jie intersection respectively). You can also take bus lines 11, 64, 126, 736, 801, 831, 920, 926, 930, and the Jinjiang Tour Bus to the Xinbeimen stop on Renmen Lu, or lines 64, 66, 929, and the Fangchuan Line to the Fuyou Road stop on Henan Nan Road. There are parking lots on Fuyou Road, Jiuxiaochang Road, and Henan Nan Road (near Dajing Road).

Travel Plan

Most tourists in Shanghai justifiably give primary status to visiting Chenghuang Miao and Yu Yuan Garden. If you have an abundant amount of time, it is worth giving yourself a full day or two to thoroughly immerse yourself in these places. However, if you are on a limited schedule, you should still set aside at least half a day to spend in the temple and the garden. You can use the rest of your day to explore the curio markets on Dongtai Lu and the Wenmiao Confucian Temple. If you have a little bit more time, you can also check out the Little Peach Orchard Mosque, The Old City Wall-Dajingge, the Shanghai Natural History Museum, and spend some time strolling through the lanes and alleyways in Dongjiadu. For those visiting Shanghai on the run, you can limit your visit to the alleys and lanes between Chenghuang Miao and Dongjiadu, representing some of the oldest lifestyles in Shanghai. Before you head out, remember take your camera, video camera, and plenty of film.

The City God Temple
(Chènghuáng Miào, 城隍庙)

Chenghuang Miao can be traced back to Late-Yuan/Early-Ming Dynasty figure Qin Yubo. An official during the troubled times of the Yuan Dynasty, Qin eventually gave up his high position, and escaped to what was then the small town of Shanghai. The Ming Dynasty was later ushered in with the ascension of its first ruler Zhu Yuanzhang who implored the talented and scholarly Qin Yubo to come back and claim an official post in his government. Qin Yubo at first refused the request, but under the threat of death, he eventually had no choice but to comply and join the Ming Dynasty rulership. After Qin's death, Zhu Yuanzhang conferred him the post humus title, Chenghuang Zhishen — Shanghai's god of the city.

Shanghai's Chenghuang Miao temple was finally created during the reign of Ming Ruler, Yong Le (1403-1424). The county magistrate, Zhang Cunyue, decided not to build a new temple from the ground up, but to have the Jinshan Spirit Temple converted into the Chenghuang Miao. To do this, the statue of Huo Guang, (the area's Guardian General) who was worshipped in the Jinshan Temple, was moved to the front of the temple and the statue of Qin Yubo was placed in the back. Over the course of history, the temple was destroyed and rebuilt a number of times, but during the temple's latest construction, not only was the temple's audience hall and central chamber rebuilt, but the rafters and ridgepoles were painted, the tiles were painted green, and the eaves colored red. Other halls such as the Royal Mausoleum, Constellation Hall, Yama's Palace, Temple of the God of Wealth, Wenchang's Palace, Immortal Xu's Hall, and Yuqing's Palace were added on to expand the temple. At the end of the Second World War, people started referring to Chenghuang Miao Temple as the Old Chenghuang Miao in order to differentiate it from the Chenghuang Miao market area at Jinlin Xilu and Lianyun Lu.

Chenghuang Miao still occupies a sacred place in the hearts of elderly Shanghai residents. At every holiday, the devout step up to the entrance of the temple, buy packs of incense and make wishes in front of the City God Temple. The curling smoke of their burning incense carries their wishes fluttering high up into the Shanghai sky.

Yu Yuan Garden

(yù yuán, 豫园)

Chenghuang Miao is the bustling marketplace and Yu Yuan Garden is literary and refined. Both are neighbors, sitting side by side, but between them are clear and definite boundaries. Yu Yuan is like the dim sum of Shanghai. There are no grand large masterpieces here, but you will find small elegant paintings around every bend and turn. When winter draws to a close, plum blossoms come into full bloom in the white snow. White walls, black tiles, withered plum branches, and luxuriant red and white plums coordinate masterfully with Yu Garden's red and black window lattices. Quiet green waters are so dark that they appear almost black. The trees are such a deep shade of green that they could be either flourishing or depressed. Mountain stone is overcast in grey, but nevertheless is full of character. Imagine a scene from ancient times when the snow's intermittent fall would leave the

Food and drink

The snack stalls and snack shops at Chenghuang Miao have a splendid reputation. Here you can find: New Year's cake, *xièkéhuáng (蟹壳黄)* crisp rolls with a sesame crust, sweet fermented glutinous rice with rice flour dumplings, stinky dry tofu, roasted sweet potato's, hot ginkgo nuts, water chestnuts, and pear syrup candy. Most of the snack stands are concentrated in the area near Chenghuang Miao and the Bridge of Nine Turnings.

Nanxiang Steamed Bun Shop

(nánxiáng mántóu diàn, 南翔馒头店)

Located on the side of the Bridge of Nine Turnings, this shop focuses its business on small crab meat filled steamed buns *(xièfěn liǎolóng bāozi, 蟹粉小笼包子)*. Everyday, you can see a long line of customers here, and piles upon piles of food steamers in front of the glass window. A steamer full of steamed meat buns costs between 20 RMB and 30 RMB. Nanxiang also has two crab meat bun set lunches that cost 50 and 150 RMB respectively.

ground wet and slick, and the air was filled with songs about beautiful young women.

The story of Yu Yuan Garden begins with a dutiful son. During the reign of Ming Dynasty Emperor, Jia Qing, Pan Xuduan, an official in Sichuan, decided to prove his filial piety by building his parents a private garden in the town of Shanghai. Construction began in 1559, and it quickly turned into a tremendous project, taking almost 20 years to complete. The layout did not fully come under control until 1577, the fifth year of Emperor Wanli. Pan Xuduan decided to name the garden with the character "Yu" from the famous saying, "Yuyue Shuangqing,Yiyang Tiannian" or "make your parents happy, and care for them in their old age". Sadly, Pan's parents died before the garden was finished.

At the beginning of the Qing dynasty, the Pan family fell on hard times. Without funds to properly manage and renovate Yu Yuan Garden, it gradually fell into abandonment and ruin. Pan Xuduan's descendants sold the garden at a low price, and the garden's serenity slipped away as it converted into management and administration center for a local guild. Between the 19th century Opium Wars and the Small Sword Society uprising, Yu Yuan Garden was heavily contested territory, and eventually became an encampment for foreign invaders. In 1958, Yu Garden was classified as one of Shanghai's major cultural preservation units, and was finally allowed to rise again after years of oppression.

Sansui Tang Hall *(sǎnhuì táng, 三穗堂)*

Sansui Tang is an important component of this "mountain forest in the city." Yangshan Tang hall makes up its bottom floor and Juanyu Lou is at the top. A water pavilion sits to Sansui Tang's rear. Follow the winding corridors and climb up to Juanyu Lou. From here you can look out on the idyllic landscape of mountains and lakes, and the speckles of duckweed floating upon the Lotus Flower Pool. Across the river stands an ornamental mountain of piled Wu Kang yellow stones shipped in from Zhejiang. Renowned Ming Dynasty horticulturalist, Zhang Nanyang, was responsible for the mountain's meticulous arrangement.

CuixiuTang Hall *(cuìxiù táng, 萃秀堂)*

Start in Cuixiu Tang and pass through the Moon Gate. Going behind a buttress of the Dragon Wall will take you to Dianchun Tang Hall. When the Small Sword Society started an uprising in September 1863, they established a government office in the Dianchun Tang.

Yuhua Tang Hall *(yùhuátáng, 玉华堂)*

The Yuhua Tang interior is decorated with a set of Ming Dynasty furniture constructed completely of red sandalwood. Its exterior is fronted by the graceful and elegant figure of exotic stone. Measuring 3.3 meters tall and weighting in at 500 kilograms, this three million year old stone is pitted with 72 small holes. Called the *Yùlínglóng*, this stone has the prized characteristics of being slim, wrinkled, and translucent — called the "three types of beauty". Yulinglong

Food and drink

Lübolang restaurant *(Lǜbōláng, 绿波廊)*

Specializing in local Shanghainese cuisine, for 20 years this restaurant has hosted such luminaries as Queen Elizabeth, Japanese Prime Minister Takeshita Noboru, Argentinean President Carlos Menem, Cuban leader Fidel Castro, American president Bill Clinton and over 40 other distinguished guests. American President Bill Clinton, who came to Shanghai in 1998, was the most recent big name to visit Lübolang. President Clinton's "working lunch" of soybeans and pickled vegetables *(xiáncài máodòu, 咸菜毛豆)* and spicy chicken cubes (*gōngbǎo jīdīng, 宫保鸡丁*) received strong praise. Despite practicing with chopsticks a full month before his visit, President Clinton went through three pairs before finishing his sweet osmanthus cake *(guìhuā lāgāo, 桂花拉糕)*. Afterwards, Lübolang publicized this visit as the "President's Set Lunch", and took advantage of the opportunity by taking the president's photo and hanging a blown-up autographed version at the restaurant entrance. This occasion has greatly increased Lübolang's publicity in Shanghai. You probably will not be surprised to hear that prices here are expensive. Nevertheless, the food is pretty good. We recommend trying the crab-meat steamed buns, minced crab meat with heart of cabbage, duck tongue in soy sauce, and other special local dishes.

Huxin Ting Tea House

(húxīntíng chálóu, 湖心亭茶楼)

This well-established tea house hosted the Queen of England during the 1980's. If you are lucky, when you visit you might be treated to a musical performance with bamboo instruments. As you would expect, prices here are not cheap, so be prepared to spend a lot of money. A cup of tea will set you back at least 50 RMB. For snacks, we recommend trying the quail eggs, *zòngzi* (*粽子*), small glutinous rice dumplings wrapped in reed leaves), and green tea sesame.

shares fame with Suzhou's Rui Yunfeng and Hangzhou's Zhou Yunfeng as one of the Southern Yangtze's "three mysterious stones". Yulinglong was originally the position of Chu Yu, owner of the Sanlintangnan Garden in Shanghai's Pudong. Chu Yu took great pride in the stone. When Chu Yu died, his stone was passed on to Yu Yuan Garden owner, Pan En, whose youngest son, Pan Yungao, married Chu Yu's daughter. The younger Pan had Yulinglong transferred into the Yu Garden.

The East Garden *(dōng yuán, 东园)*

This is a self-contained courtyard in the southeast corner of Yu Yuan Garden. Its area is small, but there is still plenty to see. Perhaps its greatest attractions are the Jiulong Chi, "Nine Dragon Pool", and ancient stage.

Address

Yu Garden is located in the Huangpu District at 132 Anren Jie. It is only a 5 minute walk from Chenghuang Miao.

Hours of Operation

8:30am- 5:30pm

Telephone

021-63283251

Tickets

30 RMB, the garden offers 10% discounts for groups of over 20. Children under 1.2 meters tall pay only 10 RMB.

Special Note

Yu Garden has opened an exhibit of rare stone carvings on its premises. Here you can see a large-scale production of a city carved in stone, and a significant collection rare stones. It you like stones, than it is probably worth a look.

Chenxiang Ge Temple *(chénxiāng gé, 沉香阁)*

Originally called Ciyunchan Temple,the Chenxiang Ge Temple was established in 1600, as a temple for Buddhist nuns. The temple was most famous for enshrining and worshiping the aloeswood Guanyin Goddess of Mercy. According the Qing Dynasty Shanghai Town Annals, Yu Garden founder, Pan Yunduan, was once supervising the transport of goods to Huaikou when he discovered the Aloeswood sculpture floating on the water. He built a pavilion next to his Yu Garden, and enshrined the sculpture inside, turning the pavilion into his personal temple. During the Qing Dynasty, the convent underwent several expansions.

The Aloeswood Goddess of Mercy was carved from the rarest water aloeswood, and was the only such sculpture that can be found in Shanghai. With her arched foot and a hand resting on her knee, Guanyin appeared lost in thought, and her pose was lifelike and natural. It was said that during times of uninterrupted rain, the sculpture would send out a pervasive long-lasting aroma. Unfortunately, the Goddess of Mercy was completely destroyed during the Cultural Revolution, and a large portion of the temple was turned into a factory. After modern restoration efforts, only one small temple courtyard remains. Nevertheless, Chenxiang Ge still retains its peaceful and secluded Buddhist style. The Guanyin statue currently found in Chenxiang Ge's Goddess of Mercy Temple was carved from Haiqiong aloeswood and donated by Hong Kong Buddhists.

Address

Located at 29 Chenxiang Ge Lu, well within reach of Chenghuang Miao.

Hours of Operation

5am-5pm

Telephone

021-63203431

Tickets

5 RMB

Food and drink

Songyue Lou Vegetarian Restaurant

(sōngyuè lóu sùcài guǎn, 松月楼素菜馆)

Located between Chenghuang Miao and Xiaoyang Lu, this restaurant is a good value and has pretty good food as well. We recommend the wheat gluten noodles, vegetable-stuffed steamed buns, orchid jellied bean curd, and Chinese crab apple cake. Songyue Lou also serves tasty vegetarian duck and sausage dishes.

Huifeng Lou Muslim Restaurant

(huífèng lóu qíngzhēn cāntīng, 回凤楼清真餐厅)

Located at 89 Henan Nanlu near the Shanghai Lao Jie archway. You will find some good Muslim cooking at Huifeng Lou.

You can also find snack stalls along Shanghai Lao Jie selling all kinds of Shanghai-style goodies. If you like fast food, there is a McDonalds on Jiuxiaochang Road next to Lao Chenghuang Miao (the "Old City God Temple").

The Shanghai Old Street
(shànghǎi lǎo jiē, 上海老街)

Originally named Fangbang Zhong Lu, Shanghai Lao Jie has undergone some dramatic changes over the last two years. It has been dressed up as an 825 meter "Old Shanghai Street" lined on both sides with early Republican-era homes. To emphasize the old street's grand style, a large decorated archway has been erected over the street's Henan Nanlu entrance. Curios and antiques in the Old Street characteristics that have carried over to modern times, and the great snack stands nearby are a windfall benefit of this area's development. If you want to relax and leave your troubles behind, the local tea houses and multi-storied opera houses can help you with that. Old establishments long disappeared from Shanghai, such as Tonghanchun, the Old Shanghai Teahouse, Deshun Tavern, Xishi Tofu House, Miss Ding's Fabric House, Laohu Kitchen, and Daughter's Red Tavern have all been reborn on Shanghai Old Street, and today, they energetically and ostentatiously beckon to passing tourists.

If time permits, take a break at the Old Shanghai Tea House *(lǎo Shànghǎi cháguǎn, 老上海茶馆)* or Danfeng Tea House *(dānfèng cháguǎn, 丹凤茶馆)* on Fangbang Zhonglu for a taste of old Shanghai. The Old Shanghai Tea House is located on the second floor of a curio shop. Covered in old paintings from the 1920's and 1930's, the storefront easily attracts the attention of passersby. The stairway leading up to the teashop is also decorated with images of beautiful women of the 20's and 30's.

Cangbao Lou Antiques Building *(cángbǎo lóu, 藏宝楼)*

Located next to the archway, Cangbao Lou, one of Shanghai Lao Jie's most famous spots and one of Eastern China's largest curio and old handicraft markets, has always received a lot of attention from antique collectors. Cangbao Lou's history can be traced back to the Qing Dynasty. At that time, the Chenghuang Miao market was a center for collecting and distributing handicraft goods, and eventually became one of the most important curio markets in the country. At the beginning of the 1980's a small antique stall formed near Chenghuang Miao on Fuyou Lu. In time it has grown from such humble beginnings into one of the Eastern China's largest curio and antique handicrafts markets with a total of over 500 stalls spread out over 13 floors.

One of Cangbao Lou's most interesting events is the "ghost market" that takes place every weekend before dawn. In the wintertime, the ghost markets become active at 4:30 in the morning. The summer ghost markets typically open as early as 2:30 am. Weekend ghost markets are packed with people from all over the country, including collectors from places like Jiangxi, Fujian, and Henan.

Coming to one of Cangbao Lou's weekend markets is a truly eye-opening experience. With a veritable cornucopia of goods spread out on the ground and in the stalls, this place is filled to capacity with porcelain, jade, bronzes, picture books, boccaro kettles, lacquer works, and much more. Potential buyers wander around armed with flashlights and magnifying glasses, hoping to discover a hidden treasure or two. Every year there are probably only a handful of people who are able to find something truly valuable here, but it is still the ultimate dream of the collectors who flood the stalls. Some spend their whole lives pouring through the markets in search of buried treasure. Closer to a curio shop than an antiques dealer, there are not necessarily any hidden treasures here. You will find mostly oddities with good and poor quality items lumped together. Quality among items tends to vary, and for the layman, the best plan of action is probably just to step back and watch the action. One more interesting thing to point out is that the stall owners are divided up according to geographical regions. People from Hebei sell Ming and Qing Dynasty period furniture, people from Shanghai sell mahogany furniture and wood carvings, and the porcelain sellers are mostly from Jiangxi's Jingdezhen. People from Henan tend to sell different types of jade.

Address

Located at the eastern entrance of Shanghai Lao Jie

Telephone

021-63281796

Confucian Temple and Secondhand Book Market

(Wénmiào& zhōurìjiùshū shìchǎng, 文庙与周日旧书市场)

Located on Wenmiao Road, Confucian Temple is the only structure in Shanghai that serves as both a center of worship and of scholarship. Dedicated to Kong Zi or Confucius, the founder of the Confucian tradition, this temple was built in the Yuan Dynasty soon after the founding of Shanghai town. At the same time, the temple also served as a school of advanced study for imperial scholars. Over the last seven hundred years the temple has relocated once, having been rebuilt at its current location during the Qing Dynasty.

Shanghai residents have cleverly linked the location of their weekend second-hand book market to the ancient school and temple, reflecting both a longing for and the continuation of an ancient educational tradition.

All Shanghai locals know that Confucian Temple is the place to go for old books. Book lovers have a special affection for this famous market. Confucian Temple is home to the largest second hand book market in Shanghai, and on Sunday, it seems that every book hunter in Shanghai clears out of their house and heads there, turning the market into a really grand scene. People in the know understand which book stalls have the good books, and crowds around these booksellers become so tight that it seems impossible for even air to escape.

Every Sunday, 230 book stalls pack into the square in front of the temple's main hall, and crowds swarm the area. Not all of the books on

sale are true secondhand books. A lot of books are in fact new books that have spilled out from a publishing company's overstocked storerooms. These are usually sold directly to small book dealers "on wholesale", and become low price deals at the Sunday market. Probably the most interesting books that can be found here are the picture story books. Almost all members of the Shanghai Story Book Association became hooked to the Wenmiao book market.

Address

Confucian Temple is located at 215 Wenmiao Lu in the Shanghai Lao Chengxiang — the Old Chinese City. It can be reached on foot from Henan Zhong Lu.

Telephone

021-63779282

Hours of Operation

The normal hours of operation are weekdays from 9am-5pm and weekends from 7:30am to 4pm.

Tickets

10 RMB for entry into Confucian Temple. It costs one RMB to enter the weekend market.

The Dongtai Lu Curio Street *(dōngtái lù gǔwán jiē, 东台路古玩街)*

Longtime residents of Shanghai view Dongtai Lu in the same way that people in Beijing see Liuli Chang. With its old style iron sheet trunk stands, Dongtai Lu sits in Shanghai's Old Chinese City, coolly watching the years go by. It is definitely worth spending a full day slowly taking in and exploring Dongtai Lu.

In the beginning, Dongtai Lu was nothing more than an obscure little street that held favor with a few cultured men of leisure. It was a place that these men would come in their free time for a cup of tea and a chat. Some come would take along small curios and antique accessories which they would display for all to see. Those who frequented Dongtai Lu began trading and dealing their curious among one another, and gradually, over time, a few antique traders set up shop along the road. Antique dealers would examine merchandise together with the tea house customers and negotiate prices, gradually forming a type of curio market with character. Deals among the tea customers were much more lively and interesting than they are today. There was no commercialism involved, and the back-and-forth bargaining always carried a small element of leisure and romance.

Another characteristic that differentiates Dongtai Lu from other markets is the phenomenon of having stalls behind stalls and stands within stands. When strolling down this narrow alley you will slowly discover that many novel small handicraft shops and quaint curio stores are found right in back of other shops. The owners of these stores were

among the first to find success on Dongtai Lu, and they usually sell objects with real collector's value. They are also outstanding and well-respected figures among of antique and curio collecting circles.

One street over from Dongtai Lu is what used to be another famous street for folk curios and crafts — Huiji Lu. With the development of Shanghai Lao Jie, many of the merchants who once occupied this street have already moved their businesses over to Fangbang Zhong Lu. A walk down this street unavoidably reminds people of how quickly things change and how unimaginably fast time flies.

Address

From Shanghai Lao Jie, Dongtai Lu can be reached on foot by traveling down Henan Zhong Lu. Bus lines 17 and 864 travel directly to Dongtai Lu. You can also take subway line one to the Huangpi Nan Lu station and walk to the Dongtai Lu entrance from there.

Hours of Operation

Roughly 10am-5pm

Little Peach Orchard Mosque *(xiǎotáoyuán qīngzhēnsì, 小桃园清真寺)*

Originally called Qingzhen west mosque and later, Shanghai Xicheng Huijiaotang, Xiaotao Yuan is Shanghai's largest piece of contemporary Islamic architecture. First established in 1917, the mosque was rebuilt at its current location in 1925. Xiaotao Yuan's domed structure is built in the West Asian Islamic style.

Address

Located off of Fuxing Dong Lu at 52 Xiaotaoyuan Jie. It can be found near the intersection of Fuyou Lu and Lishui Lu. Take bus line 923 to the final stop or line 569 to its final stop at the intersection of Henan Nan Lu and Minxing Jie.

Hours of operation

4:30am-8pm

The Old City Wall *(dàjìng gé, 大境阁)*

Built during the reign of Ming Dynasty Emperor Jia Jing, this was the only section of Shanghai's city wall left standing when it was torn down in the 1911 Revolution. Originally built as a shrine to the General Guanyu, this part of the wall is named after a horizontal board inscribed with the words, Daqian Shengjing — a wonderland of this great world — that used to hang here. The words were written by Qing Dynasty governor-general, Chen Luan.

Address

265 Dajing Lu, From Henan Zhong Lu you can easily reach Dajing Ge by walking onto Renmin Lu. You can also get there on bus line 11.

Hours of Operation

9am-4pm

Tickets

5 RMB

Shanghai Natural History Museum *(shàng hǎi zìrán bówùguǎn, 上海自然博物馆)*

The Natural History Museum was established in 1956 and currently has a collection of over 240 thousand specimens. Inside you will find exhibits of ancient human history, ancient animals, invertebrates, amphibians, mammals, reptiles, birds, fish, and preserved animal remains. A variety of special exhibitions are also held frequently. The museum exhibitions and facilities at present are not entirely perfect. The Shanghai government is currently planning to build a new museum in Pudong.

Address

260 Yan'an Donglu; Turn onto Henan Zhonglu from Shanghai Lao Jie and walk in the direction of Yan'an Lu. The Museum is only 500 meters away.

Dongjiadu Catholic Church *(dǒngjiādù tiānzhǔjiào táng, 董家渡天主教堂)*

Easily overlooked among a stretch of grey multistory buildings in the Old Chinese City, Dongjiadu Catholic Church is the oldest church in Shanghai. Conducting itself in silence, modesty, and restraint, only those who value its history are willing to arouse Dongjiadu from its slumber.

History

Dongjiadu's history traces back to the end of the Opium War, and exploring the history of this church is just like exploring the history of Catholicism in Shanghai. In the beginning, the Qing government accepted Catholicism as "a religion that exhorts people to do good," and allowed it inside China's open ports. The government would not allow Shanghai's original Catholic Church to operate, and it was later converted into shrine to General Guanyu. In February 1848, the Qing magistrate of Shanghai compensated the church with three parcels of land. Louis de Besi, Bishop of the Southern Yangtze Parish, built a new church on this land and called it Saint Francis Xavier Catholic Church in memory China's first Christian missionary.

It took six years for church construction to be completed. The foundation was laid on November 21, 1848, and the first service was held on March 20, 1853. On the day of the church's opening ceremony, a French cruiser arranged for two gun boats to anchor off of the Dongjiadu dock and fired a salvo from its guns while the church conducted its consecration ceremony. With the church's opening, Catholicism was finally able to gain a foothold in Shanghai under the missionary flag, and Dongjiadu eventually became the main church of the Southern Yangtze Parish. Dongjiadu retained this status until it was supplanted with the construction of Xujiahui Catholic Church in 1910.

Dongjiadu's church interior is imitates the style of European Jesuit Churches. The ceiling in the main hall is arched which creates excellent resonance inside. There are green panels painted onto the ceiling and a beautiful relief sculpture of China at ceiling's highest point. There are several thick columns, each measuring four meters in girth, and a spiral staircase has been installed inside one of them, leading directly to the choral level.

Spanish Missionary, Joanne Ferrer, was the church's designer. The original design was meant to be an imitation of the Roman Jesuit University's St. Ignatius Cathedral, but due to a shortage of initial funds, Ferrer was forced to give up on the original design prints and cancelled building the glass windows and large central dome on the top floor. A Baroque gable was placed two thirds up the façade as a replacement. In the very center were written three large Chinese characters Tian Zhu Tang that stand for the word "Catholic Church". At the church's highest point hangs a heavy crucifix, inspiring reverence in the hearts of the following. It is said that the crucifix weighs one ton. At the same time the crucifix is adorned with Chinese style ornamentation which is typical of early Chinese Catholic churches.

Joanne Ferrer

Joanne Ferrer's father was a court artist and accomplished sculptor in Spain. Heavily influenced by his father in his youth, the

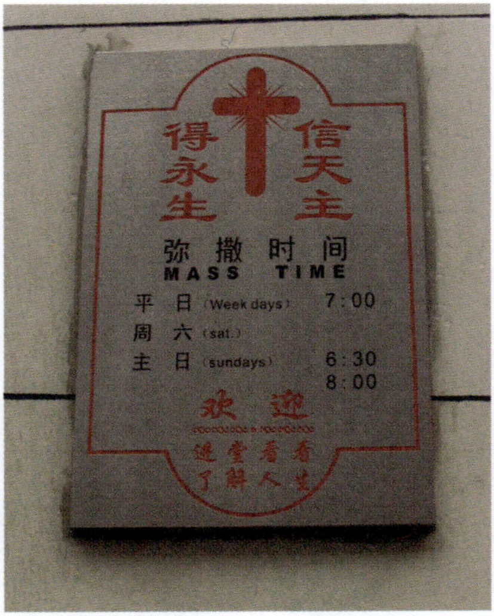

young Joanne also discovered a love of art, and followed in his father's footsteps. After arriving in Shanghai, Ferrer designed both Dongjiadu and Xujiahui Churches, finishing Dongjiadu first. After his work was complete at Dongjiadu, he decided to make Shanghai his permanent home, and established his workshop. At the time, the Dongjiadu Church required a large number of supplemental paintings and sculptures, and China lacked the personnel to complete it. Ferrer, expanded his studio to accommodate the larger workload, and started teaching classes there and later at the Xujiahui Church. He accepted a large number of Chinese students, passing on to them the skills of sculpting, painting and even engraving. During his nine years in China, Joanne Ferrer brought with him not only Catholicism; even more, he brought Western art. Unfortunately, this gifted and talented artist died young. On December 31, 1856, Joanne Ferrer passed away in Dongjiadu Church at the age of 39.

St. Francisco Xavier

The first Jesuit missionary to come to East Asia, the Spaniard, Francisco Xavier, arrived in China in 1551. Refused entry into Guangdong, he was forced onto the small island of Shangchuan near Guangdong's Taishan County. St. Xavier spent four months on and around Shangchuan where he was stricken with disease and unrelenting fever. With no medical attention, he died at the end of the year at the age of 46. His remains were shipped to India for burial. In 1662 he was canonized by Pope Gregory XV, and he is so far the only missionary to China that has ever been sainted. His burial site has become a holy place where people come to pay respects.

Address

Dongjiadu Catholic Church is located in Shanghai's Huangpu District at 175 Dongjiadu Lu. From Chenghuang Miao, you can take bus lines 324, 581, 65, 736, 305, 928, 303, 801, 868, 910, and 570 to the Dongjiadu stop. If you decide to walk, expect to travel for one and a half kilometers. On the way you will pass through the fascinating lanes of the old city. From Chenghuang Miao, walk south on Guangqi Nanlu until you reach Yujia Nong Lane. At Wanjiamatou Jie, walk east until you reach Dongjiadu. Be careful because it is easy to get lost. If you like photography or are interested in the old Shanghai style, than this route will give you plenty of opportunities to capture images of the old Shanghai.

Telephone

021-63787214

Hours of Operation

Mass is held at 7 am on weekdays and at 6:30am and 8am on Sunday.

Around Jingan Temple

(jìngān sì, 静安寺)

A quiet Buddhist temple sitting in the middle of a flourishing downtown shopping district, the name Jingan Si was once referred only to the Jingan Si Temple. Over the course of time its meaning gradually expanded to encompass the area around the temple and the western end of Nanjing Xilu. Pulling in large crowds with its prolific wisps of scented smoke, just about all Shanghai Buddhists come to Jingan Si Temple to burn incense. Aside from the temple, the Jingan Si area is also home to the Children's Palace. Constructed completely out of marble, the Children's Palace was originally the residence of the renowned Sir Elly Kadoorie.

Jingan Temple (静安寺)

Jingan Temple sits alone in the middle of the flourishing Nanjing Xilu. An island of serenity among the bustling shops and malls, Jingan Si has a history that stretches back almost two thousand years.

History: Built during the Three Kingdoms period in 247 AD, the temple was originally established, not here, but on the northern bank of the Suzhou River. It was first called Huduzhongyuan Si, and later changed its name to Yongtaichan Si during the Tang Dynasty. The temple's current name, Jingan Si, was first used in 1008 AD — the first year of the reign of Northern Song Dynasty Emperor Xianfu. In 1216, during the Southern Song period, severe damage caused by the Suzhou River forced the relocation of the Jingan Si Temple to its current address.

During the Qing Dynasty, there was a period of time when all of the Buddhist temples in Southern China fell into serious decline. Unfortunately, Jingan Temple

Transportation

Jingan Si is located at Nanjing Lu and is easy to reach by subway or bus. Take subway line number two or number seven (currently under construction) directly to the Jingan Si station. Bus lines 15, 20, 21, 01, 37, 40, 48, 45, 62, 71, 76, 94, 93, 127, 202, 506, and 824 all stop at the Jingan Si bus stop.

Travel Plan

Without a doubt, both the Jingan Si Temple and the Children's Palace can be seen in under half a day. But, if you like shopping, you may want to consider lingering around and checking out some of the markets and shopping malls nearby. You could easily spend a full day here checking out different stores. For those who like dancing, there is an old dancing hall in the area called the Shanghai Paramount Hall. Come in the evening and experience the atmosphere of early 20th century Shanghai.

Food and Drink

Jingan Si Temple Vegetarian Restaurant

(jìngānsì sùzhāiguǎn, 静安寺素斋馆)

A great stop for vegetarians, the restaurant serves both assorted vegetable noodles and mushroom noodles. Vegetarian snacks are served as well, and during the Mid-Autumn Festival you can find vegetarian moon cakes. Please note that the restaurant requires you pay before lining up to collect your noodles.

Fumao Crayfish

(fùmào xiǎolóngxiā, 复茂小龙虾)

Located at 153 Yu Yuan Lu near the Jingan Si Temple, this restaurant serves authentic Shanghai crayfish served in a dizzying variety of ways. Flavors include, curry, New Year's was no exception. Luckily, in 1741, during the reign of Emperor Qian Long, several officials assisted in Jingan Si's reconstruction, and expanded the temple by adding a fountain in the front and Baoen Yuan, the eastern courtyard. Head Monk, Master Dahai, carved a burned Song Dynasty gingko tree into the figures of 18 Buddhist saints and one of Skanda, the Buddhist temple's guardian spirit. All nineteen carvings were enshrined inside the temple and permanently preserved as temple treasures. Most of the temple was destroyed during the Taiping Rebellion, leaving behind only the solitary audience hall. Thanks to the great efforts of the abbot, Master Hefeng, Jingan Si temple was restored in 1880. In April 1881, the temple was rededicated during the Buddhist festival of "Bathing the Buddha". To commemorate the anniversary of this occasion, every year people come to the temple to burn incense and take part in what has become a lively and extraordinary temple fair.

After the World War Two, a new Tang-style temple entrance was built to the east of the original, and an ancient Indian pillar was erected on the side of the well wall of the fountain in front. This has become one of Jingan Si's identifying structures. In April of this year, head monk, Master Taixu hosted the ribbon cutting at the new Jingan Si Academy's opening ceremony. The crowd attending the ceremony included monks and layman alike, and totaled over ten thousand people, turning the ceremony into a grand occasion. In 1953, temple abbot, Master Chisong built a tantric altar in the temple interior, reviving a custom that had long since been discontinued. Without a doubt, Jingan Si has once again become a

sacred shine for people around the world, remaining completely detached from the thriving city right outside its gates.

Today: With layer upon layer of temple halls and sanctuaries, the temple has also preserved the oldest stone tablet in Shanghai. Written by Song Emperor Zhaodun while he was still a crown prince, the tablet reads, "The sunlight reflects off the Yin River waters and returns to the land". Jingan Si Temple also a Ming Dynasty bell cast from three tons of copper in 1369.

Address

1868 Nanjing Xilu

Tickets

10 RMB; 5 RMB on the first and fifteenth days of the Lunar Calendar.

Jingan Park
(jìngān gōngyuán, 静安公园)

Jingan Park is a free park across from the Jingan Si Temple. Though not large in size, it is rich in vegetation with numerous large trees. The 32 sycamore trees (French plane trees) lining the path from the main entrance stand out as some of the tallest and most imposing trees of the park. It can be said without a doubt that this is definitely a great park for the public.

Kadoorie Residence — Shanghai Children's Palace
(jiādàolǐ gōngguǎn, 嘉道理公馆)

The Shanghai Children's Palace sits at 64 Yan'an Xilu. Its main building is a spotlessly white structure constructed with marble shipped in from Italy. This magnificent building, the only marble building in Shanghai, is naturally called "the marble palace" by locals. The mansion interior has drawing rooms, both big and small, and over 20 bedrooms, each decorated with a different style and color scheme. The sumptuous furnishings and ornamentation are done in the style of ancient European palaces and are absolutely splendid. Legendary in its degree of luxury, this is a Shanghai site that you absolutely should not miss.

Food and Drink

cake, and brazed yellow crayfish. We recommend trying the crayfish New Year's cake, assorted small crayfish, assorted large crayfish, and dry-fried crayfish.

Manji Sweets Shop
(mǎnjì tiánpǐndiàn, 满记甜品店)

You will find some interesting sweets at the Manji Sweets Shop. Their selections are fresh and definitely worth a try. We recommend the Mango Banji (*芒果班戟*), the Yangzhi Sweet Dew (*杨枝甘露*), sesame paste bean curd jelly, and the snow white and black tapioca pearls. Manji is located in the Jiubai Shiji Food Market at 72 Wanhangdu Lu.

Bali Laguna

This Indonesian restaurant is located next to the lake inside Jingan Park. Expect high prices.

"The Marble Palace" (Originally the Kadoorie Residence)

This was once home to wealthy Baghdadi British Jew, Elly Silas Kadoorie. Surprisingly, construction of such an extravagant palace was not at all planned. Rather, it was

the result of an alcohol-fueled blunder. In 1919, Kadoorie's original home on Huangpi Nanlu was lost in a huge fire. Sadly, Kadoorie's wife died in the blaze when she attempted to rescue a female teacher locked inside. Distraught by his terrible loss, Kadoorie decided to temporarily return to London with his two children. Before he left, he entrusted the construction of his new house on Da Xilu (today's Yan'an Xilu) to his friend, architect Graham Brown. Little did Kadoorie know, Brown had developed

into a severe alcoholic and he was forced to pass the project along to the Moorhead & Halse Company. Once rid of his responsibility, Brown never again inquired into its progress. When the new house was finished in 1924, Kadoorie returned to Shanghai finding both "a palatial new building and Brown lying dead drunk in a hospital bed." Caring for the new house required at least 30 to 40 servants. But, the biggest shock came when the building's contractor sent over the bill. The Kadoorie Palace cost an astronomical one million pieces of silver. At the time, that was enough money to purchase 25 million kilograms of rice — enough rice to feed 140 thousand people for one year.

When the Japanese army occupied Shanghai in World War Two, the Kadoorie residence was reduced to a den of monsters, becoming part of the Japanese military institution. After World War Two came to an end, the American military arrived on the shores of Shanghai. They were able to contact Kadoorie's two sons through the Swiss embassy, and requested that they return to the marble palace. As they stepped into the house, the two Kadoories excitedly threw on all of the lights to celebrate the allied victory. While in Shanghai, they helped supply the allied troops with foodstuffs stamped with the letter K. As the story goes, the two brothers never touched the expensive food items themselves. After the Chinese Civil War, the Kadoorie family moved their enterprise out of Shanghai to Hong Kong. On May 31, 1953 Song Qingling suggested turning the marble palace into the China Welfare Association Children's Palace.

In 1979, Lawrence Kadoorie and his wife returned to Shanghai for a short trip. When catching sight of the Children's Palace, Elly's son is said to have excitedly exclaimed, "The marble building that my father loved so much has become a place of education for thousands of children".

Sir Kadoorie

At the end of the 19th century, Elly Kadoorie, like many Baghdadi Jews before him, traveled from Bombay to do business

in Hong Kong and Shanghai. Kadoorie is credited with opening Hong Kong's first consulting firm, and in 1926 the English King knighted him for establishing Shanghai's Yucai Engineering School (today's Yucai Middle school) and contributed money to build the Shanghai's first hospital for treating tuberculosis. In the 1930's, Kadoorie's two grown sons Lawrence and Horace, aided their father in expanding his enterprises. The Kadoorie family businesses eventually expanded to the point where the Kadoorie name could be mentioned in the same breath as the wealthy and renowned Sassoons and the Hardoons, two of Shanghai's most powerful Jewish business families.

In October 1938, waves of Jewish refugees from Europe began flooding into Shanghai. Kadoorie took initiative to convene an aid conference and set up Shanghai's community groups and social relief organizations inside his marble palace. Not only did Kadoorie donate huge sums of money, he also funded the construction of the Jewish Youth School, which only accepted children of European refugees. When the Pacific War began in 1941, the generous Kadoorie family suffered calamity. As the Japanese marched into the European concession, the Kadoories were kicked out of their homes and detained inside Hong Kong's Stanley Concentration Camp. Afterwards, they were brought back to Shanghai where they were shut inside the Zhabei Concentration Camp. Sustained with only a daily ashtray of rice, cold, sick, and starving, Elly Kadoorie was tormented to death. His wealth and enterprises were plundered by the Japanese, and his holdings in Hong Kong and South East Asia were wiped out.

Address

The Kadoorie Residence is located at 64 Yan'an Xilu near Huashan Lu. It is about one kilometer from Jingan Si. You can walk to the Kadoorie Residence by following Wanhangdu Lu from Jingan Si to Yan'an Xilu and turning west. You can also get there by taking bus routes 1, 48, 57, 71, 127, and 311.

Around Huangpi Nanlu

(huángpí nánlù, 黄陂南路)

Huangpi Nanlu is currently one of the hottest and most lively stretches in Shanghai. First there is Xintiandi, which has been the talk of the town for quite some time. In the 19th century, Xintiandi was a residence area for people of status, and it had a scale and a reputation that was unmatched in Shanghai. Afterwards, a large influx of lower middle class outsiders moved into the Shikumen buildings, and dramatically changed the social structure of the area. Originally created as a "one family per house" structure for people of wealth and influence, Shikumen became a place where ten families would squeeze into one residence. These buildings eventually became the inspiration for the movie 72 Tenants. Some of the movie's famous characters and places such as Tingzi room, the Ke Tang room, Xiangfang, Tianjing, the second landlord, and Baixiangren Saosao have all become part of what has evolved into "the old dream of Shikumen". Although it once represented a time of hard living, today it evokes warm and nostalgic memories in Shanghai's elderly. The newly refurbished modern day Shikumen at Xintiandi has become an enchanting and lively arena of sights and sounds.

The beautiful Sinan Lu and Rui Jin Lu roads are just a short walk away from Xintiandi. Here you can admire the old houses and residences of famous Shanghai figures. Sun Yat-sen and Zhou Enlai's old residences are here, as well as the Rui Jin Guest House, and Taiyuan Villa. These old buildings still silently capture the memories of history and the splendor of the past.

Xintiandi *(xīntiāndì, 新天地)*

Perhaps the old architecture at Shikumen is too mournful and nostalgic. Maybe the people of Shanghai's alleyways suddenly developed yearning for some western-style nightlife. With a variety of factors coming together at the right time, Xintiandi was born.

The Northern Plaza: Covering an area of 30 thousand square meters, the northern plaza of today's Xintiandi is also the location of this area's earliest alley residences. It seems that in the blink of an eye, Xin-

Transportation

Take subway line one to the Huangpu Nanlu sta tion. Leave the station from exit number two and turn left. Follow Madang Lu for about 200 meters and then turn left at the Taicang Lu intersection.

Take bus line 10 or 146 and get off at the Xingye Lu stop.

Take the Number 8 Tunnel line and get off at the Chongqing Nanlu stop

Take the lines 781 or 146 to Taican Lu, or lines 911, 926, or 42 to Huaihai Lu.

You can also take lines 2, 17, 24, 36, 41, 42, 96, 104, 128, 575, 530, 780, 786, 835, 864, 869, 933, 911, 920, 945, Tourist Line Number 10, the Number 8 Tunnel Line, Daqiao Number One Line, or the free Huaihai Lu sightseeing bus, all of which will take you here.

Shikumen
(shíkùmén, 石库门)

Its two entry doors are painted in black with large brass rings and thick granite door frames. Shikumen's layout is typical of Chinese residences found south of the Yangtze River, with a small courtyard and a pavilion room. Shikumen's special characteristics seem to have condensed so thickly that some people find them stifling. Indeed, of all the architecture in Shanghai's alleyways, Shikumen's is the most distinctive. The alleys of Shikumen flourished in the 1860's. It is similar to other architecture in Shanghai in that although the buildings in Shikumen were home to working class families, they are still clearly influenced by a western aesthetics. Connected together into rows, these residence structures includes such embellishments as Corinthian and Ionic columns.

tiandi's Northern Plaza has become one of Shanghai's most extravagant large-scale enterprises, attracting countless numbers of patrons to this area's theme restaurants, clothing outlets, painting galleries, cafes, and bars. Even renowned artist, the late Chen Yifei's studio has opened a store here, Layefe Home, selling magazines, clothing, ceramics, jewelry, and furniture. It has become one of the northern plaza's most recognizable businesses.

Stars of the Shanghai fashion world have also surged into the area. Each residence is still arranged according to the old alley structure, and its facade is still united in the old Shikumen style, but the interiors are totally different, shaped into diverse collections of bright elegant styles. No one can deny that Xintiandi's renovation has preserved the old buildings. But, it has also made them profitable and sustainable. It is a reminder of a time decades ago when Xintiandi represented the forefront of the new modern era. Grab dinner while you are here, and then sit for a while in one of the cafes along the plaza, savoring the fusion of the contemporary and the historical. Photographers will not want to miss an opportunity to wander around here. Dusk is the best time to take pictures when the sky is still awash with a subdued blue. The mood at this time is eerie and passionate, and is your best opportunity to line up your camera lens. Probably the only thing at Xintiandi worth complaining about is the numbers of tourists that have skyrocketed over recent years. The crowds have gradually become a permanent part of the scenery, and you have become part of theirs.

There is a Shikumen Museum on Xingye Lu near the north entrance to Xintiandi. The museum uses a restored residential building to bring back the authentic look of an early twentieth century Shanghai family dwelling. Tickets: 20 RMB

The Southern Plaza: It is regrettable that the Southern Plaza did not learn more from the experiences in the north and continue Xintiandi's heritage preserving development. Here you can find tall buildings, wide movie screens, a huge plaza, and glass structures stretching to the sky. These modern architectural elements seem incompatible with older alley architecture in the north.

The first National Communist Party Congress site with its grey walls sits in its deep silence. In Xintiandi it is common to reflect on history, the fleetingness of fashion and the profoundness of the ancient, the years of war and years of peace. Exiting from the Southern Plaza entrance will take you by a post office that sells early twentieth century postage items including such things as postmarks. Feel free to grab some of the free pamphlets on the post office counter. Most introduce the various enterprises in Xintiandi.

Address

Xintiandi is located in the Taipingqiao District on the eastern end of Huaihai Zhonglu. It is bordered on four sides by Taicang Lu, Huangpi Nanlu, Madang Lu, and Zizhong Lu. Xintiandi Plaza Beili is located at 181 Lane off of Taicang Lu. Xintiandi Plaza Nanli can be found at Xingye Lu's 123 Lane.

Travel plan

There is a lot to see in this part of town, so it is recommended that you set aside between half a day to a full day to explore. Afternoon is the best time to see Sinan Lu because the light at this time is gentle and warm and has just enough brightness to turn out some great photography. You can visit Rui Jin Guest House and Taiyuan Villa at any time, day or night, but you definitely want to see Xintiandi at night. Shops at Shikumen turn on their lights in the evening, filling the old architecture with an eerie and mysterious beauty. This is a great time to experience the combined atmosphere's of Xintiandi and Shikumen; at night you will not be bothered by large tour groups, but you will still run into growing crowds of people on their way out to grab a bite to eat.

The Site of the First National Communist Party Congress *(zhōnggòng yīdà huìzhǐ, 中共一大会址)*

If you do not know much about the history of China's Communist Party, than stop here for an enlightening taste of modern Chinese history. This is the spot where the Chinese Communist Party was founded, and it is now a patriotic educational site for Shanghai students. Although it looks like nothing

more than a common residential building, it has become a daily stop for large numbers of out-of-town Chinese tourists. The Chinese Communist Party's first ever meeting took place here on July 23, 1921. It was held on the first floor inside an 18 square meter living room. Among those present at the meeting included Mao Zedong, Dong Biwu and 13 other party representatives. The meeting was interrupted when the participants realized that they were being monitored by a French police station. They immediately fled the scene. The meeting was eventually reconvened on a boat off of Jiangxi's Jiaxingnan Lake, and the central leadership was elected through the party platform. Thus the China's Communist Party was born.

The memorial hall has an exhibition room filled with artifacts and mementos of the party's founding period.

Address

347 Huangpi Nanlu

Telephone

021-53832171 ext. 111

Hours of Operation

8:30 am-4pm, closed on Mondays and Thursdays.

Tickets

3RMB

The Dr. Sun Yat-sen Residence *(sūnzhōngshān gùjū, 孙中山故居)*

The former residence of Dr. Sun Yat-sen is located on Xiangshan Lu (originally 29 Moliai Lu) on the Western side of Fuxing Park. This is a quiet and secluded two- storey deep grey European-style garden home. There is a square shaped yard in front surrounded on three sides with holly, magnolia, camphor, and pine. A statue of Sun Yat-sen stands among the pine trees.

History

In 1917, Sun Yat-sen resigned from his presidential duties and organized the government for Army of Law and Protection in Guangzhou. Elected as the army's commander in chief, he rallied the troops for a Northern Expedition. In only his second year as commander in chief, Sun was forced out of office, and he came to Shanghai with his wife Song Qingling. In Shanghai, Sun was politically helpless and alone, and he found himself facing severe economic problems. This house was given to Sun and Song Qingling as a gift by four overseas Chinese who had just returned to Shanghai from Canada. Sun moved here in 1918.

Sun and his wife lived in this house for five years, and the furnishings on display today were arranged according to the recollections of Song Qingling.

Visting

When you visit, you will be allowed to tour the study, living room, washroom, and showroom. There are also several other rooms that are not open for public viewing. Walking into the living room, you will see a photograph of Sun Yat-sen hanging on the middle of the wall; it was taken when he temporarily occupied China's presidency. The image has been inlaid inside a frame of red, yellow, blue, and black pieces of wood that have been pieced together. Continuing on from the living room, you will arrive at the dining room where you will see Sun Yat-sen and Song Ringling's 1915 wedding portrait from Nanjing hanging inside the dining room's balcony wall. Moving onto the second floor, you will arrive at the study where Sun Yat-sen frequently worked. Passing

Food and Drink

Xintiandi is full of restaurants, bars, and cafes, and the establishments here are characterized by luxurious atmospheres and a variety of different moods. While they are not to be missed, do expect prices to match the high-end atmosphere.

T8 Restaurant

Famous for its decor, this western restaurant was rated by National Geographic Traveler as one of the world's fifty best restaurants. With its dim lamplight and contracted lines, the style here is very unique. Designed by a famous Japanese designer Yasuhirokoich, this is a place where trendy people come to be seen. T8 mixes eastern and western cooking styles, matching dishes from each of China's major cooking schools with western-style craftsmanship. While the atmosphere is tops, expect to pay 260 RMB for a set meal.

Paulaner Brauhaus

(bǎoláinà cāntīng, 宝莱纳餐厅)

Located in Beili, this may not be the greatest place to eat, but it is an excellent spot to kick back with a stout beer and listen to some live music. The band plays here every night, and the place really picks up after 9pm.

La Maison French Restaurant

(lèměisòng, 乐美颂)

Famous for its Moulin Rouge-style Dance performances, the underground wine cellar dining room has a lot of atmosphere.

Luna *(lùnà, 璐娜)*

Luna is one of Xintiandi's first bars, and over the years, it has become a favorite of Shanghai's bourgeoisie. But, with number of the tour groups increasing by the day, people who enjoy privacy no longer come here. Nevertheless, the action at Luna never stops. Service personnel on the second floor are almost all young Filipinos. If you are coming through an indoor balcony leads to Sun Yat-sen and Song Ringling's master bedroom.

At the time, the Sun residence did not just function as Sun Yat-sen and Song Ringling's home. It was also the main ground of operations for the revolutionary party. In 1922, Sun met with Chinese Communist Party member, Li Dacha, and on August 25 of that year he met with Hendricks Sniveled, the representative of Adolph Abramowitz Jeff, the Soviet Ambassador to China. Together they published the Sun-Jeff Manifesto. That September they carried out exploratory discussions about Nationalist and Communist cooperation on Sun's own front lawn. On March 12, 1925, Sun Yat-sen, overworked and suffering from liver cancer, died in Beijing at the age of 59.

Address

The Sun Yat-sen Residence is located at 7 Xiangshan Lu

Telephone

021-64372954

Hours of Operation

9am-4:30pm

Tickets

8RMB

Residence of Zhou Enlai

(zhōugōngguǎn, 周公馆)

Sinan Lu is a beautiful road that stands just outside the bustle of Shanghai life. The street has a style all its own, feeling neither monotonous nor lifeless, but its quietness makes it a place for silent introspection. The addresses between 51 and 95 on Sinan Lu were once called Yipin Cun. It was a gathering place of celebrities and the famous. 73 Sinan Lu was once the residence of Communist Party representative, Zhou Enlai. The front of the residence is marked with a placard reading "Zhou Residence" in Chinese and in English.

History: Simple and frugal, the Zhou Enlai residence was built between 1912 and 1936. Coming out the front door takes you right out onto the great Sinan Lu. The residence has a coarse grey stucco overcoating that fills the old structure with a firm and steady disposition. Covered in verdant green ivy, the old strong wall is a tangle of naked vines when the ivy leaves fall in the winter.

Tranquil on its surface, the Zhou Residence once served as Chinese Communist Party's main base of activity in Shanghai,

and was witness to a countless number of historical events. On September 16, 1946, Zhou met with reporters from United States, holding a local and international press conference which was attended by over 70 people. Here he met with US President special envoy, General Marshal, and on October 17 and 19 of that year he met and exchanged views with Kuomintang and third party representatives. This is also the place where Zhou Enlai met with American reporter, Anna Louise Strong, as she made her way to Yan'an.

The residence's front entrance is tall because it sits right over the building's shallow basement. Pushing open the newly painted red door and stepping into the simple interior is like watching the unfolding of an old scroll. While the light is dim, it is easy to

Food and Drink

with someone who does not speak English, watch out.

Jesse Restaurant *(xīnjíshì jiǔlóu, 新吉士酒楼)*

Located inside an old house in Beili's building number nine, this restaurant serves local cuisine. We recommend the soy braised pork, tofu and minced crab, and the silver threaded mustard greens. Expect to pay 100 RMB per person. Beware; most people tend to feel that the service at Jesse is indifferent at best.

Zen *(cǎidiéxuān, 采蝶轩)*

This Cantonese restaurant has branches all over Shanghai. Their dishes are meticulously prepared, but portions tend to run small. Expect to pay over 38 RMB for a vegetable dish. The shrimp dumplings are widely recognized as the best item on the menu.

Yandang Lu Food Street
(yàndànglù měishíjiē, 雁荡路美食街)

The food street is very close to the Huangpi Xilu subway station, and is only a short walk from Huanhai Lu. Although called "Food Street", it nevertheless seems rather desolate in the daytime and evening.

Sinan Lu, Fuxing Zhonglu, and Nanchang Lu all have a number of snack stalls and restaurants serving local Shanghai cuisine. Prices here are not too high, so do not be afraid to try a place that looks interesting. Of the three streets, most restaurants can be found on Sinan Lu.

Taihe Restaurant
(tàihéyǐnshídiàn āniángmiàn, 泰和饮食店阿娘面思南店)

Taihe Restaurant located at 19 Sinan Lu, serves Ningbo-style cuisine. Their signature dish is noodles with croaker and snow vegetables. The noodle broth is fresh and tasty and they do not skimp on the fish. A bowl will cost you 12 RMB, but you will have to pay extra for a plate of pickled vegetables. Because busi-

see everything arranged in perfect order.

Zhou Enlai's bedroom is on the first floor in a room east of the living room. It is the most highly furnished room in the house. Zhou did not live in this room for long. Because he frequently received guests, he moved into a safer and more convenient room on the eastern end of the third floor. The rooms on the second floor are spacious and receive very good light. An outdoor staircase installed next to the balcony leads into the garden. With its thicket of flowers and trees, the garden is full of vitality. A large pagoda pine tree stands in the middle of the verdant green yard. It is said that in the summer and fall, Zhou liked to stroll around tree every evening after dinner.

Address

The Zhou Residence is located at 73 Sinan Lu in the Luwan District. Only 50 meters south of the Sun Yat-sen Residence, it can easily be reached on foot.

Telephone

021-64730420

Hours of Operation

9am-4pm

Tickets

2 RMB

Special Note

The former residence of legendary Peking Opera master, Mei Lanfang *(méilánfāng, 梅兰芳)*, lies south of the Zhou Residence on the other side of his flower garden (87 Sinan lu). Mr. Mei lived here between 1933 and 1958. 517 Fuxing Zhonglu is the former residence of famed poet and intellectual, Liu Yazi. None of these buildings are open to the public. Each has been converted into civilian housing, and today are homes to a number of families.

Fuxing Park

(fùxīng gōngyuán, 复兴公园)

One of the earliest parks in Shanghai, Fuxing Park is loaded with French character. A century before it became a park, this plot was part of the Gu family's fertile farmland. Due to their abundance of land, the Gu family had a private garden built that the locals called "the Gu Residence Garden". One day in 1900, the French bought the garden and expanded it with an additional 1.66 acres of farmland. It started as an encampment for French troops, but the leisure-loving French liked it even more as a place to relax. On July 1, 1908 the French political institution in Shanghai decided to turn the Gu Residence Garden into a park, and had famous French horticulturalist, Papot, supervise the project. A year later, the park was finished and was named, the "Gu Residence Park". It was also called French Park. After World War II, the park's name was finally changed

Food and Drink

ness here is usually booming, you usually have to wait for a table. When you sit down you are then given a number and have to wait again for your noodles. Some people complain that the noodles here have too much MSG.

Shanghai Lane Restaurant

(shànghǎi lòngtáng càiguǎn, 上海弄堂菜馆思南店)

Found at 8 Sinan Lu, this atmospheric Shanghainese restaurant serves a classic soy-braised pork entree.

Yangzhou Restaurant

(yángzhōu fàndiàn, 扬州饭店)

Serving authentic Huaiyang cuisine, this restaurant makes a good minced crab and tofu. It can be found at 31 Sinan Lu.

Madame Zung Bar

Madame Zung Bar(formerly Sally's) on 4 Xiangshan Lu was one of the three first bars opened in Shanghai. The basement level is packed on weekends.

If you are willing to walk a little farther, **Fumin Noodle Shop** *(fùmín miànguǎn, 富民面馆)* at 78 Taicang Lu (in the direction of the Chang Lu intersection) serves Shanghai-style noodle dishes. Eat your fill for between 5 and 10 RMB. Another interesting restaurant is **Haoyoulai Sichuan Restaurant** *(hǎoyòulái chuāncài guǎn, 好又来川菜馆)* (78 Zhonglu near Tai Lu), which serves authentic Sichuan cuisine. You can eat well here for about 20 RMB.

Shuidu Xuan *(shuǐdūxuān, 水都轩)*

This Cantonese restaurant at the southern door of the Taiyuan Villa is the most expensive restaurant in the area. Trying just a few dishes can still set you back over 200 RMB.

Rui Jin Guest House

(ruìjīn bīnguǎn, 瑞金宾馆)

There are several restaurants and bars inside Rui Jin Guest House, and they all enjoy

to Fuxing Park. Today, Fuxing park is flourishing with vegetation and towering green trees. The last two years has seen an incursion of nightclubs, bars, and karaoke centers. With one great leap, Fuxing Park has transformed itself from a quiet park into a focus of Shanghai nightlife and a place to let yourself loose.

St Nicholas Church
(shèngnígǔlāsī dàjiàotáng, 圣尼古拉斯大教堂)

In the early twentieth century, wave after wave of post-revolution Russian aristocrats, government officials, army officers, and clergy, fearing persecution from Soviet Union, fled from Russia into Shanghai. At one time, Shanghai was home to 50 thousand of these White Russians who brought their rich Russian culture with them into this port city. China's earliest ballet school was opened in Shanghai by a Russian resident, and China's earliest nude model was a White Russian girl who was hired by famous art educator, Liu Haisu. At the time, the hiring caused quite an uproar. While all of this action was taking place, the new and unfamiliar Eastern Orthodox Church began quietly taking root in Shanghai.

Facing a massive new religious community, the construction of one or two eastern orthodox churches was not enough to carry the burden for handling so many people. Therefore in 1928, a plan was initiated to open a grand new church. 100 thousand silver pieces were raised on the French Concession's rue Corneille. A lot of passion and religious devotion was poured into the project and a beautiful place of worship was created. The grand white dome at the center of the structure came to occupy a central place in peoples' field of vision. Its half-circle crests come symmetrically off the top in the front, back, left, and right, like a slowly blooming lotus. On March 31, two years after beginning construction, St Nicholas was completed and its opening ceremony was held. Both fresh and elegant, the structure was a masterpiece that architects would come to view and study. Every Sunday, the church would be filled with Russians, and during the major holidays, the crowd spilled out the front of the church and into the surrounding streets.

During the Cultural Revolution, St. Nicholas suffered a fate similar to that of other churches in China. The spire on the top of the roof was heartlessly torn down, and the church was turned into a factory. St. Nicholas was finally fully restored at the end of the twentieth century, and the church spire has been rebuilt. For a while, the church had been converted into the restaurant Ashonti, which was once considered one of Shanghai's best French Restaurants. But today, the church doors are locked tight, and a security system has been installed to keep people out. St. Nicholas has devolved into a place of little interest to anyone.

Families now live in the courtyard behind the church, and the corners of many of their houses still retain sculptures that have been left behind. If you want to have a look at these sculptures, you need to first get permission from the landowner. Continuing down Gaolan Lu will lead you to the beautiful garden houses nearby. This is a nice place for photographers to wander around for a day taking pictures. If you come in cloudy weather, you had better bring a tripod. The old homes are painted in dark colors.

Address

The church is located in the Luwan District at 16 Gaolan Lu. It is a short 50 meter walk from the Sun Yat-sen Residence.

Food and Drink

good reputations in Shanghai. **Xiaonanguo** *(xiǎonánguó, 小南国)*, serving local Shanghai cuisine, is pretty easy to find. The food here is exquisite, with moderately sweet and salty flavors. Expect to pay between 100 RMB and 150 RMB per person.

Face Cafe

Located in building number 4, this, one of Shanghai's most famous cafes is decorated in mysterious and bewitching Thai, Indian, and Pakistani colors. Here you will find elegant Shanghai women speaking in perfectly fluent English, and listening to bossa nova and other fashionable music. You can be just like them, sinking into an "Opium Bed" and propping your feet up on a "five color" sofa. Enjoy a different world of peace and comfort under the lazy sun, seemingly miles away from the clamor and noise of Xintiandi. Face's freshly ground coffee in the afternoon is classic, and one cup runs at a cool 35 RMB. The food menu focuses on mainly Thai cuisine.

There are also two Southeast Asian restaurants in building four. One is called **Hazara** *(哈扎拉)*, the other is **Lan Na Thai Restaurant** *(兰纳泰国餐厅)*. Prices at these two establishments are definitely on the high side.

The stretch of Taiyuan Lu near the Marshal Villa has a lot of snack stalls. Mustard greens and pork tenderloin steamed buns are practically everywhere you turn. One place you should try is **Old Shanghai Yangchunmian** *(lǎoshànghǎi yángchūnmiàn, 老上海阳春面)* at 236 Taiyuan Lu. This restaurant focuses on traditionally flavored Shanghai snacks and noodles. The vegetable soup noodles and ribs cost 10 RMB. The **Marshall Bar** inside the Marshal Residence plays European and American golden oldies all day long. The bar is run by two women who are both warm and welcoming. Expect to spend between 30 RMB and 50 RMB per person.

Rui Jin Guest House
(ruìjīn bīnguǎn, 瑞金宾馆)

With its thick iron railings and dark colors the Rui Jin Guest House is a distinctive place. Tall trees and a diverse collection of flowers can be found within the hotel wall. Stepping through the wide entrance, you will immediately look upon the imposing courtyard and the grand refined western-style buildings in the garden. This venerable old garden hotel was once the most eminent and reputed private residence of 1930's and 1940's era Shanghai. Built in the 1930's, the most storied sections are without a doubt buildings number one and number two. Chiang Kaishek and Song Meiling were once frequent guests here as were Zhou Enlai, Chen Yi, and Lin Biao. The five villas, each with its own style, are all built in the European fashion, and create an extremely comfortable living environment. The man who was responsible for these fantastic buildings was none other than the legendary British explorer and businessman, H.E. Morris.

Morris was one of the first western explorers to come to the Far East, arriving in Shanghai in 1867. An inveterate gambler, Morris loved to bet on horse races. Luckily for Morris, he was blessed with excellent luck and ended up winning a fortune at the race track. With his newfound wealth, Morris invested in real estate, buying up

land and building houses for rent, and he eventually bought into Shanghai's North-China Daily News newspaper. Many of the homes in Shanghai's alleyways begin their names with the Chinese character, "ma". Short for Morris, this is a sign the British explorer was involved in the house's construction or sale.

Rui Jin Guest House's number one building was originally meant to be a residence built exclusively for Morris. However, when construction was completed, Morris decided he did not want to live here. Supposedly, he did not particularly care for the building's lighting and colors, feeling that they were to dark. Not long after the building was

After the founding of the People's Republic, buildings one through four were united (they were originally independent homes) to form the National Hotel which was used exclusively to receive foreign heads of state and VIP guests.

Rui Jin Guest House is excellently preserved, and has been utilized as a setting in many Chinese films such as Chen Kaige's Temptress Moon *(fēngyuè, 风月)* and Man Kit Poon's Shanghai Grand *(xīn shànghǎitān, 新上海滩)*. As it is portrayed on film, Rui Jin Guest House is really one of the most beautiful old structures in Shanghai.

Rui Jin Guest House sits on the atmospheric Rui Jin Er Lu. When you walk down this road, tall Chinese parasol trees will restrict your line of vision with their long branches. Both sides of the road are densely packed with stores, which have turned Rui Jin Er Lu into a small bustling commercial road. Loaded with authentic modern Shanghai tones, if you arrive in the evening, Rui Jin Er Lu will allow you to deeply experience Shanghai's unique charm.

If you decide to stay at Rui Jin Guest House, stay in one of the deluxe double bedrooms. The rates are 990 RMB a night and you need to book in advance. Telephone: 021-64725222. Before you book a room, be sure to ask if the hotel is running any discount rates.

finished, Morris sold it and began working on new house nearby. Morris's new house would eventually become Rui Jin Guest House's building number three. The design of this new building was, as expected, different from the first. Mounting materials incorporated marble, copper and glass, and the color scheme was much brighter as a result.

In 1945, Morris's house was incorporated into part of the Kuomintang headquarters, and Song Meiling was frequently seen coming and going from this building. A rumor at the time stated that Huang Jinrong had purchased the building for Song Meiling as a birthday present.

Address

Rui Jin Guest House is located on 118 Rui Jin Er Lu. It is a five-minute walk from Huaihai Lu and a ten minute walk from the Huangpi Lu subway station. Traveling by bus, you can take lines 14, 24, 42, 96, the 146 Loop Line, the 401 Southern Line, 786, and 304 to the Huangjiner Lu or the Rui Jin Hospital bus stop.

The Marshall Residence — The Taiyuan Villa

(tàiyuánbiéshù, 太原别墅)

Most people fall in love with the Marshal Residence at first sight. Today, you can still hear people mention how this elegant building so finely reflected General George Marshall's graceful disposition, and how the building and the man were both equally unforgettable.

On December 20, 1945, General Marshall took a specially chartered plane to Shanghai and moved into this house on 160 Taiyuan Lu.

Passing through the dark green iron gates and following the tortuous small path into the grounds, you will come upon this romantic French Renaissance-style villa. Its simple clean lines and gentle brownish-yellow and grey powder colors give this house a warm and comfortable feel. The villa architecture is graceful and elegant; its four-sloped rooftops are covered in green tile, and five Napoleon helmet-styled windows mark the meeting point between the roofing and the eaves. Directly under the eaves lies a succession of white brackets. The ground level porch is supported by three classical Greek Doric columns, and an open-aired balcony sits on top.

In its former life, this was an independent garden villa belonging to the French colonials. In 1940 the property was sold to the son of Cen Chunxuan, the viceroy of Guangzhou and Guangxi under Wang Jingwei. After World War II the property was taken over as "illegal property", and in 1953 it was turned into a VIP Hotel used exclusively in entertaining foreign dignitaries. Today, the villa is part of Rui Jin Guest House and known as the Taiyuan Villa.

General Marshall's Mission to China: Anyone familiar with modern Chinese history is probably familiar with General Marshall's visit to China. On November 27, 1945 American president Harry Truman allowed Patrick Hurley to resign from his post as Ambassador to China. On December 20, he sent the army general chief of staff, George Catlett Marshall, as the president's special envoy to China to help mediate the military conflict between the communists and the nationalists, and help Chiang Kai-

shek speed up deployment of the Civil War. On the 22nd, Marshall arrived in Chongqing and on the 27th negotiations between the Communists and the Nationalists resumed. On January fifth 1946, an agreement was reached called the "Agreement On Ending Internal Military Conflict". Marshall eventually returned to the United States, frustrated by what he saw as a hopeless attempt to compromise between both parties.

Address

The Marshall residence is located at 160 Taiyuan Lu (originally called Route Rene Delastre). You can get here by walking from Huangpi Nanlu or Huaihai Zhonglu. You can take bus lines 41, 42, 45, 96, 104, 128, 301, 327, and 864. Be sure to get off the bus at Yongjia Lu or at Jianguo Xilu and walk over.

Special Note

The Tang Enbo Residence is located at 200 Taiyuan Lu, and its architectural style is very similar to that of the Marshall Residence. Tang Enbo was a high-level Kuomintang officer before China's liberation. Although it is not frequently open for tours, if time allows, you can still have a look around the building grounds. The Marshall Residence has two doors. The main entrance is labeled with the words "Taiyuan Villa", the other is labeled only with a street number. If the guard at the door asks what you are doing, you can say that you are going in to have a cup of coffee. More often than not, no one will prevent you from going in. The residence is about one kilometer away from Rui Jin Guest House and takes about 20 minutes to walk over. Along the way you will pass by Yongjia Lu. This road has a few residential areas you can visit, and some have architecture worth seeing. Most of it is British-style residential architecture.

Around Huaihai Lu
(huáihǎilù, 淮海路)

Huaihai Lu is one of the most important roads in Shanghai, and the place where Shanghai residents have traditionally come in pursuit of fashionable goods and flashy lifestyles. Constructed in 1901, Huaihai Zhonglu became a place where Shanghai's bourgeoisie once flocked in droves. Beginning in the East at Renmin Lu, Huaihai Lu stretches West to Kaixuan Lu. One of the French Concession's main roads, in 1915 it was given the name Avenue Joffre, named after French Marshal Joffre. At that time,

Avenue Joffre was considered one of the best places in the Shanghai. Noblemen and noblewomen could frequently be seen strolling in the drooping shade and pervasive aroma of the Chinese Parasol Trees.

With the arrival of the 1920's, came a flood of Russian refugees who entered the French Concession and took over the central section of Avenue Joffre. As this new Russian community began settling in, large numbers of Russian stores sprang up along the roadside. By the 1930's, Avenue Joffre had developed into a thriving commercial street dealing in middlebrow western clothing, fashionable outfits, jewelry, shoes, hats, and cosmetics, and was dotted with cafes, bars, and western restaurants.

Today's Huaihai Lu is still nostalgic for the shadows of Avenue Joffre. How many old Shanghai folk still dream about the old days — carrying around old records, mulling over chapters from Zhang Ailing's Red Rose White Rose, and lingering away the days on Huaihai Lu. Even more romantic are the young whose silhouettes can be seen splashed under the shade of the Chinese parasol trees. On Huaihai Lu you can stop in at the Shanghai Library and visit the villas and residences that once belonged to an early generation of Shanghai celebrities. Huaihai Lu also has a number of interesting old Shanghai houses like the Sheng Xuanhuai residence which was built in 1900 (today it is the Japanese Consulate in Shanghai). You can also see the French castle-like sky-rise apartment buildings constructed in 1910, and classical style Wu Kang apartment buildings built in 1942. Most of these buildings are not opened to the public, but you can still enjoy the dimension that they give to this street's atmospheric backdrop.

Transportation

Take the subway number one line to the Shaanxi Nanlu or Changshu Lu stations. If you exit at Shaanxi Nanlu head west. Walk east if you exit from Changshu Lu. You can also take bus lines 02, 42, 926, 24, 126, 320, and 911 to the Shaanxi Nanlu and Changshu Lu bus stops. If you plan on going to the Cathay Theater, the Parkson Shopping center, or the Shanghai NO.2 Department Store, then get off at the Shanxi Nanlu stop.

Travel Plan

Huaihai Lu has two can't-miss sites, and both can be enjoyed in just a few hours or less. One site is the Hengshan Moller Villa, which we strongly suggest you visit at night. The other is the Huaihai Lu commercial street--a shopper's paradise. If you love shopping, please refer to the chapter on shopping in Huaihai Zhonglu.

Food and Drink

Huaihai Lu has an impressive number of eateries. Shanghai Times Square, Hong Kong New World, and the Hong Kong Plaza all team with restaurants and food joints. Of the choices offered there, Kakatei Japanese Restaurant and Ebi Sushi are both popular choices. Ebi Sushi is the cheaper of the two. Vegetarians will probably want to check out The Vegeatery on the third floor of Shanghai Central Plaza (381 Huaihai Zhonglu). The Vegeatery has a 38 RMB lunch buffet, and the food there is pretty good.

Rosso Ristorante

(luósù huáihǎidiàn, 罗素淮海店)

Located at 381 Huaihai Zhonglu on the third floor of Shanghai Central Plaza, this French

If you like shopping, you can check out Maison Mode and the Shanghai Pacific Department Store. Come and discover the hidden gems and unique character of Huaihai Lu which has enchanted Shanghai for two centuries.

Eastern Orthodox Church
(dōngzhèng dàjiàotáng, 东正大教堂)

New and old, eastern and western, Shanghai has always been tolerant of diverse architectural styles and architects have historically been given free reign to exercise their creativity. Sitting on Route P. Henry East at the intersection of today's Xinle Lu and Xiangyang Beilu, the Orthodox Eastern Church is both refined and unrestrained, resembling a large palace stretching down from the sky. Along with the towering Chinese parasol trees of Xiangyang Park, the Orthodox Eastern Church has dramatically increased the appeal of this street that had previously experienced nothing more than several lackluster centuries of existence.

In 1928, Orthodox Eastern Archbishop Simon of Shanghai decided to construct a church on this piece of land inside the French Concession. His plan was thorough, but when he began collecting money for the endeavor, he discovered that most Russian refugees had barely enough money to survive much less contribute money for a church. Archbishop Simon decided to raise money through the issuance of "church bonds" which began circulating in 1930. When Archbishop Simon died of illness, and Archbishop Victor took over responsibility for the fund raising and church construction. The church was completed in February 1936, and it eventually became the seat of the Orthodox Eastern regional bishop of Shanghai.

The church interior is plain with little decoration other than grease paint adornments which are frequently found in Russian churches.

Closely linked to the fate of Shanghai's Russian community, the church blossomed

Food and Drink

restaurant has a 58 RMB lunch time buffet. The prices here are also pretty reasonable.

Coco Yifan Wu

(COCO yìfānwū huáihǎidiàn, COCO一番屋淮海店)

Located at L209, 688 Huaihai Zhonglu (near Sinan Lu), this cheap Japanese-style restaurant primarily serves noodles. Prices there average out to about 40 RMB per person.

Qichun Restaurant

(qǐchūn cāntīng, 起春餐厅)

Located at 124 Jinxian Lu (near the Maoming Nanlu intersection), Qichun serves up authentic Shanghainese food. The restaurant is small and is always packed. Expect to spend 40 RMB per person.

Linglong Restaurant

(línglóng cāntīng, 玲珑餐厅)

The atmospheric Linglong Restaurant is located at 57 Shanxi Nanlu. While not very large, Linglong serves tasty, saucy, red-colored Shanghai-style entrees. Portions are large, service is fast, and the price is right. Business here is always humming, and despite its small size, Longling is still one of the most famous eateries in Shanghai. We recommend the soy-braised pork, the water spinach in fermented bean curd sauce, and the ribs and potato soup. Prices average out at about 40 RMB per person.

Jinlong Fast Food Restaurant

(jīnlóng kuàicān, 金龙快餐)

Jinlong is a street-eats style restaurant located next to the Eastern Orthodox Church and is always packed with customers.

Boona Cafe

This relaxing cafe is located at 88 Xinle Lu. It is a nice place to relax after a day shopping and sightseeing, and the prices here are reasonable. There are magazines and books on the book shelf if you want to read, and wireless internet service is also available.

under the community's rise and tall with their disappearance. In 1965, the passing of Shanghai's last Eastern Orthodox Bishop led to the church's total abandonment, turning it into an unmanaged orphaned building. Later, the church enjoyed a brief resurrection as the Shanghai electric vacuum parts institute and much later became the Aluoha Music Dome Restaurant. Today, the church has been abandoned once again. Unfortunately, the general public is not allowed to tour the church interior. Tourists must appreciate the church from the outside.

There is a model train store right next door to the Orthodox Eastern Church selling miniature replicas of every train that has ever been used in China. Expect to pay between 100 RMB and 200 RMB per unit. The store also carries curious little trains that move on their own. If you are not a model train enthusiast, you will still get a kick out of the store's personnel who are all dressed in train attendant uniforms.

The Eastern Orthodox Church

Since the separation of the church in the eleventh century, in the 16th century the Russian Orthodox Church became the largest church in Eastern Orthodoxy. When the Eight-power allied forces invaded China, the Qing government agreed in a humiliating treaty to allow Czarist Russia to establish churches in China. In 1920, Russia received the right to establish churches in Shanghai. After the October revolution of 1917, waves of Russian refugees flooded into northeastern China and Shanghai. Shangha's White Russians settled in the Chabei District and onto Avenue Joffre turning it into a center of Russian activity.

Address

Located in the Xuhui District on 55 Xinle Lu (at the intersection of Xiangyang Beilu), you can reach the church from the Shaanxi Xilu subway station. After you exit the station, walk in the direction of Xiangyang Park and pass through the first intersection.

Xiangyang Park

(xiángyáng gōngyuán, 襄阳公园)

Xiangyang Park is located at the head of Xiangyang Beilu. This is a small park with a lot of history. Many Shanghai locals reminisce about it when they are away from home. Opened as Dumei Park in the 1940's, this has always been a favorite spot for Weiqi players and enthusiasts. Famous Chinese Weiqi players such as level 9 masters, Chen Zude and Qian Yuping, level 8 masters, Rui Naiwei and Wang Qun, and child prodigy, Chang Hao, have all reputedly spent significant time in Xiangyang Park playing Weiqi. Unfortunately Xiangyang Park's golden days of Weiqi are over. If you go for a stroll in the park today, you can still occasionally see a couple of Weiqi players here and there, but you will find mostly Shanghai locals going about their common daily activities.

Special Note

Weiqi is a common board game found in East Asia. It is known by the Japanese and many westerners as go.

Moller Villa

(mălè biéshù, 马勒别墅)

One evening in 1926, a young British girl living in Shanghai had a mysterious dream. In her dream, she imagined she owned her own Hans Christian Anderson-style fairy tale castle. Charmed by his daughter's imagination, the girl's father, Eric Moller, decided to build a home in the image of his daughter's dream castle. This new home not only recreated his daughter's dream, but also incorporated elements commemorating Moller's former life of adventure. He hired

Food and Drink

There is also a cafe inside the Hengshan Moller Villa that sits across from a large velvet lawn. Stop in here for a cup of coffee for an extremely satisfying experience. The Moller Villa's hotel restaurant serves local Shanghai cuisine in a setting that will remind you of an old Shanghai movie. Expect to pay around 150 RMB per person. You can also find a lot of restaurants right outside the hotel entrance.

Xinjiang Uigur Restaurant

(xīnjiāng fēngwèifànguăn wéiwúér cāntīng, 新疆风味饭馆维吾尔餐厅)

Located on Shaanxi Nanlu, entrees at the Xinjiang Uigur Restaurant are packed with Xinjiang flavor, though prices are not cheap. After seven pm you can enjoy Xinjiang music and dance performances.

an architect and invested a huge amount of capital into designing this Northern European-style castle villa. Located on Shanxi Nanlu, the house was completed in 1936.

The villa's main door is deceptively small, and when you walk inside you may not be prepared to be dazzled by the rich fairytale colors. Complete with Norwegian-style steeples, gothic pinnacles, Chinese style glass tiles, Tiger windows, Taishan face brick, and colored ornamental floor slabs; you will see niches for Buddhist statues collected together in one hall, and exquisitely carved decorations can be seen all over the house. Stained glass is inlaid into the domed ceiling and pagoda peaks of different heights, creating mysterious and marvelous contours. Coming to the Moller Villa is like visiting a magical North European village.

Today, Moller's Villa has become the Hengshan Moller Villa hotel. The hotel lobby, found on the first floor of the main building, is decorated in a tasteful and exquisite manner. Generally speaking, the hotel will not give you any trouble if you want to come in and tour the building, and you should definitely stop in for a visit if you have the time. Moller furnished this dream villa to look like a luxury ocean liner. You will find wooden carvings of nautical scenes, and even the floor is decorated with fine strips of wood, arranged to look like seaweed and kelp. The finest of these wooden strips are only a few millimeters wide.

The villa stairway is separated into not two, but three sections. You can climb the stairs on one side and come down the stairs on the other. If you are not familiar with the layout of the hotel it is easy to get lost in this stairway maze. Each stairway is built to the same width, and each gets narrower the closer you get to the top.

If you are not a hotel guest, one thing you are not allowed to do here, unfortunately, is visit the hotel's rooms, which are furnished with aristocratic-style furniture from the 1930's. If you are not in a rush, you should take some time to sit in the hotel's cafe. As the afternoon stretches into evening, walk to the yard in front of the building and gaze upon the villa under the lights. Moller Villa is definitely the most beautiful at this time. It is truly a world out of your dreams.

The Moller family was not in Shanghai

long before World War Two arrived on their doorstep. In 1941, the Japanese army entered the foreign concession. Moller's entire family was forced into concentration camps, and Moller's villa was converted into a Japanese club. After the war, the Kuomintang turned the villa into a general office, and today it is a hotel with rooms that you can book. If you would like to experience this hundred year old dream world for yourself, expect to pay 780 RMB for a standard double room. In the off season you can probably knock the price down about 20%. Telephone: 021-62478881. Website: www.mollervilla.com

Eric Moller

A British citizen, Moller arrived in Shanghai in 1919. Like many western explorers of his time, Moller made his fortune at Shanghai's race track. When his prized horse died, he had a bronze statue made and placed in the corner of his garden as a token of memory. Moller was also fond of dog racing and proved to have equally good luck in that arena.

Two or three years after arriving in Shanghai, Moller assumed a post at the horse racing assembly and became involved in shipping and real estate ventures. He eventually founded the Moller Machinery and Ship Building Company, Ltd. Moller's old factory is now Shanghai's Hudong Shipmaking Factory. From the hotel's entryway, you can see photographs of Erik Moller across the hallway.

Address

The Moller Villa is located in Shanghai's Jingan District at 30 Shaanxi Nanlu. You can get there by taking bus routes 24, 104, 304, 71, 49, and 127. Be sure to get off at the Shanxi Nanlu stop.

Around HengShan Lu
(héngshānlù, 衡山路)

On Hengshan Lu you will find blue-green French parasol trees, garden villas with mahogany colored roofs, European-style gazebos, and cozy cafes. In the evening you can enjoy live music and laidback nightlife.

Built in 1922, Hengshan Lu was originally a famous street in the French Concession known as Avenue Petain. Measuring at 2.3 kilometers in length, in October 1943, the road officially changed its name to Hengshan Lu.

Shanghai locals love coffee, and cafes can be found on virtually every street. In its early days, Hengshan Lu was steeped in coffee culture. Number one on Hengshan Lu, today's Xiangzhang Garden, is home to the Hengshan Café. This simple museum-like place has some historical significance; established in 1985, it was the first café to open in Shanghai after the Cultural Revolution. Over its 20 years of operation, it still retains its original look. Many people come to appreciate the nostalgic feel of the place. It is a popular spot for first dates.

It is recommended that you visit Hengshan Lu in the evening and enjoy its quiet and restrained nightlife. Dim lamps, flickering candles, and the quite soft tones of music and singing will bring you into this comfortable new world. If you come during the daytime, you can visit the Community Church, the Xujiahui Catholic Church, or pass through one or two small roads to the Song Qingling Residence. If you feel so inclined, this is also the place to visit the Shanghai Library where you can quietly spend part of the day exploring its enormous collections.

Transportation

The Xujiahui Catholic Church is located at 158 Puxi Lu. To get there, take subway line one to the Xujiahui station. You can also take bus line 56 and get off at its final stop, Nandan Donglu (Jianguo Hotel), or take lines 122, 732, and 770 to their final stops at Tianyaoqiao Lu. Buses that pass by Xujiahui include lines 02, 15, 42, 43, 44, 50, 72, 93, 205, 401, 548, 572, 593, 806, 814, 820, 824, 830, 847, 864, 872, 920, 923, 926, 927, 931, 946, the Daqiao number six line, airport line 3, tourist line number 10, the Xumin line and the Xu Chuan line.

You can also take the following bus lines to Huaihai Zhonglu: 44, 48, 72, 113,126, 138, 506, 548, 911, 920, 923, 926, 945, 946, and tourist line number 7.

Travel Plan

Take the subway to the Xujiahui station. First visit the Xujiahui Cathedral and the Xujiahui Library before heading over to La Villa Rouge inside Hengshan Park. You can walk or take a cab or bus to the Community Church and from there, pass through Wulumuqi Lu toward Huaihai Lu. Check out the Song Qingling Residence and then move over to the Shanghai Library. Head back over to Fenyang Lu to see the Little White House and other pieces of outstanding colonial architecture.

If you are short on time, you do not need to visit any site in particular, just stroll down Hengshan Lu, Fuzing Xilu, and Fengyang Lu. At the intersection of Fenyang Lu and Hengshan Lu you will find a bronze statue of Russian poet, Alexander Pushkin.

Xujiahui Catholic Church — St. Ignacious Cathedral

(xújiāhuì tiānzhǔ jiàotáng, 徐家汇天主教堂)

Xujiahui Catholic Church's two brick-red spires pierce the blue horizon. Though their color is a bit faded these days, they are still a startling sight in this thriving downtown area. To get to the church's main entrance, you need to walk down a small road in back of Xuguangqimu Plaza. Home to an art gallery and lined with gardens, you will rarely see many people on this quiet and secluded road; although, you may occasionally come across a person or two hustling through.

Western missionaries started their activities in Shanghai at the beginning of the 17th century. In 1847, Jesuit missionary, Claude Gotteland, chose to build a small Jesuit church at the northern face of Xujiahui cemetery. With the support of one famed Ming Dynasty official, Xu Guangqi's, descendants and an other local chrisitan named Lu, in 1904, he was able to obtain a portion of land to build a newer larger church. The church's official name was Church of the Virgin Mary for Mother of God. It was designed by W.M. Dowdall and built by the French Shanghai Construction Co. At the time, this was the best architectural team working in Shanghai. The church's base was constructed in the shape of a cross — the main entrance facing east — and fresh flowers were planted around the church's sides. Sitting serenely over the alter, the divine statue of the Virgin Mary with baby Jesus was shipped over from France before Easter Day in 1919. The opening ceremony and first mass were held when the church was finally finished on October 22, 1910.

First-time church visitors are usually shocked by its grand scale and its magnificent ornamentation. When the church was initially built, it was considered the Church's buttress in China, and the premier church of the Far East. Over several decades, as the Church continued to develop, a monastery, museum, library, astronomical observatory, and orphanage were all built to the church's side. These brand new structures have helped cement the church's status as the central church of the Southern Yangtze missionary district.

The church's main entrance is not usually kept open, but if you claim to be here for a church service, you will be allowed to enter through the side door. The people watching the doors are always a little bit suspicious of new visitors. No photography is allowed inside the church.

Xu Guangqi

Xujiahui is located at the meeting point of the Puhui Dike, Zhao Family Brook, and Fahua Jin waterways. Ming Dynasty scientist, Xu Guanqi used this small virtually uninhabited hamlet to build a small farming village and conduct agricultural experiments. An official from Beijing, Xu Guangqi was also one of Shanghai's first Catholics. In his old age, Xu Guangqi returned to his hometown of Shanghai. Xu and his parents are buried in the Xujiahui cemetery (on the grounds of today's Guangqi Park).

Address

Take the subway to the Xujiahui station. Exiting the subway station will take you right to the Xujiahui Catholic Church.

Telephone

021-64382595

Hours of Operation

Every Saturday and Sunday from 1pm to 4:30pm. Church members will show visitors around the church.

Xujiahui Library

(xújiāhuì cángshūlóu, 徐家汇藏书楼)

Walking 10 meters north from Xu Guangqi's cemetery will take you to the library. Built by French Jesuits, this, the first modern library in Shanghai, provided books to Shanghai's Catholic missionaries for reading and on loan. It was the largest library in early Shanghai, and in modern times it has become incorporated into part of the greater Shanghai library. Xujiahui Library is open on Saturdays from 2pm to 4pm. Groups are allowed in for fifteen minutes at a time and are lead inside by workers on the premises.

Food and Drink

You can find Japanese cuisine, Dongbei Daxian Dumplings, Xinxin Little Kitchen *(xīnxīn xiǎo chúfáng, 欣欣小厨房)*, Argentinean Barbecue, Bifeng Tang *(bìfēngtáng, 避风塘)* and other restaurants near the Wanping Lu entrance.

Yifang Clay Pot Porridge

(yìfāng shāguōzhōu, 一方砂锅粥)

Located at the intersection of Huaihai Lu and Wanping Lu, this restaurant cooks up all kinds of rice porridges. Most of the porridges are seafood-based and cooked in clay pots. The portions are large, but because each portion is made from scratch, cooking times tend to be long. Expect to pay about 50 RMB per person.

Visitors must register their name, wear tags, and put their cameras in their bags. No photography is allowed.

Song Qingling Residence

(sòngqìnglíng gùjū, 宋庆龄故居)

Over the course of her life, Song Qingling lived in this house for the longest period of time. To Song Qingling, Shanghai was her place of birth, and she is quoted as saying, "I go to work in Beijing, but I come home to Shanghai." Song returned to Shanghai for the final time during the Spring Festival from December 1979 to February 1980. After spending her holiday here, Song returned to Beijing. She fell ill and died on May 29, 1981 at the age of 88.

Passing down a long outdoor corridor will take you deep into the heart of the Song Qingling residence. Lined with luxuriant old camphor trees, this path is cool and comfortable in the summer time. Emerging from the corridor takes you right into the memorial plaza. A white marble statue of Song Qingling can be seen here, and it coordinates well with the surroundings. The residence's main building is a three storey milk-white structure shaped like a ship.

Built at the beginning of the twentieth century, the structure was built by a Greek ship captain as his own personal dwelling. After the end of World War Two, the property was confiscated by the Kuomintang Central Trust Bureau as property of the enemy regime. In a letter to a friend, Song Qingling once wrote that she wanted to leave the Sun Yat-sen residence and have it turned into national monument, a memorial for people to visit and look upon with reverence. Chiang Kai-shek gave personal orders to have this former Greek property authorized for Song Ringling's use. In 1948, she moved out of the Sun Yat-sen building and into her new home.

Today the residence shows Song Ringling's house just as it was when she lived there. The rooms are decorated simply but gracefully with gentle tones. There is a restaurant next door that Song visited frequently. An avid reader, Song had two studies on the first floor where she would often work and write. Sometimes she would do nothing, just sitting quietly and looking out on the property. You do not need to set aside a large amount of time to see the whole residence, but the garden outside is a nice place to linger and enjoy the silence.

There are all kinds of Song Qingling books, postcards, and other materials on sale at the entrance.

Address

Located at 1843 Huaihai Zhonglu. You can get here on foot from Hengshan Lu. It will take you about 15 minutes to walk from the Hengshan subway station.

Hours of Operation

Monday through Friday 1pm to 4pm.

Tickets

8 RMB

Shanghai Library
(shànghǎi túshūguǎn, 上海图书馆)

Just a five minute trip from the Song Qingling residence, follow Huaihai Zhonglu toward Fuxing Xilu to reach the huge Shanghai library. Built in 1952, the main building is made up of two large high rises and a group of smaller buildings along its sides. The two buildings to the east and west are in the shape of multi-dimensional platform-style blocks, and are meant to symbolize both a foundation of accumulated cultural achievements and humanity's endless search for knowledge. Library collections include over 13 million books, making it the second largest library in China and one of the ten largest libraries in the world. The Shanghai library is widely known for its family histories, letters, contemporary Chinese and English periodicals, rare edition English works, and rubbings of stone inscriptions. You can also find selections of classical and contemporary music, opera records, and tapes. Over 20 reading rooms are separated by subject area including: ancient books, integrated collections, cultural and literary documents, social sciences, natural sciences, foreign languages, and compact discs.

Reserve the books you want to check out over the internet, and a small trolley will bring your selection out from the stacks. You can follow the following link to the library's Chinese website: www.libnet.sh.cn. The website introduces the library and its collections. Unfortunately, no English language website is available.

Address

1555 Huaihai Zhonglu at the intersection of Gaoan Lu.

Telephone

021-64455555

Hours of Operation

8:30am-8:30 pm

Special Note

If you want a temporary library pass to get into the reading rooms, you will need to bring your passport and 10RMB. The library stops processing reading room passes after 5pm. For a one-year library card you will need to bring your passport and long-term Shanghai residence permit. Fees range between 10 RMB and 50 RMB depending on which collections you plan to use, and you may be asked to give a 100 RMB or 1,000 RMB deposit if you plan to check books out of the Chinese and foreign language collections, respectively.

The Shanghai Community Church *(guójì lǐbàitáng, 国际礼拜堂)*

A diverse nightlife has started making incursions into Hengshan Lu's romantic splendor. More and more people come here to enjoy the early evening mist but overlook the living history on both sides of the road. The Shanghai Community Church is found on the central section of Hengshan Lu. A tall crucifix hides the front entrance. During the springtime, a thick blanket of ivy covers the wall like a green cape.

In the 1920's, a group of American Christians organized a choir group on Route Doumer (today's Donghu Lu). Deciding that they needed a more permanent place to conduct their choral activities, they had their first church built. Completed in 1920, the Americans constructed their church, Unity Church, on Donghu Lu, and most of the church goers were Americans. In 1923, a more diverse group of internationals decided to build a church on Hengshan Lu. Construction was finished on March 8, 1925 and the church was called Shanghai Community Church. The church's neutral name reflects the church's tolerant nature and multi-denominational nature.

Shanghai Community Church's main entrance faces north. Its top is decorated with intersecting roof trusses, and its red brick structure, recalls old German pastoral architecture. When you walk inside you will be able to fully appreciate a more complete panoramic view of the structure. Both sides of the church have corridors with pointed arches and arched window frames. As the sun sets, golden shadows of light pour in through the windows. A walk out onto the polished stone terrace allows you to experi-

ence the church's countryside simplicity.

As Shanghai Community Church's fame continues to spread, famous figures have begun showing up at church services. Among the long list of notables are former US president Jimmy Carter and his family. Moreover, religious figures like British Archbishop of Canterbury, Dr. Robert Runcie, famed warrior of peace, South Africa's Arch Bishop Desmond Tutu, and famous American evangelical, Dr. Billy Graham have all held religious services here. Today, church activities remain pretty typical, but it is still active with weekly Sunday services. The church's graceful musical tradition has also been preserved with a sixty member chorus. They perform peaceful worship music every Sunday as well as on Christmas and Easter. If you can make it to a Sunday service, you will have an opportunity to hear their moving and delightful sounds. We suggest taking a discrete recording device so that when you leave, you can take the music with you. Services are conducted by foreign nationals in English.

Address

Located at 53 Hengshan Lu in the Xuhui District (at the intersection of Hengshan Lu and Wulumuqi Nanlu). Walk north from the Hengshan Lu subway station to get here.

Telephone

021-64376576

Hours of operation

The church is usually open. Church members will throw open the doors and welcome you in for Sunday services. Fixed Sunday service times at 7:30 am, 10:00 am, and 7 pm.

La Villa Rouge
(xiǎohónglóu, 小红楼)

La Villa Rouge towers loftily over its green, sunny, lazy corner of the Xujiahui Park. Created by the EMI Record Company, this was also home to China's first record company. EMI arrived in Shanghai at the end of the nineteenth century, bringing with it its fashionable new gramophone. In 1921, EMI bought a lot at 1434 Xujiahui Lu (today's 811 Hengshan Lu), and established the "Eastern EMI Record Company", building Shanghai's first recording studio. For a while, this was also China's best recording studio. Today, the company's recording rules and regulations, inscribed in 1983, are framed on the wall of the building's first floor. Starting here, the symbol for Pathe-Marcont, EMI's French subsidiary, quickly spread throughout China and Southeast Asia. There is a record cutting machine at the doorway of the building's first floor. This is China's oldest phonograph.

La Villa Rouge, formerly a red building, is now painted grey, and it is both grand and refined. Nowadays, the building houses a French Restaurant with a Malaysian owner and a Japanese chef. The ownership wisely did not ignore the building's history when they designed the restaurant. If you come for dinner or just want to come in and relax for the evening, the restaurant plays records on its old gramophone, adding new layers to its rich atmosphere. La Villa Rouge serves a buffet and a la carte style entrees, and the chef focuses on innovative cuisine. Here you will sample entrees that cannot be found anywhere else.

Address

La Villa Rouge is located at 811 Hengshan Lu (inside the Xujiahui Park).

Telephone

021-64316639

Hours of Operation

11:00am to 2am. The polite service people at the door will let you look around, but photography is not allowed.

Ai Lu *(àilú, 爱庐)*

Now part of the Shanghai Music Conservatory Middle School, the building at 9 Dongping Lu was once home to two of the most famous people in the world — Chiang Kaishek and Song Meiling. When the couple was married in 1927, Song Meiling's older brother, Song Ziwen, bought this building for his sister and Chiang as a wedding present. When the newlyweds returned to Shanghai from their honeymoon in Hangzhou and Mogan Mountian, they moved into this property, making it their long-term residence. Chiang Kai-shek owned many properties in Shanghai, but this one was his favorite. He carved the characters for the word ailu ("love cottage" in Chinese) in the ornamental hill outside, and you can still see them there today. Chiang was not able to stay here for very long. He was always on the move, rushing from one place to another. Song Meiling often traveled at her husband's side, but, nevertheless, was able to spend more time at their home.

The Conservatory Middle School does not have a large campus, and Ailu is easy to find next to the school's main gate. The house looks older than ever, and the hanging vines are flourishing. Dark red-colored flat tiles on the roof are extremely well preserved, and the black, white, and yellow cobblestones in the wall are as beautiful as before. Music only adds to the spirit of this little house, and you can hear the sound of string instruments reverberating here all day long. A practice studio now occupies the house's first floor and the other rooms have been converted into classrooms. The structure still preserves a secret escape route that, in special circumstances, can be used to escape to the outside. But if you ask the guards around the building, they will not be able to tell you where the secret stairwell is.

Before the building was absorbed into the middle school, it was occupied for a while by Mao Zedong's wife, Jiang Qing. Old men and women who tend to linger around the building chat tirelessly about the peculiarities of history surrounding the building and its inhabitants.

Address

The Music Conservatory's middle school is located at 9 Dongping Lu. It is within walking distance of the Hengshan Lu subway station.

Director of the French Concession Chamber of Industry Mansion

(zǒngdǒng guāndǐ, 总董官邸)

This residence is in the middle of a large courtyard surrounded by high walls. Tall trees form an effective second wall in the courtyard interior. When you walk onto the property you will be able to see a small ribbon-like stream. It is said that when the courtyard was built, there was a Venetian statue sitting in the stream, but sadly, after the Cultural Revolution, all traces of the statue have disappeared. Built in 1905, this refined and secluded house was originally the residence of the French Concession's Chamber of Industry Director. Sitting on the green lawn, this white palatial structure looks a lot like the White House in Washington, DC. Many locals like to refer to it as the "Little White House".

The high-powered general director's mansion was constructed on Fenyang Lu, originally known as Route Pichon. Route Pichon was a one kilometer long road situated in what was then a remote stretch of Shanghai. Surrounded on all sides by farm houses and intersecting stretches of farmland and rivers, this was not where the action was, and indeed, the mansion was supposedly situated here in order to help the general director find some peace and quiet outside the bustling streets of urban Shang-

hai. It was also said that the director feared trouble in the French Concession, and hid here in Shanghai's safer outlying regions. Safety in the French Concession was a valid concern considering the huge disturbances that occurred there during the 1870's and 1880's.

It took a total of five years to build the mansion, and its design reveals the French spirit of art and romance. At once dignified and ornate, careful and artistic, the grand main building is fronted by a large artistic French yard. The doors and windows have ornately carved relief sculptures, and the lobby's floor and ceiling are covered with marble finishing. Exquisite sculptures also decorate the ceiling. Today, the building is occupied by the Shanghai Museum of Arts and Crafts. You can admire the museum displays and beautiful residential architecture at the same time.

French Municipal Council: The French Municipal Council was very similar in function to the International Settlement's Municipal Council, and was the French Concession's largest municipal government organization and leadership organ. It was created in 1860 when the Taiping military entered Shanghai, and the various International Settlements united together to protect their territory and to fight back the Taiping army. Originally, the organization was called the French Concession Ministry of Works, but it later changed its name to the French Municipal Council. From this point on, the Consul General was also Director of the French Concession's Chamber of Industry, making him the most powerful person in the French Concession.

Address

The General Director's residence can be found at 79 Fenyang Lu (at its intersection with Taiyuan Lu). To get there you can take bus lines 96, 42, and 45. If you are coming from Hengshan Lu, you can come over on foot. Just walk down to the Dongpin Lu intersection and than turn onto Fenyang Lu.

Hours of Operation

9am-11 am; 1pm-4pm

Around Sichuan Beilu

(sìchuān běilù, 四川北路)

Shanghai locals who grew up on and around Sichuan Beilu will always carry nostalgic feelings for this road. Today's flourishing prosperity mirrors the thriving bustle that Sichuan Beilu experienced in the past. It is both sweet and loaded with Shanghai style. Here you can find Yingzi Photographic Shop, Xinhua Book Store, Sixin Dim Sum Shop, Xihu Hotel, Yanji Western Food Association, and Di Qi Department Store. For many Shanghainese people, this is the place where they had their first picture taken, the place where they spent their first Christmas, and the place where they tasted Western Food for the first time.

Originally called Szechwan Lu (North), Sichuan Beilu runs from the Suzhou River and the Sichuan Lu Bridge in the south to the Hongkou Park in the north. Stretching a total of 3.7 kilometers, this is Shanghai's third major commercial street after Nanjing Road and Huaihai Lu, and it was one of the first roads constructed as Shanghai developed into a city. When the United States' concession was created in 1848, the southern portion of Sichuan Beilu became the part of the concession's border. When the northern portion of the road was completed, it was considered a "border crossing construction". At that time, it was a spot where Shanghai's foreign residents would come to socialize together, especially Shanghai's Japanese residents. Afterwards, it became one of Shanghai locals' most loved commercial areas.

After Sichuan Beilu's reconstruction in 2005, not a trace of its original appearance remains. All that can be seen here now is brand new high-rise buildings and new store fronts facing the street. Perhaps these newer modern buildings will continue to

Transportation

Transportation to Sichuan Beilu is convenient. You can get there on bus lines 13, 17, 21, 18, 19, 70, 65, 21, 47, 592, 848, and 863. Be sure to get off the bus at Sichuan Beilu. You can continue on foot to Duolun Lu.

You can take the subway number three line to the Hongkou Football Stadium and then take lines 18, 21, 97, 139, 231, 854, 79, 939 or the take subway line number three and get off at the Lu Xun Park. Continue on to Lu Xun's Residence from there.

Travel Plan

Most people find Sichuan Beilu friendly and approachable. It is well within reach of Duolun Lu, and home to Lu Xun Park, the Lu Xun residence, and a number of other attractions all within a one kilometer circumference. Duolun Lu has a lot of old houses, and sculptures of famous and important Chinese figures from the last century. The area may seem a little touristy, but that does not make it any less interesting. When you leave Duolun Lu, you can walk to the Lu Xun Residence only 300 meters away. Lu Xun Park is only 500 meters, one bus stop, from the Duolun Lu or Lu Xun Park. Half a day's time is enough to see all of the attractions here, but if you like photography you can stay a little while longer to take some pictures. There are a few small lanes and alleys worth visiting where you can see how regular Shanghai people live. When the weather is good, you can see people stretch bamboo poles out of their windows to dry their clothes in the sun, a classic Shanghai scene. These are great places to spend time with your camera.

expand up and down the street, changing the face of this famous road. One thing will never change though; everything on Sichuan Beilu is here for the common man's consumption. Baleno, Metersbonwe, and other brands popular with Chinese masses have set up shops on this street. Sichuan Beilu is also known as a good place to window shop despite the famous advertising slogan, "go window shopping everywhere else, but come buy at Sichuan Beilu."

If you do not care for shopping, there are plenty of interesting things to see here just the same. One hundred years ago, Chinese literary figures were active along the nearby Duolun Lu, and Lu Xun's former residence, Lun Xun's memorial site and tomb can all be found along Sichuan Beilu. You can also wander the ancient alleys and appreciate some typical traditional Shanghai residential architecture. You will have the opportunity to come away from this stop with a much better understanding of Shanghai.

Duolun Lu *(duōlúnlù, 多伦路)*

The words, "一条多伦路，百年上海滩" "One Duolun Road: a witness to one hundred years of Shanghai history," are painted onto the side of a colorful motley wall. A Lu Xun statue stands by its side.

Duolun Lu (originally Doulean Lu) was once a relatively anonymous Shanghai street snuggled up next to the bustling Sichuan Beilu. With Lu Xun Park located to the street's north, Duolun Lu is small enough that it has difficulty making its way on to some maps. This sleepy stretch of road is a place that exudes calmness and serenity. The large archway at the intersection with Sichuan Beilu marks this place as a tourist site, and, indeed, the street is lined with shops selling curios, stationary, and souvenirs. But, the people who walk this street are mosthy the Dunlun residents themselves. When the weather is good, you can see them sitting on benches taking in the sun, chatting, or walking their dogs in their nightgowns and flip-flops. If you could go one hundred years back in time, perhaps you would run into literary giants Lu Xun or Mao Dun on the street. Maybe you would see Guo Morou, Ye Shengtao, or Shen Yimo, or perhaps even Rou Shi or Ding Ling. Over one fleeting century of time, Shanghai began as a sleepy fishing village with flat bottomed boats, saw an invasion of foreign firms in the 1930's, and evolved into the thriving metropolis of today. As this city has changed, Duolun Lu has toiled in obscurity while guiding a generation of Chinese writers. Despite its general absence from literary writings, Duolun Lu has definitely attained "a key position in the sphere of modern literature".

Most of the famous literary residences along Duolun Lu have long since been converted into common residential housing, and most do not openly welcome visitors. But, do not let this seeming lack of attractions dissuade you from coming. Duolun Lu is home to a series of small private collectors' museums that will surely excite collector fanatics out there. Here you can find the Chopsticks Museum (191 Duolun Lu), the Timepiece Museum (193 Duolun Lu), Writing Style and Strange Rocks Museum (189 Duolun Lu), not to mention places like the Book and Ticket Collection Gallery, Newspaper Clippings Museum, and Ancient Pottery Collection Gallery. There is also a hard-to-notice underground market (the 8 Duolun Lu Curios Market) next to Gongfei Cafe. Here you can find stands working in curios, coins, and books; though there are not too many places here to go shopping.

Food and Drink

Wangjia Restaurant

(wángjiā xiǎocài, 王家小菜)

Located at 1755 Sichuan Beilu on the fourth floor of the Baixia Hotel, this well reputed restaurant serves local dishes and slashes prices in the evening. Expect to pay 40-50 RMB per person.

Chanshenxian Goose Gizzard Hotpot's

(chánshén xiān écháng huǒguō, 馋神鲜鹅肠火锅)

Located at 1888 Sichuan Beilu, this restaurant specializes in goose hotpot. The hot pot is quite fresh and includes lots of bamboo shoots. It tastes pretty good. Expect to pay about 40 RMB per person.

Dongfeng Xiuxian Plaza

(dōngtài xiūxián guǎngchǎng, 东泰休闲广场)

Located at 2002 Lane on 17 Sichuan Beilu, this plaza has a number of good restaurants such as the **Duck King** *(yāwáng, 鸭王)*. **Alishan Hot Pot** *(ālǐshān huǒguō, 阿里山火锅)* is also good and certainly worth a try. **FeiLong-Fried Baozi** *(fēilón gshēngjiān bāozi, 飞龙生煎包子)* on the first floor sells fried stuffed steamed buns at 3RMB a piece, chicken wraps for 5 RMB, and four small minced crab meat steamed buns for 8 RMB. Beef and rice vermicelli noodle soup costs 5 RMB a bowl. The food here is good, although there is almost always a long line.

Youzi Laoya Glass Noodle Soup

(yóuzǐlǎoyā fěnsītāng, 游子老鸭粉丝汤)

From Sichuan Beilu walk down Jiangxi Beilu. Stop at 579 Wuchang Lu for this great snack restaurant with a lot of character. Even during the 39 degree summer days, you will find undeterred customers lining up here under the hot noon sun. The duck and rice vermicelli soup is served in bowls filled with large quantities of duck gizzards and duck intestines. 5

Hong De Tang

(hóngdétáng, 鸿德堂)

One of the most eye-catching buildings on Duolun Lu is Hong De Tang at 59 Duolun Lu. Hong De Tang is a church housed inside a traditional Chinese building. Originally home to the American Presbyterian Mission Press, the structure was later transformed into a large scale printing and publishing house. In 1925, the American Presbyterian Church donated ten thousand dollars, which was combined with numerous Chinese donations to found the church. Its design adopted traditional Chinese architectural elements such as corbel brackets and up-turned eaves. Construction finished in 1928 and the church was given the Chinese name, "Hong De Tang". At the time, the first floor housed a virtue cultivating primary school and the chapel was located on the second floor. Today, the Suzhou Embroidery Gallery occupies the first floor lobby.

Jingyunli *(jǐngyúnlǐ, 景云里)*

This is Lu Xun's first long-term residence in Shanghai, and is also the place where he and Xu Guangping met and fell in love. A little over 10 meters in length, this street also housed Lu Xun contemporaries Mao Dun, Ye Shengtao, Zhou Jianren, Ping Xuefeng and Rou Shi.

Tang Enbo Residence

(tāngēnbó gōngguǎn, 汤恩伯公馆)

Located at 250 Duolun Lu, this Spanish style garden villa was once home to Kuomintang Commander in chief, Tang Enbo. Today it is a coin museum with Asia's largest exhibition of ancient coins.

Kong Xiangxi Residence

(kǒngxiángxī gōngguǎn, 孔祥熙公馆)

Located at 250 Duolun Lu, the Kong Xiangxi Residence once belonged to the Kong family, which was once one of the four most powerful families in China. This building was designed in the Islamic style and is inlaid with Arabic-style porcelain tiles — white but with dark colored patterns. Its flamboyant appearance can still be appreciated today.

Bai Chongxi Residence

(báichóngxǐ gōngyù, 白崇禧公寓)

Located close by on 2023 Lane at 35 Sichuan Beilu, this was once the apartment of Kuomintang Defense Minister Bai Chongxi. Today the residence has been converted into a hospital. According to Bai Chongxi's son, famed Taiwanese writer Bai Xianlong, the table where he once played table tennis can still be found there.

Some of the other local homes, the China University of Art, Shanghai Art Opera Troup, Neishan Book store and museums are all worth strolling through and examining for a few hours. Lu Xun was once a frequent customer at Gong Cafe found on the underground floor of a tall building at the head of Duolun Lu.

League of Left Wing Writers Memorial Gallery

(zuǒlián jìniànguǎn, 左联纪念馆)

Located at 145 Duolun Lu, this building looks unremarkable indeed. This is the locale where famous Chinese writer Ye Shengtao edited Novel Monthly, and Mao Dun wrote his first novel Huanmie. Ding Ling finished his work Meng Ke here, and Ba Jin wrote Mie Wang. This is also the

Food and Drink

or 6 RMB will be enough to fill you up. Even if you are not crazy about what is in the soup, know that this is indeed a well-loved Shanghai dish. If you really want to enjoy it, you need to overcome your aversion to eating blood.

Kankyoshuten

(xiánhāng jiǔdiàn, 咸亨酒店)

Korean barbecue and other cuisines are served in this converted Japanese-style house. Prices range about 40-50 RMB per person. This is a restaurant worth visiting.

Old Film one Cafe

(lǎodiànyǐng kāfēi guǎn, 老电影咖啡馆)

This converted western-style building is now an old cinema-themed cafe. Classic Shanghai films are constantly rolling here, and old movie star, Zhao Dan's, mountain and sea scroll paintings are on display. You will also be able to see a memoir by Gu Yelu about his experience working together with film star Zhou Xuan as well as a 1920's era German film projector.

Wanshou Zhai *(wànshòuzhāi, 万寿斋)*

Located at 123 Shanyin Lu (between Sida Lu and Jixiang Lu), Wanshou Zhai is a well-reputed Dim Sum restaurant. "Three freshness" *(sānxiānxiàn, 三鲜馅)* wantons have always been this restaurant's specialty. These savory wantons are filled with pork, shrimp, and dried bamboo tips, i.e. the "three freshness". A bowl of ten wantons costs 4 RMB. Classic small stuffed steamed buns cost 4 RMB for a set of 8 RMB, but they are not as authentic as those served at Nanxiang Xiaolong.

Shanyin Noodle Shop

(shānyīn miànguǎn, 山阴面馆)

Located at 51 Shanyin Lu 208 Nong (near Tianaizhi Lu), this is another fine place to eat noodles. You can eat well here for between 5 RMB and 10 RMB.

place where the League of Left-Wing Writers and Shanghai's Art Opera Troupe were established. The memorial gallery includes literary and writing related displays. There are also exhibitions of ten of China's great cultural figures including Lu Xun, Mao Dun, Qi Qiubai, Guo Moruo, and others.

League of Left Wing Writers
(zuǒlián, 左联)

The League of Left Wing Writers or "Zuolian" was formed in Shanghai on March 2, 1930. This was a revolutionary writers group under the leadership of the Communist Party, and it was that era's only Chinese literary movement and ideological trend. "Zuolian" was initiated by the likes of literary luminaries such as, Lu Xun, Guo Moruo, Mao Dun, Xia Yan, Tian Han, Yu Dafu, Rou Shi, and Ding Ling, and they lead the movement with their early works. The Zuolian Movement's written works have already become well sought after by collectors. The most representative works from that period include Lu Xun's Fake Free Book, Guo Moruo's Three Volumes of Drift, Yu Dafu's Chenlun, Mao Dun's Spring Silkworm, and Lin's Family Shop.

Address

Duolun Lu is located in the Hongkou District. Though short, Duolun Lu has a tortuous zigzagged shape. Both of the road's entrances are located on Sichuan Beilu.

Lu Xun's Residence
(lǔxùn gùjū, 鲁迅故居)

In October 1927, Lu Xun moved from Guangzhou to Shanghai. Living first in Jing Yun on the Hongkou District's Huangbin Lu, he later moved to today's 9 Shanyin Lu 132 Nong (originally Shigaota Lu's Dalu Cun). Lu Xun resided at Shanyin Lu until he died in 1936 at the age of 56. At Shanyin Lu he published 9 collections of essays and the historical novel, Old Stories Retold. He also edited several published works includ-

ing Yu Si, Ben Liu, Chao Hua, Sprouts, Front Post, Cross of the Street, Translator, and translated a number of foreign works.

The residence at today's 9 Shanyin Lu is nothing more than an ordinary small grey building, and it has completely mingled with the lives of the people in the marketplace. Aside from the eye-catching sign, "Lu Xun Residence", it is absolutely indistinguishable from anything else in the neighborhood.

Built in 1931, the three story Dalu Xincun was considered a new style alleyway building. When Lu Xun was still living in 23 Jingyun, he would visit his Japanese friend, Uchiyama Kanzo's, book store every day to read and buy books. Uchiyama Kanzo was Lu Xun's loyal and committed friend, and was always looking out for Lu Xun's safety. In April 1933, Lu Xun was able to move into his new residence under the pretense that he was a worker at Kanzo's book store. Everything in his residence today is arranged exactly as it was in Lun Xun's life. Much of it was arranged personally by Lu Xun's wife, Xu Guangping. Most of Lu Xun's valuables were taken with Xu Guangping when she moved into her new house the Huaihai Fang on Huaihai Zhonglu. When Lu Xun's residence was established as a memorial site in 1950, Xu Guanping donated all of the valuables to the site to share them with all who loved and admired her husband.

When you visit Lu Xun's residence, guides will take you around the house providing you with explanations and tidbits of history. Groups are split up and lead inside a few people at a time. Photography is not allowed. The house's second floor has Lu Xun's bedroom and study. The calendar on the wall near the window is still turned to its original page at October 19, the 25th year of the Republic of China (1936). The alarm clock on his dressing table has stopped at 5:25. This is the date and time of Lu Xun's death. You can still see Lu Xun's medicine lying on the cupboard in the storage room. Lu Xun struggled with lung disease, but he refused to go to the hospital. Much of the medicine he used, he made himself at home.

In his last year of life, Lu Xun's body weight fell to 37 kilograms. Nevertheless, he spent most of his time tirelessly working on the publication and translation of his friend, the late Qi Qiubai's Collected Narrations Written at Sea. The time he spent on Qi's works reflected the deep feelings he felt for his deceased friend. Mao Dun lived in building number six, right next door. Lu Xun's Japanese friend Uchiyama Kanzo also lived nearby. Qu Qiubai's residence is also in the area, but none of these homes are open to the public.

Lu Xun *(lǔxùn, 鲁迅)*

(September 25, 1881 — October 19, 1936), is one of the giants of modern Chinese literature, and the founder of the New Literary Movement. He was born into a declining feudal family in Zhejiang's city of Shaoxing. His original name was Zhou Shuren (and was also known as Yucai). He studied medicine in Japan, and when he returned to China, he published Diary of a Madman under his pen name, Lu Xun. Lu Xun's life's work totals 20 volumes. Among them are Diary of a Madman, Kong Yiji, Medicine, and The True Story of Ah Q. Lu Xun's work opened the window to China's new literary history, and heavily influenced both Chinese and international writers. His other works include collections of essays like Er Xin Ji, Er Yi Ji, and Hot Wind. These writings are still enthusiastically received by young Chinese literary buffs.

Address
Located on 132 Lane at 9 Shanyin Lu in the Hongkou District.
Telephone
021-56662608
Hours of operation
9am -4pm
Tickets
8 RMB

Lu Xun Museum
(lǔxùn jìniànguǎn, 鲁迅纪念馆)

The Lu Xun Residence was once part of the old Lu Xun Museum, but they were separated when the new museum was built in Lu Xun Park at 2288 Sichuan Beilu. The museum has over 200 thousand cultural artifacts and virtually all are related to Lu Xun's ten years in Shanghai. The collections include about 10,000 valuable pieces including drafts of written works, poems, and translations, books and periodicals, items he used in his daily life, and wood carvings that he created in the 1930's. The exhibition is not large; most of what you can see is limited to about 1,000 items. You can learn more at the museum's web page at: www.luxun.Chinaspirit.net.cn.

When you visit the museum, it is common to run into tour groups. You can avoid them by going early in the morning or later in the evening. If you still happen to run into a tour, just wait for them to leave. These group tours do not usually linger for very long.

Lu Xun passed away on October 19, 1936 and his remains were buried at what was then known as Wanguo Public Cemetery. In 1956, on the eve of the 20th anniversary of Lu Xun's death, a Lu Xun tomb was built in the corner of the Hong Kou Park, and Lu Xun's inner and outer coffins were solemnly transferred to this site and reburied. Today, the grass yard in front of the tomb is decorated with a sitting statue of Lu Xun, and Lu Xun's coffin and remains are buried under his gravestone. The two Chinese cypress trees on both sides of the grave were planted by his wife, Xu Guangping, and his son, Zhou Haiying.

Address

2288 Sichuan Beilu in the Hongkou District. You can walk to the park from the Lu Xun residence in just a few minutes.

Telephone

021-56669711

Hours of Operation

9am-4pm

Tickets

For tickets to the Lu Xun memorial: Adults 9 RMB, Children: 6 RMB.

Around the City

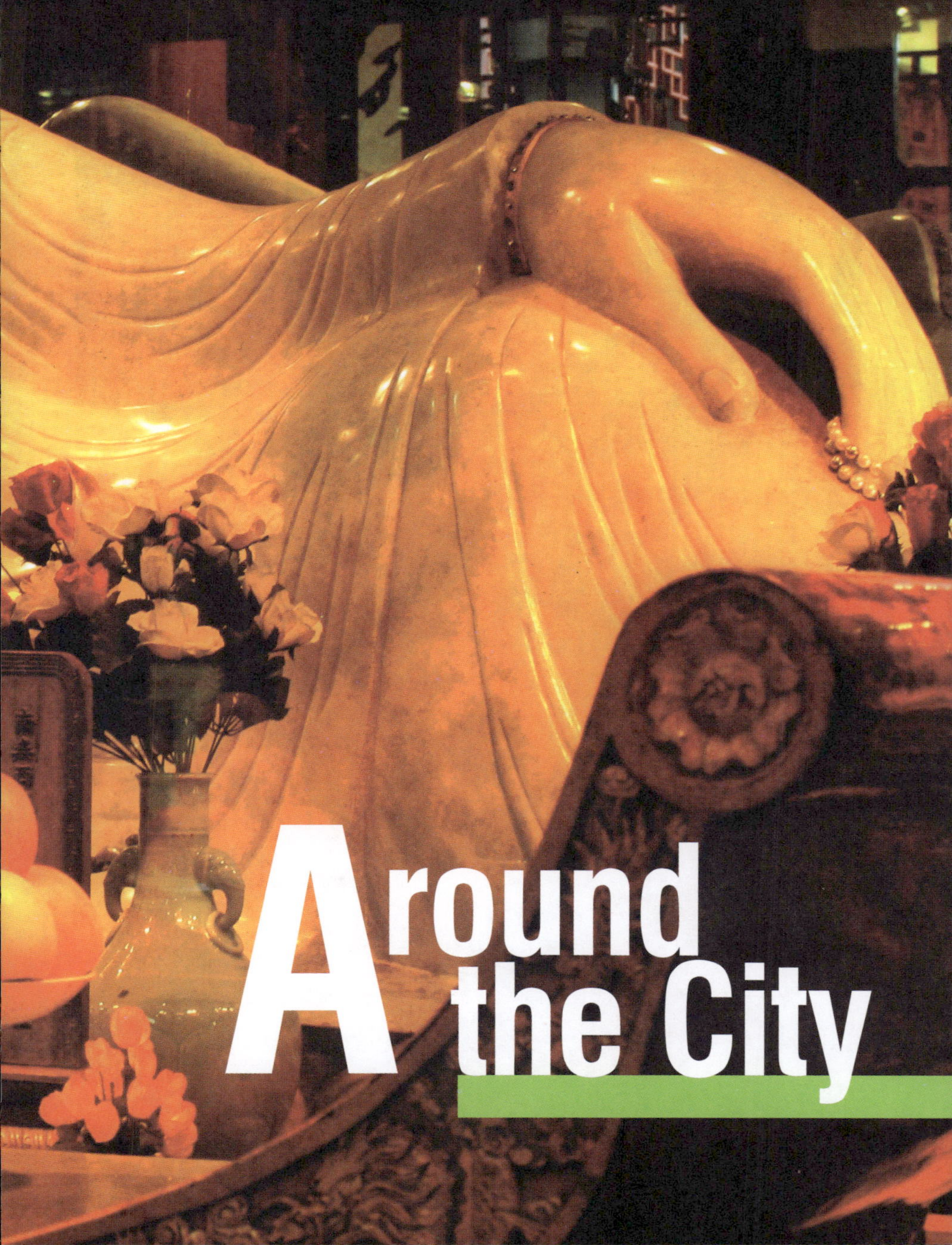

Temples

Jade Buddha Temple
(yùfósì, 玉佛寺)

Most people travel out to Yufo Si Temple to see its two charming jade Buddhas. When they arrive though, visitors are thunderstruck by this huge 7,737 square meter architectural complex, complete with Song Dynasty style.

Walking past the temple's Great Emperor Hall, will take you by the Precious Hall of the Great Hero, the Jade Buddha Building, halls on both sides devoted to "Guanyin", the Goddess of Mercy, the Copper Buddha Hall, the Reclining Buddha Temple, the Temple of Benevolence Hall, the meditation room and refectory. Climbing up to the second floor of the Jade Buddha Building will take you to see the first of the famed Jade Buddha statues. The second is located in the Reclining Buddha Temple.

The statue on the second floor of the Jade Buddha Building is known as the "treasure of town and temple". A representation of the seated Siddhartha Guatama (founder of Buddhism), at only 1.95 meters tall, the statue is not particularly large. Only one single giant piece of jade was needed to carve almost the entire statue you see here. Fringes of the jade Buddha's kasaya, or Buddhist monk coat, and the bracelet on his right arm are decorated with a hundred small pieces of jadeite, agate, and other precious stones. Sitting cross-legged, the Buddha's left hand rests on his left leg, and his palm faces upwards denoting the tranquility and concentration of his meditation. His right hand falls naturally at his side, fingers touching the ground, in a position called "touching earth". This slight gesture is rich in meaning, indicating that only the Earth can testify to all of Buddha's benevolent acts and his contributions to all creatures. Sending off a sparkling crystal-clear luster, the Buddha's eyes are half open and his lips are closed in composed serenity with a slight temperate smile. No matter from what angle you view him, he is always serenely and attentively watching you.

The Reclining Buddha Temple statue depicts the Buddha, Siddhartha Guatama, posed, naturally, in a reclining position. Called, "Siddhartha Guatama Obtains Nirvana," this statue portrays the eighty-year old Siddhartha as he achieves parinirvana (the highest state of Buddhism) under two Sal trees in the outskirts of the Kushinagar. Intricately carved from a single large piece of white marble, the Buddha's right hand supports his head as he lies on a couch of mahogany wood. His face reveals a slight smile of peace and tranquility.

Yufo Si Temple owes its existence to these two Buddhist statues. During the

eighth year of Qing Emperor Guangxu, Master Huigen of Putuo Mountain, set off on a journey through the Wutai and Emei Mountians on his way to Tibet. From Tibet, Huigen continued on to India and Myanmar. In Myanmar he came upon a mountain with a quarry of beautiful jade. With the support of the Myanmar King and the local Chinese-Burmese people, Huigen cut a large amount of jade out of the quarry and hired skilled Tibetan craftsmen to have it meticulously cut and polished. When their work was finished Huigen was left with a total of five jade statues. Seven years later, Huigen returned from Myanmar to Putuo Mountain. He had the statues shipped inland by river and as a result, was forced to pass through Shanghai. At the time, the Shanghai investment bureau did not have a boat with an attached crane, and they where unable to continue this shipment of over one ton of jade. The father of Qing Dynasty railway minister, Sheng Xuanhuai, was at the scene, and earnestly requested that Huigen leave the Jade behind. Huigen relented, leaving behind two statues, and the Yufo Si temple was constructed to accommodate them.

Once you have seen the jade Buddhas, the temple's other precious artifacts are worth visiting. The Precious Hall of the Great Hero has an ancient bronze statue of the standing Siddhartha Guatama Buddha cast in 491 AD during the reign of Northern Wei Dynasty Emperor Taihe, and a stone sculpture of the Medicine Buddha carved in 543 AD, the first year of Eastern Wei Dynasty Emperor Wuding. Both sculptures are subdued in composition, but created with great artistry. A Ming Dynasty statue of the Goddess of Mercy, cast in copper, sits in the Guanyin Goddess of Mercy Hall, and a Ming Dynasty bronze Amitabha Buddhist statue can be found in the Copper Buddha Hall.

Yufo Si Temple was moved from its original location in 1918, when Zen monk, Master Ke Cheng, built a new temple on Anyuan Lu. Yufo Si Temple Abbot, Master Yuanjian, founded the Shanghai School of Buddhism inside this new temple in 1942.

Today, the Jade Buddha Temple remains an essential stop for Shanghai visitors who desire to burn incense and pray. Included among the countless numbers of temple visitors are former United States presidential first lady, Nancy Regan, Britain's Princess Marguerite, Former French Prime Minister Pierre Mauroy, the Governor General Sir

Ninian Stephen of Australia, the Governor Generals of Hong Kong and Macau, and eminent monks from Hong Kong, Macau, Taiwan, and all over the world. This is a place where people from all over the Buddhist world can come together despite differences in language and race. Magnificent smiles abound at Yufo Si, making the temple feel somewhat like heaven.

Address

Yufo Si is in located Shanghai's Putuo District at 170 Anyuan Lu. To get there, you can take bus lines 13, 19, 24, 36, 54, 63, 68, 76, 105, 106, 112,113, 138, 206, 223, 506, 516, 550, 563, 738, 768, 830, 837, 866, and 922.

Telephone

021-62663668

Hours of Operation

8am-5pm; Buddhist practitioners come here to pray and burn incense on the first and fifteenth days of the Lunar Calendar. On those two days, the temple is open until 5:30pm.

Tickets

Usually 10 RMB, but it's only 5RMB on the first and 15th days of the Lunar Calendar.

Food and drink

The Yufo Si Temple Vegetarian Restaurant can be found on the eastern side of the Buddhist supply shop. Their vegetarian fare has a long history and is well known in Shanghai. Prices here are also reasonable. Expect to pay about 30RMB per person. You can also buy vegetarian snacks here. Their Jingsu Moon cakes are a classic. Made with expert care and attention to every detail, the moon cakes have a crisp shell and fruit and nut fillings. These exquisite treats are famous all over Shanghai.

Zhenru Temple

(zhēnrúsì, 真如寺)

Zhenru Zhen is a typical small suburban Shanghai town, and is home to one of greater Shanghai's most ancient temples. Before the temple was constructed, there was little of anything that could be found here. As the temple developed and its drifting incense permeated surrounding areas, a small market was created nearby. Zhenru Zhen town was eventually born out of the temple and the growing market.

Zhenru Si Temple's main hall is one of the best preserved wooden Yuan Dynasty monasteries in China's Southern Yangtze Region. Originally called Wanshou Si, or "The Big Temple", by commoners, the temple was built in the Southern Song Dynasty during the reign of Emperor Jiading, and rebuilt in 1320, during the seventh year of Yuan Dynasty Emperor Yanyou. After the Yuan Period reconstruction, the temple was renamed Zhenru Si. Today, it is Shanghai's oldest wooden architectural structure. In the beginning, the temple was packed with priceless artifacts. But, over the years they gradually fell into ruin. Nevertheless, you can still appreciate the ancient Yuan-style main hall and the ancient gingko trees out front. During the new renovation in 1992, the Four Lokapalas (temple guardians) were enshrined in the Great Emperor Hall — Hufa Protector of Law, Weituo Buddhist Guardian Spirit, Bodhisattva, and a copper Maitayra donated by the Shanghai Museum. Singaporean, Master Xing Ren, also donated three jade Buddha statues to Zhenru Si. In 1994, a Hall dedicated to "Guanyin", the Goddess of Mercy, was built in the center of the Precious Hall of the Great Hero as was a library of Buddhist scriptures. Today, the library's 11,970 Buddhist texts are open to the public. Unfortunately, there are few English language texts for perusal.

Most of the buildings in today's temple are newly constructed, but the ancient Yuan Dynasty pagoda at the northern end of the hall has great artistic value and is an uncommon treasure of Buddhist art.

Address

Located in the Puluo District's Zhenru Zhen Town at 5 Houshanmen Lu. To get there you can take a number of bus lines including line 6, airport line 6, and the Beian line.

Telephone

021-62971581

Hours of Operation

8 am- 4pm; open at 5 am on 1th and 15th days of the Lunar Calendar.

Longhua Temple

(lónghuásì, 龙华寺)

Longhua Si is the oldest and largest monetary in the entire Shanghai municipality. Located well outside the city, you will have to travel quite a ways if you are looking to come here to visit the temple or pray. Longhua Si is located inside Longhua Town, and, like Zhensi Zhen, the town owes its existence to the presence of the monastery. The lifestyle here is drastically different from that of urban shanghai. Short on glitz and modern fashions, Longhua town is long on authentic traditional Shanghai atmosphere. It is a fascinating place to visit.

One of the more popular legends about the Lonhua Si's construction takes place during the Three Kingdom's period of China's history. Sun Quan, King of the Wu Kingdom, built this monastery to out of respect for his mother. The name Longhua comes from the Longhua Tree, which according to the Buddhist scripture, is the place where Maitreya Bodhisattva attained Buddhahood. Another legend places Longhua Si in the Five Dynasties period when it was built by the Wuyue King, Qian Liu. Whatever the case, the temple is old enough to have been captured by Tang Dynasty poet, Pi Rixiu, in his poem, "Longhua Yebo". Having seen many rises and falls over the course of its existence, today it is easy to see that the monastery is quite old. Qing Dynasty Emperor Guangxu had the temple and pagoda renovated, and the complex was renovated once again after China's civil war. Today, Lonhua Si's monastery, pagoda, and Wanzhong Bell are all hot tourist attractions, drawing people from all over to see them.

Pass under the monastery archway and through the main entrance. Walking along the monastery's central axis will take you straight into the Maitreya Hall. Here is where you will find Maitreya, "Buddha of the Future," enshrined as a statue. Continu-

ing along the axis will take you next into the Great Emperor Hall, containing four meter high statues of the Four Lokapalas along both walls, and a statue enshrining the "Tianguan" Crowned Maitreya in the center. The Tianguan Maitreya statue portrays Maitreya Bodhisattva practicing Buddhism in the Tusita Heaven courtyard. In the back you will find the statue of Weituo placed into a niche carved in the wall.

Longhua Si is a temple dedicated mainly to Maitreya. That is why you can find two statues of Maitreya here — unusual for a Buddhist temple. While the Maitreya statue in the Great Emperor Hall portrays him as a Bodhisattva, the one in the Maitreya Hall shows Maitreya as one of his other incarnations, commonly called, "Buddha with a Cloth Sack" or "Laughing Buddha".

Following the temple's central axis will take you next to the Precious Hall of the Great Hero where you will find Vairocana Sambhoga-kaya Buddha enshrined in the center. On the temple's left and right sides you will see statues of Manjusri and Samanatbhadra Bodhisattva, and you can find representations of the 20 heavens and arhat (saints) along both walls. To the hall's back is an island with the Goddess of Mercy and her assistant, Shancai Tongzi — "the boy who attracts wealth". Continuing forward will take you past the Hall of Three Sages and the abbot's room before finally arriving at the library.

Longhua Pagoda

The Longhua Pagoda towers above like the Longhua Si Temple giant. You will be able to spot this ancient weathered pagoda from a long distance as you approach. The seven octagonal wood and brick tower was built in 977 AD and stands 40.4 meters tall. Though Longhua Si is filled with Tang, Five Dynasties, Ming and Qing Dynasty writings, gold seals, and Buddhist Statues, the pagoda may be the temple's biggest and most important ancient artifact. It is also one of Shanghai's best preserved ancient pagodas.

Longhua Bell

A bell is a major Buddhist instrument and an extremely important part of a temple. It is customary for monks of all temples to ring bells and beat drums in the mornings and evenings to frighten away evil demons and spirits. Longhua Si Temple's Wanzhong Bell is well known and was one of the eight great Ming and Qing Dynasty Shanghai sites. The drums and bells on the eastern and western sides of the temple interior are particularly magnificent with 6.5 ton bronze bells cast during the reign of Ming Dynasty Emperor Hongwu. When the Longhua Bell is rung, it not only signals the beginning of a new day, but it is also meant to cleanse the hearts of the commoners. At the beginning of the Spring Festival (Chinese New Year), the Longhua Wanzhong bell sounds 108 times, bidding farewell to the passing year and welcoming in the new. Many Shanghai residents come to the Longhua Si on Chinese New Year's eve to make wishes, and welcome the New Year with the sound of the bells. It is a lively and boisterous scene.

Longhua Revolutionary Martyrs Cemetery

Walking west from the temple will take you to the Longhua Revolutionary Martyrs Cemetery. Before it was turned into Xianhua Park in 1928, this piece of land was once a peach orchard. Its name was later changed to Longhua Park before becoming part of what is today the Martyrs Cemetery. The cemetery was once the site of the famous Kuomintang Songhu Garrison Headquarters and prison. Operating in 1928, the prison occupies a dark corner of modern Chinese history; countless numbers of early Communist Party members were killed and imprisoned here in the early twentieth century. After undergoing renovation, the garrison's male and female prison area and martyr field (execution ground) have been opened for public viewing. You will not find any explanatory or identifying markings around the old prison site. In the gravesite outside, you can find the graves of many old Communist party leaders, revolutionaries, and patriots like Liu Yiyi, Yun Daiying, Li Bai, Zhou Taofen, and martyrs from the Left Coalition of Writers. International tour groups can often be found touring the cemetery. It is also a nice place to enjoy some peace and quiet.

Address

The Longhua Si Temple is located in the Xuhui District at 2853 Longhua Lu. To get there, you can take bus lines 41, 44, 104, 718, 734, 809, 304, and 933 to the Longhua tourist city. You can also take lines 56, 111, 326, 714, 720, 770, 847, 857, 932,the Hushen line, and the subway number three line. Be sure to get off the train at Longcao Lu.

Telephone

021-64566085

Hours of Operation

7am- 4:30 pm

Tickets

10 RMB

Special Note

Longhua Si also has several other important activities worth experiencing. There is New Years incense burning in February, and the March temple fair grave sweeping ceremonies in April. In October you can take the lucky Longhua tour, and listen to the evening drum beats. Longhua Si swarms with people during these activities and holidays. It can be quite an imposing site.

Universities

Fudan University

(fùdàn dàxué, 复旦大学)

Fudan University represents the pinnacle of aspiration for many top Chinese students. Located in Shanghai's suburbs, the university has no tall buildings and is completely surrounded by wide-open spaces. It immediately gives one the impression that it is a great learning environment. When you enter the campus, you will notice that it is covered with street signs. If you follow the signs all the way around campus, it will take you three hours to circle back to the university entrance.

One of China's oldest universities, Fudan

was founded in 1905 as the Fudan Public School. It became a private university in 1917. In those times, Sun Yat-sen closely followed and supported Fudan's development. He even contributed a written address for Fudan's 1923 yearbook. Over the next decade, such illustrious figures such as Lu Xun, Guo Moruo, Zao Taofen, Lao She, Zhu Kezhen, and Ma Yinchu were all demonstrated their academic and literary talents in Fudan's classrooms and corridors. University founder, famous contemporary Chinese educator, Ma Xiangbo, named the university after a famous line from "The Book of Yu and Xia" out of The Great Tradition of the Book of the Elder: "Ri Yue Guanghua, Danfu Danxi — The light of the sun and the moon will never stop shining". The line is meant to encourage the continuous striving for improvement, to entrust Chinese intellectuals to be the master of their country's education, and to create a strong country through education.

It is best to avoid touring Fudan at noon and when classes end or you will get stuck in the mobs of students pouring out of classrooms. At other times, you will find the campus to be extremely quiet. Walking around during these silent times will give you a chance to reminisce about your own student days — wandering around your school campus with your backpack and textbooks. Fudan has a lot of nice attractions to visit including the Xi Yuan Garden with its safflower, green lotuses, running water, kiosks, and young scholars passing through in groups of twos and threes. The words of teacher Zhu Dongrun are etched into stone at the front of the garden: "Hear the sounds of books turning and students reciting". On the other end of the campus you can find the Yan Yuan Garden with its remote quiet scenery and more concentrated feelings of spring. As you continue onward inside the university campus, you will reach the front of the Xianghui Hall with its large grass square, grey architecture, and the condensed poetic charm of Fudan University.

There are several stretches outside the Fudan campus that are lined with interesting bookstores. Many of these roads are worth exploring.

Luming Bookstore

(lùmíng shūdiàn, 鹿鸣书店)

Located on Guoquan Lu, Luming was once praised as one of the Shanghai's most tasteful bookstores. The only problem with the store is that it never discounts its books. Most people go to Luming to browse the new releases, and then go to other bookstores to buy them on discount.

Qingyun Bookstore's Discount Center *(qìngyún shūdiàn tèjiàbù, 庆云书店特价部)*

From the university entrance, walk along Guonian Lu in the direction of the number six teaching building. There, in an extremely inconspicuous nook, you will find Qingyun Bookstore Discount Center. Specializing in discounted original edition foreign language books, Qingyun is made up of two rooms, less than ten square meters each, stacked to the ceiling with foreign language books and magazines. The store's tight passageway allows only one person to pass through at a time. Discounts here can reach as high as 70-80%, meaning that you can walk away with many books costing as little as 5 to 10 RMB.

Xinping Bookstore
(xīnpíng shūdiàn, 心平书店)

Located at Guonan Lu, the name on this bookstore's storefront was written by Ji Xianlin. Xinping was once known as the famous Yangpu Technology Bookstore and has a history that spans ten years. One-color academic books are sold here and everything is offered on a 15% discount. Another bookstore nearby, Zuoan Bookstore (左岸书店), has a nice booklist and 20% discounts.

Student Bookstore
(xuérén shūdiàn, 学人书店)

Located on Fudan's promenade, this bookstore has a large inventory. Novels by contemporary writers can usually be found here before they arrive in other book stores. Qingyun Bookstore also has a branch here offering 70% discounts and brings in large shipments of new books on an irregular basis. The refined atmosphere here is also a plus.

Address

Fudan University is located at 220 Handan Lu. To get here you can take bus routes 329, 139, 133, 59, 960, 942, 828, 854, 850, 812, 966, and the Chuanhong special line.

Food and drink

There are many restaurants and cafes along Fudan University's Promenade. Students make up these restaurants' biggest clientele and prices are reasonable.

Tongji University
(tóngjì dàxué, 同济大学)

From Fudan University's gate, pass through Guoquan Lu and then turn onto Siping Lu. Continue along for several hundred meters and you will arrive at Shanghai's other venerable center of learning, Tongji University. Founded in 1907 as a German language medical school for German doctors, the school was called "Tongji" meaning cooperate and work together. In 1912 an engineering school was added, and in 1923 it was turned into a full-fledged university. Tongji University finally became a national university in 1927.

On the Tongji University campus, the Tongji University Press's sales room, located in the university classroom building, is the most notable attraction. Here you can find almost every work published by the university press, and there are frequent discounts. Further on inside the campus, you will find a lot of modern classrooms and dormitories — nothing that will particularly excite your imagination.

Address

Tongji University is located at 1239 Siping Lu and is only a 15 minute walk from Fudan University. You can get there on bus lines 55, 61, 937, 142, 147, and 910. Be sure to get off at the Siping Lu-Tongji University stop.

East China University of Politics and Law
(huádōng zhèngfǎ xuéyuàn, 华东政法学院)

Quietly keeping watch over Suzhou River's bank, the dark profound marble stone tablet marked with the university's name, sits across from the university's main gate witnessing the baptism of time. Located on the original site of Saint John's University, the Politics and Law University is China's first western-style institute of higher learning. Originally founded as St. John's, a religious secondary school, in the late nineteenth century, it became a full-fledged university in 1905, and in 1952, the Chinese Military and Political Committee allowed the university to change its name from Saint John's to East China University of Politics and Law. The campus has an artistic atmosphere with simple and unsophisticated architecture, huge trees that stretch up to the sky, and is filled with the gentle rising and falling sound of bells floating over from the Taofen Building.

The school's campus straddles the Suzhou River, and both halves are commonly referred to as River East and River West. Entranced with the exquisite Suzhou River scenery, university founder, Bishop Samuel Scherschewsky, was struck with inspiration to found a school here. The University's most beautiful attractions are concentrated on River West side of the campus.

River West Tour: After you enter through university's main gate, walking forward for two minutes will take you by the Friendship Building on your right and the University President's building and a small yard on your left. The red Friendship Building fuses Chinese and Western architectural styles. A complex and exquisite structure with a colored domed roof, the president's building was originally the office building of Saint John's University President Scherschewsky.

Continue on by the President building and you will see the red library and Liusan building. The red faculty and graduate student library is over 100 years old. Winding along the side of the Liusan building, a small path will lead you back on to the main avenue connecting the president's office and library. As you pass the Taofen building and its famous bell tower, the Huazheng Commemorative Monument will enter into your field of vision. A small white building, the civic activities center sits next to the Taofen building where a small path leads to the basketball courts and the gymnasium. A pocket-sized garden near the gymnasium connects to the Shuren Hall, and the Dongfeng building sits to its right. If you take a left out of the Dongfeng Building, you will walk right to the campus bridge.

Moving along on the small path will take

you to one of the campus's more defining structures, the Huazheng Commemorative Monument, which was built to celebrate the fiftieth anniversary of Saint John's University. Tennis courts are on the left of the monument, and the resplendent Simeng Hall and the dignified Gezhi Building stand to the side. Both buildings are venerable hundred year old structures. Right in the back of the monument, you will find the Taofen Building. Originally called Huaishi Hall, the Taofen Building has a square shaped clock tower on the roof complete with a chiming clock. Today the Taofen Building still has an old mock courtroom, which is frequently used for instruction.

Address

East China University of Politics and Law is located at 1575 Wanhang Dulu. It can be reached by bus lines 13, 921, and 922. You can also take subway lines number two and three to the East China University of Politics and Law stop (华东政法学院).

Special Note

There is a small snack street near the campus bridge. Here you can find lamb kebab, spicy peppery soup, ground meat sandwiches, fried strong-smelling preserved bean curd, *yóu dūnzi* (油墩子), and any other kind of Chinese snack you could possibly want to find. The university often shows off the snack street to prospective students. The friendship building has accommodations. A normal room runs 150 RMB and 180 RMB is what you will pay for a standard room. Normal rooms have all of the standard facilities such as air conditioning, separate bathroom, and shower. Standard rooms have better facilities and decor. Their telephone number is: 021-62071663.

Others

Art Archives and Warehouse —50 Moganshan Lu

(yìshù cāngkù, 艺术仓库)

50 Moganshan Lu is right off the bank of the Suzhou River. Once known as the Shanghai Chunming Rove Factory, the site was founded in 1917 and is currently filled with industrial architecture dating from the 1930's to the 1990's. In 1999, artist Ding Yi rented a warehouse at 1131 Suzhou Xilu for his art studio, and Xue Song opened a studio at 50 Moganshan Lu in 2000. Not long after, Ding Yi's art galleries', "Biz Art Art Center", "Shanghart Art Gallery", and "Eastlink gallery" were established here, one after another, and the area changed its name to Chunming Art Industrial Park (春明艺术产业园). Without a doubt, this warehouse occupies a preeminent position in the mainstream of Shanghai art.

Most people in Shanghai are unfamiliar

with Chunming Art Industrial Park's formal name. However, if you mention the "big storeroom" or "that warehouse" you will probably elicit a nod of general understanding. Today, the area around Moganshan Lu has already been developed into a brand new residential area. Only the "big storeroom's" huge dark red warehouse, broken down old homes and attention-grabbing smokestacks refuse to assimilate into this sparkling sea of modernity. The Art Warehouse is occupied by a collection of 70-80 artists from 11 different countries.

As you walk through the warehouse complex, you will notice signs directing you to different artist studios. Each studio also exhibits the painter's works. The price of each piece of art varies according to its size and dimensions; though, artists will let you browse even if you do not plan on buying anything. Some studios also sell albums of their works so that you can gain a more comprehensive understanding of the creative trends among cutting edge artists. Aside from the art collections found here, the factory has some ancient machinery that is worth taking a look at. In building number five, you can find some motley 1930's era German power distribution equipment made by Siemens. This dust covered industrial equipment is a type of living history — a rather amorphous type of avant-garde artwork, neither artificial nor affected, with a cloak of realism and tinge of artistic flavor. They are truly eye-catching constructions.

Address

Take subway line number one and get off at the Shanghai Zhan Railway Station. When you leave the station, follow Tianmu Xilu across the Changshou Lu Bridge and Aomen Lu. Walk a little bit farther and you will arrive at Moganshan Lu.

大库 BIG WAREHOUSE

MChoice
麥創

Special Note

Mogan Lu is pretty far removed from Shanghai's city center. There is a cafe at the Art Park entrance and a few cafes and bars scattered around inside the complex, but no restaurants. If you want to catch a bite to eat, you will have to find something around the Moganshan Lu area. Most of your choices here will be limited to Shanghai-style snacks. Larger sit-down restaurants are few and far between.

Shanghai Botanical Garden

(shànghǎi zhíwùyuán, 上海植物园)

The Shanghai Botanical Garden has 17 different exhibition areas that are open to the public. They include the herbal medicine garden, magnolia garden, peony garden, azalea garden, rose garden, sweet-scented osmanthus garden, bamboo garden, pine and cypress garden, fern garden, and environmental botanical zone. Here you will also find a memorial hall devoted to Yuan Dynasty textile innovator, Huang Daopo. The botanical garden's greenhouse covers a total of 558 square meters including 20 thousand annual potted plants, and 50 thousand flowers. Aside from the plants and flowers, the greenhouse also cultivates miniature plants.

Address

Located at 1111 Longwu Lu, you can take bus lines 56, 131, 714, 720, 820, 824 and the Longwu Line.

Telephone

021-54363369

Hours of Operation

7 am- 5:30pm; Greenhouse: 8:30 am- 5:30 pm

Tickets

15 RMB for entry; a 40 RMB combo ticket includes entry fee and the greenhouse. Groups of 30 and above receive a 20% discount. Seniors 70 and up receive 30% discount.

Shanghai Zoo

(shànghǎi dòngwùyuán, 上海动物园)

Originally known as the Shanghai Western Park, the Shanghai Zoo is big enough for you to spend half a day here. Here you will find almost 6,000 animals including over 600 rare and endangered species. Notable attractions include the David's deer, the giant panda, golden snub-nosed monkeys, white-lipped deer, Northeast Chinese tigers, Chinese alligators, giraffes, kangaroos, penguins, hippos, sea lions, ostriches, cougars, African lions and more. There is also a plentiful number of birds. You will no doubt notice that after a long term of captivity, none of the animals seem particularly lively. When you see the polar bears, you can not help but wonder if they would not be better off back at the North Pole. Nevertheless, the museum still attracts large numbers of children during summer and winter vacations and on weekends. For a number of Shanghai residents, this old zoo symbolizes a period of their childhood and a lot of young adults come here to rediscover their youth.

The museum is also home to the first science education center ever built inside a mainland Chinese zoo. This is the place to catch elephant performances and other trained animal performances.

Address

2381 Hongqiao Lu. To get here, take bus lines 57, 91, 505, 831, 911, 92, and tourist line number 4.

Tickets

30 RMB. Buy a 40RMB full-value ticket if you want to catch an elephant performance. Primary and Middle school students enjoy a 20% discount, and seniors over 70 years old enjoy 30% discount. Children under 1.2 meters in height are allowed in free of charge.

Shanghai Film and Television Amusement Park

(shànghǎi yǐngshì lèyuán, 上海影视乐园)

If you are interested in film or in old Shanghai lifestyles, than is an important place to visit. Although the amusement park is located in the Shanghai's suburbs, it is still easy to reach with public transportation. For those who are into old Shanghai nostalgia, you can find replicas of 1930's era Nanjing Lu, ancient Shanghai alleyways, and recreations of old Shanghai urban life. This movie and television city was created by the Shanghai film studio, and over thirty films and hundreds of television series have been filmed here. Today, many Shanghai film studio films are still shot here, and when you visit, you may actually catch a film shoot. If you do not, you can still admire the elegant costumes and film sets on display. The wax statues of movie stars are worth a look, as are the recreations of Shanghai sights.

Shanghai Movie and Television Amusement Park is divided into four large stu-

dios and three small studios including, Old Urban Shanghai, Amusement Park of the World, Chenghuang Miao, Cartoon World, Plaza of the Stars, Reading Center, World of the Silver screen, Stunt Place, Wharf and the Harbor District. However, many people find the shooting area small and narrow, and a lot of what is on display are replica items. This gives some people the feeling that everything here looks rough or unauthentic.

When you have had enough of the replicas and sets, you can take the electric streetcar for a ride around the grounds, and catch one of the two daily performances at 10:30 am and 1:30 pm. Each performance lasts half and hour, and both the morning and noon performances are the same. Performances mostly recreate scenes from famous movies like Bruce Lee's Chinese Connection. Sometimes audience members are allowed to take part in the performances and are asked to mimic a scene. It is usually pretty funny to see. Participants are usually rewarded with a souvenir t-shirt and hat. Once in a while, the performances are acted out by Shanghai film studio stunt actors, allowing you to take in exaggerated two and three person wrestling or boxing performances. These stunt shows also involve such standards as stuntmen falling off building roofs.

Address

The Shanghai tourist line bus leaves everyday from the Shanghai Stadium at 8:40 and returns at 1:30 pm. A round trip ticket costs 55 RMB. You can also choose to take the Jiaoqu Bus from the Shanghai West Bus Station (上海西区汽车站) or the Jinjiang Leyuan subway station, and get off at the Chedun Stop. All-included tickets can be bought at Shanghai tourism distribution center. The latest bus back to the Shanghai Bawanren Stadium leaves at 3pm in the afternoon. At first you may worry that the tight bus schedule does not leave you enough time to explore the entire 200 hectare park, but, in reality, you may find that at 2 pm you have run out of things to do.

Hours of Operation

8 am-5pm

Tickets

50RMB

Special Note

The amusement park is not in the most convenient location, and is not that easy to find. You may find that you need to ask for directions while you are on the road. The park's facilities are not terrific. There are places that serve food, but little that could pass for a proper lunch. We suggest packing your own water and snacks.

Outside the City

Around Jiading District
(jiādìngqū, 嘉定区)

Two of Shanghai's most famous cultural and historical towns, Jiading and Nanxiang, reside in Shanghai's Northwestern Jiading District. If you are drawn to the bucolic images of small bridges over flowing streams, residential lanes and alleys, and the sounds of Shanghai's spoken dialect, than these two towns are definitely worth a look. Naturally, the environment here is worlds away from the bustling streets of Shanghai. While most places of interest here are historical and cultural heritage sites like Gu Yiyuan, the Jiading Confucius temple, and the Yunxiang Si twin pagodas, food is definitely the star attraction in Jiading. Nanxiang is the home of Nanxiang "xiaolong bao" (small stuffed steamed buns) so get ready to fill up when you come. One of the best things about Jiading is that few tourists come here. You will probably have the beautiful scenery all to yourself.

Guyi Yuan Garden
(gǔyīyuán, 古猗园)

Every one of Guyi Yuan's wayside pavilions and arched bridges shows summersault-like grace. Those who are particular about atmosphere and mood say that Giyi Yuan is the place to come when your mind is serene and you have the time to slowly savor its scenery. If you feel impatient or are in a rush you will probably not be able to appreciate the garden's elegance. You will probably need half a day to slowly walk around the garden and appreciate it with the even temper and good humor the experts prescribe.

Built during the reign of Ming Dynasty Emperor Wanli, Guyi Yuan is over 400 years old. The garden is small, and was first established as the personal garden of Henan assistant prefecture magistrate, Min Shiji. Originally named Qi Yuan, the garden's throngs of bamboo precipitated its eventual name change to "Guyi" (Ancient Beauty), inspired by the line "Lüzhu Yiyi — the mellow beauty of green bamboo" in the Book of Poetry.

With its verdant bamboo, terraces and pavilions, winding paths and corridors, ornamental mountains, and ponds, the garden is both extremely beautiful and manages to

Transportation

Nanxiang Zhen *(nánxiángzhèn, 南翔镇)*

Nanxiang Zhen is eighteen kilometers away from the People's Square. You can take bus line 517 from the Shanghai Zhan railway station, the 562 line from Jingsi, and 822 from the intersection of Haining Lu and Xizang Beilu. Line 6A, the Beijia line (from the northern bus station to Jiading), the Xianghua line to Huacao,Xianghuang line to the American Dream Park, the Hunan line to Zhang Miao, and the Luonan line to Luodian all leave from the Shanghai Stadium.

Jiading Zhen *(jiādìngzhèn, 嘉定镇)*

Take the tourist 6A line, the Beijia line, or line 837 from the Shanghai rail station, and line 6A from the gymnasium (6:30 am-5pm). The Beijia line from the northern bus station (5am-7pm) goes direct to Jiading. Renmin Square (369 Chengdu Beilu near Nanjing Lu, 6am-6pm), Shanghai Zhan rail station (the western end of the Hengfeng Lu bridge near Jidian Dasha), and the Shanghai Exhibition Center (6 am-9:30 pm) all have lines running direct to Jiading.

Food and Drink

Qinghe Lu, known as "Jiading's Little Nanjing Lu" and Meiyuan Lu are bursting with restaurants. You can find anything here from Sichuan flavors, to seafood, to local benbang Shanghai specialties.

Dingwei Hotpot
(dǐngwèi huǒguō, 鼎味火锅)

Located at 2 Chengzhong Lu on the southern side of Legou; telephone: 021-69523677. The pickled vegetables and fish broth is loved by Dingwei's hungry customers. Portions are large and the flavors are good. Expect to pay 45 RMB per person.

capture the poetic spirit of ancient Chinese gardens. History and archeology enthusiasts will be interested in seeing the two Tang Dynasty Buddhist pillars, each of which is over 1,000 years old.

Xi Pool is at the center of Giyi Yuan Garden. On the pool's western side is the Ming Dynasty White Crane Pavilion, and a stone boat-shaped pavilion called Buxidan lies to its north. Located across the water from the Buxidan is a floating bamboo skinned pavilion flanked by a bamboo mountain. A Plum Blossom Hall lies at the pool's eastern end. The hall and its flower path outside are carved with plum blossom designs, and plum blossom flowers lie in every direction. The exquisitely carved Song Dynasty Putong Pagoda sits in the center of the Lotus Flower Pool, and Buddhist stone pillars rest in front of the Southern Hall and Weiyin Ge Pavilion.

When the Japanese army invaded China's three northeast provinces (Jilin, Liaoning, and Heilongjiang) in 1931, a group of Nanxiang Zhen's patriotic citizens raised funds to build a square pavilion on top of a large dirt hill inside the garden. The pavilion roof was built with only three corners, missing the corner in facing the Northeast, alluding to nation's territory that had fallen into enemy hands. The pavilion is built to be a reminder of this national humiliation and a symbol of China's determination to reclaim its lost territory.

You can visit a tea house located inside the bamboo forest on the edge of the water. The tea house is usually not very busy. A cup of Longding tea costs 15 RMB and a cup of Longjing green tea runs 12 RMB. The tea leaves used are of good quality.

Address

Located in the Jiading District's Nanxiang Zhen Town at 218 Huyi Lu. Parking in the Guyi Yuan Garden parking lot costs 10 RMB, but you can park along the street for free.

Hours of Operation

5 am-7 pm

Tickets

12 RMB per person and also includes entry fee to the Yunxiang Temple.

Food and Drink

There are many restaurants serving *xiǎolóng bāo* (小笼包, small stuffed steamed buns) along Guyi Yuan Lu. There is also a restaurant serving *xiǎolóng bāo* inside the garden. Eat at the garden's restaurant for the great atmosphere. Expect to pay 10 RMB for 20 buns. You can also buy soup made with laver — a type of purple vegetable — and small shrimp for 2 RMB a bowl. Take note: the *xiǎolóng bāo* served here and along the road have thick skins and are not very authentic.

Yunxiang Temple
(yúnxiángsì, 云翔寺)

From Guyi Yuan, turn right and follow Wuyi Lu until you reach Jiefang Jie, and then take another right. Turn right yet again when you reach Renmin Lu, and then turn onto Nanxiangzhen Dajie which will take you right to Yunxiang Temple. Yunxiang Temple is another pleasant patch of open space in Nanxiang. Parking here is free, and there are few tourists. It is a nice place to enjoy some peace and quiet.

While Yunxiang temple is quite large, people usually come here to visit twin pagodas. Of all of Shanghai's ancient pagodas, these two treasures of Chinese brick pagoda

Food and Drink

Xi Shengyuan Wonton Restaurant
(yíshèngyuán húntún diàn, 熙盛源馄饨店)

Located at 389 Fengzhuang Lu (near Caoan Lu). This popular traditional spot serves famous Wuxi xiaolongbao steamed stuffed buns and wontons. Flavors here are terrific. Expect to pay 10 RMB per person.

Long Fei Restaurant
(lóngfēi cānyǐn cāngchǎng diàn, 龙飞餐饮仓场店)

Located at 422 Cangchan Lu; telephone: 021-59987777; there is no one in Jiading who is not familiar with Long Fei. Good food and low prices make it a popular spot. Long Fei serves local Shanghai specialties. The garlic ribs, Guifei pork shanks, and Shunde Eggplant are all recommended. Expect to pay 50 RMB per person. Longfei has another branch at 285 Meiyuan Lu.

Dongshan Yugang
(dōngshān yúgǎng, 东山渔港)

5551 located in the Anning Zhen Town at 5551 Angong Lu; telephone: 021-59571818. Although a little bit out of the way, Dongshan Yugang has a terrific atmosphere with seafood and mild flavors. Expect to pay about 100 RMB per person.

Xinwangfu
(xīnwángfǔ jiǔdiàn, 新王府酒店)

Located at 2199 Qilianshan Lu (near the Caoan Lu intersection; telephone: 021-69187777. This luxury restaurant serves exquisite dishes, but portions are small. Recommend dishes include Dongpo stir-fried beef tenderloin and dry-fried xieniang noodles. Expect to pay about 80 RMB per person.

architecture are the venerable old men. Built between the Five Dynasties period and the beginning of the Northern Song Dynasty, the pagodas were originally built on each side of the White Crane Nanxiang Si Buddhist temple. According to legend, during the reign of Southern Dynasties Emperor Liang Tianjian (502-519 AD), a farmer once discovered a stone in his dusty field. When he retrieved the stone, he discovered that two cranes would often come over to stand on it. Seen as a sign of good fortune, a monk collected alms to build a temple on this site. When the temple was built, the cranes flew south and never returned. The temple was named Nanxiang Si or "Flying South Temple" in memory of the two cranes. During the Southern Song Dynasty the temple's name was changed Yunxiang Temple.

In 1766, during the year of Qing Dynasty Emperor Qian Long, a huge fire burned the ancient temple to the ground. All that remained were the two pagodas. In 1982, the two pagodas were completely restored. Restoration work was done in accordance with the remaining structure, vestiges, and materials found under the ground.

Tickets

8 RMB. Tickets from Guyi Yuan Garden can also be used to gain entrance and burn incense.

Eastern Paris Golf Village Club *(dōngfāng bālí gāoěrfū xiāngcūn jùlèbù, 东方巴黎高尔夫乡村俱乐部)*

Located south of Nanxiang Zhen, the Eastern Paris Golf Village Club is an 18-hole two-level golf course with a total of 48 fairways. At nighttime, the golf course is completely illuminated. This is a par 61 course. The first nine holes stretch out for 1,870 yards, and the next 9 holes are 1,637 yards, combining for a total of 3,507 yards. Grass type: Baimuda. Total Area: 27 Hectares. Eastern Paris has a complete range of facilities including a practice range, restaurant, pro shop, and shower/dressing room.

Address

277 Nanxiang Yangzi Lu. Driving south five minutes from Nanxiang should take you there.

Telephone

021-59126888

Jiading Confucian Temple
(jiādìng kǒngmiào, 嘉定孔庙)

Confucian Temples were once built all over China to commemorate Confucius, founder of the Confucian tradition. The Jiading District Confucian Temple is located at Jiading Zhen's Nan Dajie. Built in the Southern Song Dynasty during the rule of Jiading (1219), it was first called Wenxuanwang Temple and known as "the premier temple" of Eastern Wu.

Three ceremonial stone pillar archways sit in front of the temple. Xing Xian, the archway on the east, was constructed in 1249 during the reign of Song Emperor Chunku. Yu Cai, the archway on the west, was built in 1353 during the reign of Yuan Emperor Zhi Zheng. The central archway, Yin Gao, is nine meters tall, and was built in 1586 during the rule of Ming Dynasty Emperor Wan Li. Following the archways are stone pillars topped with 72 stone lions in varying postures. These lions represent Confucius's 72 devoted disciples. Walking along Yin Gao archway's central axis line will lead you through a series of constructions including the Lingxing Gate, the Panchi Bridge, Confucian Gate, and the main hall. The temple's Confucian hall is the

Accommodations

Because the Shanghai International Circuit is located inside the Jiading District, many racing fans choose to spend a night or two in Jiading Zhen. There are a number of reasonably priced hotels found in both Jiading and Nanxiang towns.

Ying Yuan Hotel
(yíngyuán fándián, 迎园饭店)

Located in Jiading Zhen at 150 Qinghe Lu; telephone: 021-59520952. This is a four-star hotel with all of the appropriate amenities and good service. Standard and single rooms run 600 RMB a night. Discounts are usually available.

Jiading Hotel
(jiādìng bīnguǎn, 嘉定宾馆)

Located in Jiading Zhen at 100 Bole Lu; telephone: 021-59534341. Room rates run between 360 and 588 RMB. Huilong Pond and the Confucius temple are located to the hotel's south. This is a nice place to set up camp when you head out to see the Jiading sites. The environment here is also good. All rooms are equipped with air-conditioning, refrigerators, telephones, color TV, hot water, broadband internet, and satellite television.

Shanghai Yingyuan Zhi Xing
(yíngyuánzhīxīng, 迎园之星)

Located in Jiading Zhen at 221 Meihuayuan Lu; telephone: 021-59520123. Located within close distance of the eateries along the Qinghe Lu restaurant street, Shanghai Yingyuan Zhi Xing offers clean rooms and all the facilities you need. Expect to pay between 128 RMB and 180 RMB for a standard room and 240 RMB for a suite. This is a popular spot with tour groups, so it would be best to call in advance and make sure there are rooms available before you go.

fourth largest in China, and is now home to the Jiading Museum. The artifacts on display here relate mainly to the Imperial Civil Service examination system. If you find the exhibits a little bit dry, than quickly move on to the Jiading Museum's collection of calligraphy-inscribed steles. The museum's calligraphy collection spans five imperial Dynasties, from the Tang to the Qing. The stele gallery is right next to the Danghu School of Classical Learning (on the temple's eastern side, right in front of the Minglun Hall). Here you can find the extremely valuable inscribed works of Huang Tingjian, Shen Zhou, Wen Zhiming, and Dong Qichang — each of whom are renowned craftsmen of calligraphy and painting.

Address
183 Nan Dajie, Jiading Zhen Town
Telephone
021-59530379
Hours of Operation
8am-5pm
Tickets
10 RMB

Pool of Convergent Dragons *(huìlóngtán, 汇龙潭)*

Located near the Confucian Temple, Hui Longtan was carved out of the ground in 1588 during the reign of Ming Emperor Wan Li. The pond adds an extra dimension to the Jiading Temple scenery, with its graceful beauty of mountains and water. Most other Confucian temples generally lack the type of scenery that Hui Longtan provides. The name, Hui Longtan, comes from "Wulong Xizhu", the traditional Chinese image of Five Dragons Chasing the Pearl. The five streams that feed into the pond represent the dragons in the image. A mountain-island in the middle of the pond, Yingkui Mountain, was built in 1460, the fourth year of Ming Emperor Tianshun. There is a small pavilion at the mountain top, called Lingyun Pavilion, that offers panoramic views of Hui Longtan.

Address
299 Tacheng Lu, Jiading District
Telephone
021-59529604
Hours of Operation
8am-5pm
Tickets
5 RMB

Qiuxiapu Garden *(qiūxiápŭ, 秋霞圃)*

Qiuxiapu is one of Shanghai's five great ancient gardens. Built in 1502 during the Ming Dynasty, this was originally the private garden of Gong Hong, the Ming Dynasty minister of public works. Today you can still enjoy the garden's four scenic areas,

rather simple display.

It is commonly known that the Yinzhuajia fish from the Qingjing pool are absolutely delicious. Qing Emperor Qian Long once caught wind of these famous fish, and he ordered that several be brought back to his palace from Qiuxiapu. Qian Long praised the fishes' excellent flavor, and their fame eventually spread outside Imperial palace, becoming known far and wide.

Address
314 Dong Dajie, Jiading Zhen Town
Hours of Operation
8 am- 4:30 pm
Tickets
5 RMB

the Peach Blossom Pool, Nixia Pavilion, Qingjing Dike, and the district temple. If you like creative views, then come in the autumn when the trees rustle in the air, the fall wind is soughing, and the scenery inside and outside the thatched cottage has a unique, natural, and unrestrained pizzazz.

As you enter the garden, you will notice that the garden is centered on a clear pond, and stone mountains and ancient trees can be found on all sides. Ningxia Ge Pavilion sits on the eastern side of the Peach Blossom Pool, forming the main scenic area of the garden. A well-preserved Chenghuang Miao (City God Temple) Hall and mausoleum sit in the garden's east. It was built during the Southern Song under the reign of Emperor Jia Ding, and transferred into Qiuxiapu during the reign of Ming Emperor Hong Wu. Moving onto the Yimiao Scenic Area, there is the former Chenghuang Miao Hall, now the Shanghai Folk Culture Gallery. In gallery you will find an exhibition room entitled "portraits of Shanghai local customs". It is a

Fahua Pagoda

(fǎhuá tǎ, 法华塔)

Fahua Pagoda (also called Jinsha Pagoda) is located on Jiading Zhou Qiao's "Old Street" — Lao Jie. Lao Jie is a scenic road lined with bridges, pagodas, and rivers. This particular pagoda, built in the Song Dynasty under Emperor Kai Xi, is one of Lao Jie's oldest. During the following dynasties, Fahua underwent several different levels of renovation. In January 1996, the pagoda's shrine, housing numerous Buddhist relics, was cleaned and excavated revealing valuable treasures from the Song, Yuan, and Ming Dynasties. Artifacts included Buddhist statues, written works, ancient coins, and jade. That same year, the temple was renovated in the Ming Dynasty style.

Telephone
021-59525688

Around The Fengxian District

(fèngxiánqū, 奉贤区)

If you find yourself craving the ocean breeze, the Fengxian District is the place you want to be. Second only to Shanghai's Chongming Island, Fengxian is a coastal region located in southern Shanghai right off the Hangzhou Harbor. Not only does it have 31.6 kilometers of coastline and 13.7 kilometers of riverbank, Fengxian also has an artificial beach and the first man-made gulf in Chinese history. It is an interesting place to visit.

Fengxian is not just sand and waves, though; it also has a long and impressive history. According to legend, a disciple of Confucius named Yan Yan came to this place to teach and lecture. Later generations gave Fengxian its name out of respect for the sage. (Fengxian is a short form of the phrase Jingfeng Xianren, or "Pay respects to the virtuous man"). Fengxian's history stretches back four thousand years, and has one of Shanghai's largest collections of ancient artifacts. Here you can find the ancient Song Dynasty Tongjin Bridge, Ming Dynasty Wan Fo Pavilion, and the Qing Dynasty Stone Embankment. Fengxian is also a farming belt, producing a wide variety of agricultural products, the most famous of which are Shang He Pai jujube dates and Fengye honey pears.

Transportation

Fengxian is about thirty kilometers from Shanghai's city center. From Shanghai you can take the Shenhai Line running from the Shen Zhuang subway station to Nanqiao and the Haiwan Tourist area; Shen Shao Line which starts at the Shen Zhuang subway station and moves on to Nanqiao, Qingcun, Fengcheng Zhongxin Zhen, Hong Miao, before coming to Shaochang; the Nanhai Line goes from the Honghai Nanlu subway station to Nanqiao; the Tanghong Line starting at Pudong Tangqiao and moving on to Fengcheng Zhongxin Zhen and Hongmiao; the Lianzhuang Line goes from the Lianhua Lu subway station to Nanqiao and Zhuang Xing. Traveling along any of these lines will take you only a little longer than an hour. You can cross the Fengpu Daqiao Bridge into Fengxian, or take ferries from the Xidu and Wuqiao Ferry docks, which all run across the Huangpu River.

Wanfo Ge Pavilion
(wànfógé, 万佛阁)

Wanfo Ge is located on Fengcheng Zhen town's Beijie. There is a run-down alley right outside, but it does nothing to detract from the ancient temple's dignity. Walking down the alley, you will immediately spot this temple straddling both town and the ocean. The three characters of the temple's name, "Wan Fo Ge," hang at the entrance.

Wanfo Ge is one of Shanghai's largest temples for Buddhist nuns, and it was founded before the Ming Dynasty. In 1386, a high Ming Dynasty official, General Tang He, supervised the construction of a wall to protect the coast against incursions of Japanese pirates. Wanfo Ge pavilion was enclosed inside the north gate bastion. The coastal wall eventually came to be known as the Fengcheng Town Wall. Wanfo Ge's dimensions are not nearly as large as it once were. Today's temple is made up of three main buildings: the Wanfo Lou Building, the Bell Tower, and the Drum Tower. Stepping through the temple complex's front entrance will bring you first to Maitreya Hall. As you move on from there, you will see three to four storey towers standing in front of you. Wanfo Lou stands in the middle and the drum and bell towers are to its left and right. All three buildings are newly restored. Tathagata Buddha is enshrined in the Wanfo Lou's main hall. Circling around the back will take you to another large hall. Surprisingly, this second hall has an elevator which travels all the way up to the building's top floor. The light in this hall is excellent, and a sitting statue of Siddhartha Guatama is in the center. As many as ten thousand images of the sitting Siddhartha Guatama line the hall's four walls, and countless cup-shaped lamps are fixed to the walls' faces. Wanfo Ge temple derives its name from this hall (Wanfo Ge — thousand Buddha pavilion), and the lamps in this room are dazzlingly brilliant. A classroom can be found on the Bell Tower's second floor, where you can frequently see young Buddhist nuns attending class. In the back of the Wanfo Lou is a hall dedicated to the Guardian of the Earth Bodhisattva.

Buddhist nun, Master Xin Liang is in charge of the temple. She is over eighty years old. If you wish, you can pay her a formal visit.

Tickets

5 RMB

Fengxian Bay Tourist Area
(hǎiwān lǚyóuqū, 海湾旅游区)

China's first man-made bay, the Fengxian government spent 300 million RMB to build it. Located at the Fengxian District's southernmost point, this is also Shanghai's only bay. Seven kilometers away from Fengxian's central new urban area, the bay overlooks the deep water harbor to the east and the East China Sea (Hangzhou Bay) to the south. It also faces across from the Zhejiang Province's coastal regions. Even though the bay is artificial, it still attracts residents from in and around Shanghai, and you can always see families here on the weekends

The bay's newly constructed flood-prevention wall measures 2.6 kilometers long, and there are artificial dunes on the beach where people often indulge in different leisure activities. The most famous activity here is kite-flying, which has become somewhat of a local tradition. Every November,

Food and Drink

There are a lot of good restaurants in Fengxian. Most of them serve seafood and local countrystyle dishes.

Laobayang Restaurant (老八样奉贤店) is located in Nanqiao Town at 317 Huancheng Donglu (near Yunhe Beilu). Telephone: 021-57411777. Laobayang is the restaurant that Shanghai locals traditionally go to for ceremonial occasions such as weddings and funerals, and to celebrate holidays like Chinese New Year. The eight delicacies found on the menu (the restaurant's "bayang") are Baoyu, Kou Sansi, oil fried shrimp, Zheng Sansi, Baiqie Yangrou, river carp braised in soy sauce, Shuisun seasoned pork, and peasant family sweet meat. The mutton here is good and worth trying. Expect to pay 60 RMB 0to 70 RMB per person.

Da Zhai Men Restaurant (大宅门餐厅) is steeped in Chinese atmosphere. It is not cheap, running over 100 RMB per person, but the atmosphere is excellent with rich classical Chinese surroundings. Da Zhai Men is located in Nanqiao Town at 718 Huancheng Donglu. Telephone: 021-67108777 or 67108778. We recommend the garlic zebra shrimp, steamed cod and snow vegetables, and fried baozi (stuffed buns).

If you are in the mood for coffee, try out **Dio Cafe** (迪欧咖啡) on Jiefang Lu inside Nanqiao Town's Guhua Park. Telephone: 021-617187608. The park is on the western side of the cafe and provides some excellent scenery. You will find a large crowd here every day of the week. Dio also serves simple western dishes. Expect to pay about 50 RMB per person. There are plenty of other restaurants along Huancheng Lu and Jiefang Lu. If you stick to simple fare such as noodles and fried baozi, than you should be able to eat well for about 20 RMB.

the bay hosts an International Kite festival and attracts crowds of kite enthusiasts from around the world.

Address

From the Shen Zhuang subway station, take the Shenhai line straight to the bay. The bay is the last stop on the route. Tickets cost 7 RMB. Expect to travel for about two hours. From Fengxian's Nanqiao Town you can take the Meiba line. If you are driving, take the Shenfengjin Expressway (A4), get off at the Zhelin Town exit, and take the Fengzhe Highway directly to the shore. Alternately, you can get off at the southern end of Lupu Daqiao Bridge and take the Puxing Highway to the bay.

Tickets

Entry into the vacation area is free. The kite festival has a 20 RMB entry fee. It costs 3 RMB to get onto the beach.

Special Note

The vacation area has become a street loaded with restaurants, hotels, and entertainment, and is extremely convenient. Shanghai Normal University's Fengxian campus can be found on Fengpao Gonglu not far from the vacation area. You can find plenty of internet bars and snack stalls in and around the campus.

Eryan Temple *(èryán sì, 二严寺)*

Also known as Fo Ge, Eryan Si was built during the Yuan Dynasty and is made up of such structures as the Precious Hall of the Great Hero, Great Emperor Hall, and the Jade Buddha building. There are two ancient gingko trees inside the temple. Known far and wide, these luxuriant trees were planted during the Song Dynasty. There was also once a thousand arm thousand eye statue of the Goddess of Mercy carved out of camphor wood, though it was unfortunately destroyed during the Cultural Revolution.

Eryan Si's name originated from a section of text in the Buddhist text, Niepanjing. Niepanjing's 17th saying describes "two types of dignity". One is Zhihui, wisdom; the other is Fude, virtue. Together they formed the Fuzhi er Yan from which the name Eryan Si was derived. The temple is not far from Fengxian Town, but there not a whole lot to see here. If you are on a tight schedule, do not feel to badly if you have to pass it by.

Address

Eryan Temple is located in Nanqiao Town at 1749 Huhang Gonglu. To get there, you can take the Shenhai Line or the Shenshao Line from the Shen Zhuang subway station or the Nanmei Line from the Hongmei Nanlu subway station. From the Lianhua subway station, take the Lianzhuang Line. Each bus line will take you to Nanqiao Town.

Tongjin Bridge
(tōngjīn qiào, 通津桥)

If you are an ancient tree buff or stone bridge architecture enthusiast then this might be an interesting stop to make. If not, than beautiful countryside scenery here is another great draw. Tongjin Bridge is located in Xintang village just outside the town of Xinsi. Built in 1216, this is the most ancient arched stone bridge in the Fengxian District, and one Shanghai's few Song Dynasty era arched stone bridges. Two one thousand year old gingko trees stand at the bridge's

Accommodations

Fengxian Nanqiao is Fengxian's urban center, and accommodations here are generally pretty cheap. If you want something upscale, than try **Sentosa Hotel** *(shèngtáoshā dàjiǔdiàn, 圣淘沙大酒店)*, at 1 Fengxian Nanqiao Lu, 021-57429999. A standard room here runs at about 450 RMB. You can also try out the hotel's Southeast Asian and French Restaurants.

The Guhua Garden Hotel *(gǔhuá shānzhuāng, 古华山庄)* is established inside a traditional Chinese building. Located at the Fengxian Nanqiao's town center, a standard room at the Guhua Garden Hotel will set you back 406 RMB.

Hongda Country Villa *(hóngdá shānzhuāng, 宏达山庄)*, 021-57523284, is a two-star hotel located in Fengcheng Town at 49 Nanfeng Gonglu. Loaded with country style, this is a great place to enjoy a Chinese home-cooked country-style meal. Accommodations here are also quite comfortable.

Special Note

The Fengxian District has a tourist information center located in Naniqiao Town at 276 Jiefang Zhonglu. Information here is rather limited. Telephone: 021-57424780

end. Planted at the beginning of the Song Dynasty, these trees are two of just seven one thousand year old trees found in and around Shanghai. They are truly among Shanghai's Gods of Longevity. The bridge and the trees sit quietly in the countryside next to a running stream. They form quite a picturesque scene.

Address

From Pudong East Hospital, take the Puwei Zhuanxian special line to Xinsi Zhen. You can also take the Shenhai, Shenshao, or Lianzhuang Lines to Nanqiao and then switch over to the Fengshao Line or the Meituan Line. Be sure to get off the bus at Daxin Si. Many people also make this trip by bicycle from Shanghai and Hangzhou. If you are up for it, take road one and follow the road signs. The signs are all pretty clear and are written in English, so if you follow them carefully, you should not get lost.

Special Note

The Wild Chestnut Foodstuff Factory (野荸荠食品厂) can be found near Tongjin Bridge. If you are interested, go take a look. It is an old store.

Huatingdong Stone Embankment

(huátíng dōngshítáng, 华亭东石塘)

In the first year of Qing Emperor Yong Zheng's rule, the ocean tides repeatedly and violently surged, bombarding the embankment along Hangzhou Bay and the Fengxian shore, and eventually leading to its destruction. Emperor Yong Zheng personally gave the orders to build a new stone embankment and put forth efforts to make sure it was properly supervised. Construction on the stone embankment began in the west at Jinshanzui and continued eastward to Huajiajiao (Today's Fenghai Village just outside Zhelin Town). The embankment took a full ten years to build, and when it was finished, it was called the Shili Jincheng "the 20 kilometer impregnable wall".

Address

The stone embankment is located south of Fengxian's Zhelin Town. To get there, take the Shenhai Line from the Shen Zhuang subway station, and get off the bus at Zhelin Zhen.

Around Songjiang District (sōngjiāng, 松江)

Songjiang, also called Rongcheng, is located in Shanghai's southwest. Once an ancient city, Songjing is over two thousand years old. Songjiang was historically a textile center, and as a result, it is commonly referred to as the "old textile capital". Shanghai's history really begins with Songjiang. It was founded as Huating Xian County in 751 AD, during the reign of Tang Dynasty Emperor Tian Bao. (In 2001 Songjiang celebrated the 1250th anniversary of the county's founding) When Shanghai County was established at the end of the Yuan Dynasty, Songjiang had already risen to the status of a prefecture. Many ancient pagodas, pieces of architecture, temples, gardens, and artifacts can be found within the city today. Here you can find Zuibai Chi, one of Shanghai's five great gardens, as well as She Mountian, Shanghai's only true mountain landscape. During holidays and on weekends, She Shan mountian manages to draw large crowds of Shanghai residents out of the city center.

Zuibai Chi *(zuìbáichí, 醉白池)*

One of the five great Shanghai gardens, Zuibai Chi is arranged around a central 600 square meter pool. From the water's edge you can see Chinese-style winding hall pavilions everywhere. It is an extremely creative arrangement. The wall on the southern end of the pool has the stone carving, Great Figures of Yunjian (Songjiang). It is engraved with the portraits of over 100 famous village scholars and country sages from various counties of the Ming and Qing period Songjiang Prefecture. The Old Tree Building, the thatched cottage above the pool, and Mandarin Duck Pavilion, each add to the overall beauty of the landscape.

Zuibai Chi was originally the private residence and garden of Song Dynasty jinshi (a successful candidate in the highest imperial examinations), Zhu Zhichun. The garden was then known as Guyang Yuan. In 1650, famed Qing Dynasty painter Gu Dashen transformed this garden residence into his own personal villa. Centered around a 700 square meter rectangular lotus pond, Gu

Transportation

The Songjiang District is located 40 kilometers outside of urban Shanghai. To get there you can take Tourist Line 1A from the Shanghai Stadium (7am-5:30pm), and the Husong Line from the Western Shanghai bus station direct to Songjiang (5am-7pm). The People's Square (at the intersection of Songshan Lu and Yan'an Donglu), Shanghai Indoor Stadium's Shuniu station (7:30am-5pm), and Jinjiang Amusement Park (6:30am-10pm) all have bus lines that run direct to Songjiang. If you want to drive, take the Humin elevated road to Humin Lu and follow the Huhang Expressway (A8 road) to Jiufeng Lu. Follow Ledu Lu for the rest of the way. It will take you about forty minutes to get there by car and about an hour by bus.

Food and Drink

Little Sheep *(xiǎoféiyáng sōngjiāngdiàn, 小肥羊松江店)* is extremely popular in Songjiang. This is the famous countrywide hot pot chain that uses soup made with medicinal herbs. Their hotpot is known for its strong but delicious flavor. Although the focus at the Little Sheep is on cooking meats, you can also cook vegetables and tofu. The restaurant draws a large crowd every day. Expect to pay 50RMB per person. It is located at 648 Songhui ZhongLu (Near Guyang Lu). Telephone: 021-57820177.

Xiao Tian Yuan *(xiǎotiányuán sōngjiāngdiàn, 小田园松江店)*, is located in the Xincheng District at 1027 Guyang Beilu (near Sixian Lu). They serve classic Hangzhou fare with its mild flavors and emphasis on seafood. The service here is exceptional. Recommended dishes include the green eggplant *(qīngqiézi, 青茄子)* and Tianmu Lake fish head *(tiānmùhú yútóu, 天目湖鱼头)*. Telephone: 021-67738419. There are a lot of restaurants near the Songjiang

Dashen contracted the pool's bank with irregularly symmetrical horticultural skill. It included bamboo, plum trees, ornamental mountains, and rare stones, each complimenting and contrasting with each other, melding together into one organic whole. The garden's name, Zuibai, was inspired by Su Shi's poem "Zuibai Tangji", which tells of Han Qi, a Song Dynasty chancellor who builds Zuibai Tang Hall to express his envy of the drunken Tang Dynasty poet, Bai Juyi. Gu Dashen was a fine painter and poet, but he also envied Bai Juyi's alcohol-fueled joy. He therefore named his villa, Zuibai, after Han Qi's Zuibai Tang. While not very large, Zuibai Chi Garden is exquisite. Have a seat here and whittle away the time. Normally there are not too many visitors, but crowds form on weekends and during major holidays.

Address
64 Renmin Nanlu, Songjiang District
Telephone
021-57814763
Hours of Operation
7 am-5pm
Tickets
12RMB

Square Pagoda
(fāngtǎ, 方塔)

Xing Shengjiao Temple Pagoda has always been a prominent symbol of Songjiang. The tower's structure imitates Tang Dynasty brick pagoda architecture, and it is commonly referred to as Fang Ta or "the Square Pagoda". Over nine hundred years old, the

square pagoda was built during the Northern Song Period sometime between 1068 and 1093 A.D. Xing Shengjiao Temple is even older, constructed in 949, during the Five Dynasty's Late Han period. The form and structure of the pagoda is extremely elegant. If you are willing to pay a negligible fee of 5 RMB, you will be allowed to climb to the top. Although, perhaps it would be best to save your money and help protect this cultural relic by admiring it from the ground.

Right next to the Fang Ta pagoda you will find another piece of Songjiang history, a Zhaobi or ancient decorative wall. Built in 1370, the wall once stood across from the main entrance to Songjiang Prefecture's Chenghuang Miao (City God Temple). It is beautifully carved and is one of greater Shanghai's largest and most exquisite pieces of brick sculpture art. While you are visiting the Fang Ta, you should definitely stop by the Zhaobi and take a look.

There is a rather mysterious story concerning the wall and the pagoda. During World War Two, the Japanese exercised wanton and indiscriminate bombing throughout Songjiang. All of the ancient buildings around the Square Pagoda suffered from the attacks. During one Japanese raid, witnesses claim that bombs blasted the pagoda over fifty meters in the air. But, after the cloud had passed and the dust had settled, the pagoda was still standing loftily in its original place. A rumor soon spread that the pagoda was protected by spirits. When the bombing finally ended, the Square Pagoda and decorative wall proved to be the only ancient structures that remained standing. All of the other historical architecture was leveled.

In 1978, a large portion of this ancient site,

Food and Drink

University town. Expect low prices and simple facilities.

Lesvila Theme Restaurant is located at 152 Jiaowenhui Lu. They serve pizza at reasonable prices. Expect to pay 20 RMB to 30 RMB per person. Their telephone number is: 021-67796277.

The Lake View *(yuèhúxuān, 月湖轩)*, located on the fifth floor of the Le Meridien Sheshan Shanghai Hotel *(shìmàoshéshān àiměijiǔdiàn, 世茂佘山艾美酒店)*, is one of the most luxurious restaurants in Songjiang. Come during the summer and enjoy some of their exquisite offerings. The food here emphasizes mild flavors; try the shangtang shengmian noodles and the shiitake mushrooms with tofu. The restaurant is located at 1288 Sheshan Linyin Xin Lu. Prices are high, as you would expect. Plan on paying around 200 RMB to 350 RMB per person.

Accommodations

Le Meridien Sheshan Shanghai is located at 1288 Sheshan Linyin Xinlu. This five-star hotel has an excellent ambiance, and is a nice place to spend a holiday. A standard room costs 1,254 RMB. Telephone: 021-57799999.

Shanghai Sheshan Forest Hotel *(shànghǎi shéshān sēnlín bīnguǎn, 上海佘山森林宾馆)* is located at Sheshanta Nongkou. The environment here at the eastern foot of She Mountain is fine, but the hotel facilities are a bit dated. A standard room costs 300 RMB. Telephone: 021-57651160.

Lansun Shanzhuang Hotel *(lánsǔn shān zhuāng, 兰笋山庄)* can be found near the Sheshan Forest Hotel. Constructed right next to the mountain, the hotel is secluded and quiet. Standard rooms run 240 RMB.

including a large concentration of ancient structures, was turned into the Square Pagoda Garden. The Xing Shengjiao Temple Pagoda is definitely the garden's centerpiece, but there is still plenty of other things to see, for example: the Song Dynasty Wangxian Bridge, Ming Dynasty Lanrui Hall, Qing Dynasty Empress Palace Hall, and the two famous stones, Wulao Feng and Meinü Feng. However, all of these artifacts have only retained part of their original ancient structures. The rest has been reconstructed with new materials. Needless to say, none of the artifacts are still imbued with the classical beauty they once had. The Square Pagoda Garden is large and may seem a little bit chaotic, but its eastern section has a quiet and secluded bamboo forest. It is quite atmospheric.

Visitors can also be frequently seen in the central grass yard flying kites and soaking up the sun. You may choose to paddle a boat on the garden's lake, but do not expect to be moved by its scenery. Hand paddled boats can accommodate up to four people, and cost 20 RMB per hour.

Address
1 Fangta Nanlu, Songjiang District
Telephone
021-57822157
Hours of Operation
8 am-5pm
Tickets
12 RMB

The Toroni Sutra Stela
(tángjīngchuáng, 唐经幢)

This, Shanghai's most ancient construction, is certainly not its most eye-catching, and its location is even more baffling — inside the campus of Songjiang County Seat's primary school. If you want to visit Tang Jingchuan, you will have to call the school and make arrangements ahead of time. Of course, you can try to catch the gate keeper napping and sneak in. Once you are inside the school grounds, no one will give you any trouble.

The pillar was built in 859 AD, the thirteenth year of Tang Emperor Da Zhong, and is inscribed with the full text of the Buddhist work: Fo Ding Zun Sheng Tuo Luo Ni Jing. Tang Jingchuan has been preserved as a national cultural protection unit. Standing at 9.3 meters tall, Tang Jingchuan has a total of 21 levels and eight sides. The pillar's pedestal, bands, and baldachin are finely

engraved with the images of ocean waves, pearls, clouds, heroes, gods, Bodhisattva, enshrined figures, coiled dragons, sitting lions, and images of the Buddha with lotus flowers. The carvings are exquisite, with proficiently engraved polished lines. Tang Jingchuan is truly a beautiful work of art. According to legend, the pillar was created to cover up an ocean water well. Buddhist practitioners believe that the pillar contains supernatural powers. Supposedly, virtue collected inside the pillar is enough to help souls rise from purgatory. As a result, officials once came to the Tang Jiangchuan every autumn to execute criminals in the hopes that the pillar would have an uplifting influence on their souls.

Address

Zhongshan Donglu Primary School in the Songjiang District.

Telephone

021-57822157 (call in advance to arrange your visit; entry is free)

Songjiang Mosque
(sōngjiāng qīngzhēnsì, 松江清真寺)

The Songjiang District is known not only for its prevalent Buddhism, but also for its rich Islamic heritage. Songjiang Mosque is the oldest mosque in the greater Shanghai area. Originally built during the reign of Yuan Emperor Zhi Zheng (1341-1368), the mosque was founded by the Muslim county leader known by his Mongolian name, Daluhuachi. Emperor Yong Le gave the order to rebuild the mosque in the Ming Dynasty, and it was renamed, Songjiang Huihui Fen, and was known as "Songjiang Muslim Prayer Temple". Looked after by later rulers, the mosque underwent several reconstructions. Despite all of the later period renovation, the mosque still retains its Yuan and Ming era temple-tomb style.

Songjiang Mosque faces North. The decorative wall in front reads Qingmiaowuzhen, and two characters, Chi Jian ("built by imperial order"), are displayed on a horizontal board above the door, indicating the mosques noble status. Qing Zhen Si, the Chinese characters for the word "mosque", are written on the door inside the wall. In the past, the mosque's surrounding area was used as a Muslim cemetery, though most of the gravesites have already been transferred to other places. If you walk down to the south of the mosque you will find the tomb of Yuan Dynasty leader, Daluhuachi on the right hand side. Continuing on will take you past the main hall, the Yao hall, the Northern and Southern lecture halls, Bangke Door and Water rooms. The Yao hall and Bangke Door are key rooms to visit. The inner brick wall inside the Yao Hall is ornately carved. Wooden beams were not used during the hall's construction, and it is frequently referred to as the "hall without beams". When touring the mosque, you must be sure to dress appropriately. Females are not allowed access to the worship hall.

Address
21 Gong Be ng Xiang, Xima Lu, Songjiang District.
Telephone
021-57823684
Hours of Operation
8 am-4pm
Tickets
5RMB

Yi Yuan Garden *(yíyuán, 颐园)*

Yi Yuan Garden is not very well-known and does not usually see a lot of visitors, but considering its significant collection of Ming Dynasty artifacts and architecture, it would be a shame to pass it by. In its earlier life, Yi Yuan was known as the Luo Family Garden. Changing hands many times over the course of its history, the garden belonged to the Gao family during China's Republican era. Garden owner, Gao Tianmei, was a prominent member of the Southern Society, and many society gatherings were held in the Gao Family Garden. Much of the garden's original scenery has been destroyed. Remaining sites of interest include the Guanjia Lou, a multistory building, ornamental mountains, a pool, winding hallways, and a stone bridge with three bends.

The Southern Society *(nánshè, 南社)*

Founded in 1909 and disbanded in 1923, the Southern Society has a history that spans just over a decade. With a membership of over 1,100 people, the Southern Society was a famous group of Republican Era writers. The Southern Society membership included a great deal of celebrated contemporary literary talent with such figures as Li Yazi, Su Manshu, Lin Gengbai, Ma Junwu, Zhou Guisheng, and Bao Tianxiao.

Address
Located in the Songjiang County Seat at Xiuye Qiaoxi. It can be found inside Shanghai's Number Four Welfare Institution (上海市第四福利院).

She Shan National Holiday Resort

(shéshān guójiājí lǚyóudùjiàqū, 佘山国家级旅游度假区)

She Shan Mountian is a favorite travel destination of Shanghai residents. Not by any means a large mountain, when holidays arrive, it completely fills up with people. She Shan is also not very tall, and from northeast to southwest, it has twelve peaks and stretches for only thirteen kilometers. Because the Songjiang District is often called Yunjian, you can frequently hear people refer to She Shan as Yunjian Jiu Feng or Nine Peaks of Yunjian (In China the number nine is considered a lucky number so it is used instead of the number twelve). Today the mountain is split up into eastern and western regions. The She Mountian Forest Park can be found in the east. Because the mountain is also used to domesticate birds, a giant net has been put in place to keep them from flying away. The net is grimy with dirt and one cannot help but feel sorry for the birds and plants caught inside.

Compared to the eastern mountain, the western part of She Shan Mountain has a bit more culture to offer. At 97 meters tall, here you can find China's first Astronomical Observatory and the She Shan Cathedral.

Walking between the eastern and western portions of the mountain will lead you to a Northern Song Era pagoda that was built for ascetic monks. It is said that when the pagoda was first built, a Buddhist monk used it as a secluded retreat. The pagoda later caught fire, killing the monk, but the pagoda itself survived.

There is a cable car that runs between the two halves of the mountain, so if you are not in the mood for a hike, you can wiz by in the sky.

She Shan was once honored with the good favor of Qing Emperor Kang Xi. In the spring of 1720, Emperor Kang Xi personally inscribed the board for She Shan Mountain reading Lan Sun Shan. He had local officials bring the imperial sign to the mountain. This is one of the few Chinese mountains to be named by an emperor.

She Shan Cathedral *(shéshān tiān zhǔjiàotáng, 佘山天主教堂)*

At first glance, most people are dumbstruck by the brilliant majesty of the She Shan Cathedral. To reach the church, you must first pass by the 14 pavilions of bitterness on the way up the mountain. Each pavilion is decorated with relief sculptures of the suffering Jesus Christ. In addition to the fourteen, are also three Holy pavilions and a middle hall. It is said that when Catholics come to the mountain on pilgrimage, they stop at the pavilions as they make their way to the top to remind themselves of Christ's suffering. When you reach the top of the western mountain the church will immediately come into view. Standing tall and upright in the middle of a grass field, the huge church inspires a reverent heart. She Shan's Catholic Church is somewhat different from the ones that you will find in urban Shanghai in that it is open for public visits and sells tickets for entry. This means that you can tour the church and take in this baroque work of art at your leisure. Built in 1871 by French missionaries, the cathedral has undergone several reconstructions in its lifetime.

The structure you see today is the final result of a church expansion in 1925. Aside from the church's typical baroque styling, you can also see traces of Greco-Roman and Gothic architectural influences. The church adornments and building materials also reflect traditional Chinese building techniques, making She Shan Cathedral a giant intercultural monument.

An astronomical observation platform can also be found at the western end of She Shan Catholic Church, and it is outfitted with the latest facilities and observation system. This is a favorite spot of Shanghai's amateur and professional astronomers.

The She Shan Catholic Church is huge and can accommodate 4,000 people. In 1942, the Pope conferred it the status of a

"holy place", and it has become a pilgrimage site for Chinese Catholics all over the country. Every May, the month of the Holy Mother, Catholics from every corner of China head this way on pilgrimage. The crowds at that time can get pretty intense, so you may want to avoid this period if you schedule a trip.

She Shan Mountain Astronomical Observatory

(shéshān tiānwéntái, 佘山天文台)

Astronomy buffs cannot miss She Mountain's Astronomical observatory. Built by French Missionaries in 1899, this is the earliest modern astronomical observatory in China, and has China's oldest astronomical telescope. Today, it is still a functional astronomical research center.

She Shan Mountain Earthquake Prediction Platform *(shéshān dìzhèn jīzhǔntái, 佘山地震基准台)*

Sitting at western edge of She Shan's eastern foot, the Earthquake prediction platform is surrounded by bamboo forests. This hundred-year-old building originally functioned as the Shanghai Observatory. Here you can learn more about earthquakes in Japan, and China's terrible earthquake disaster at Tangshan. The platform is also a repository of hard-to-find earthquake reference materials. If you have time, you can watch the video, Earthquakes and Animals. Hours of operation: 7:30am-4:30pm

Address

Located 30 Kilometers outside of urban Shanghai, She Shan Mountian is located off of the Waiqingsong Highway. From Shanghai Stadium, you can get here on the Tourist 1B Line. If you leave from the West Shanghai Bus Station, then take the Huchen Line or the Hu She Kun Line direct to She Shan Mountian. There are also direct tourist lines from Nanpu Daiqiao, the Shanghai Indoor Stadium, the northern district bus station, and Shanghai Xizhan the Western Railway Station. Songjiang, Qingpu, Jiading, Jinshan, and Fengxian all offer direct bus routes.

Telephone

021-57653235

Hours of Operation

8am-5pm.

Tickets

Eastern She Shan Mountian Park (includes sand sculptures, bird park, and butterfly garden) 30 RMB, Western She Shan Mountain Park (includes cable car, astronomical observatory, and church) 40 RMB. The Yue Hu Lake Ecological Park 50 RMB, Tianma Shan Garden 10 RMB, Xiao Kunshan Garden 6 RMB, She Shan Mountain Slide: Located on the eastern mountain's northern face.

30 RMB; Children 15 RMB.

Special Note

The newly constructed Yue Hu Lake Ecological Park is located at the foot of She Shan Mountian, though it is not very interesting. If you are on a tight schedule, do not feel bad about missing it.

Heavenly Horse Mountain *(tiānmăshān, 天马山)*

Located to She Shan's southwest, Tianma Shan is the largest and tallest mountain among She Shan's twelve peak mountain range, and at 99.8 meters above sea level, it is the highest point in the greater Shanghai area. The only thing that Tianma Shan lacks is notoriety. In ancient times, Tianma Shan was called Gan Shan, and according to legend, during the Spring and Autumn Period the Wu Kingdom's famed weaponsmith, Gan Jiang, forged a mighty sword here. Afterwards, the name "Tianma Shan" became popular due to the mountain's shape — resembling a heavenly horse stretching out its wings. Tianma Shan was once a famous Buddhist location, and today, the mountain is still dotted with Fangong Buddhist Temples. During the spring time and the first and fifteenth days of the agricultural New Year, pilgrims climb the mountain to burn incense in the temples. It is therefore no surprise that Tianma Shan is also called "Incense Mountain".

Huzhubao Guang Pagoda
(hùzhū băoguāngtă, 护珠宝光塔)

Built in 1079 AD during the Northern Song Dynasty, the leaning Huzhubao Guan Pagoda was once the most important pagoda in Tianma Shan's largest temple — Yuanzhijiao Si. Yuanzhijiao Si's head abbot donated a five-colored Buddhist relic in 1157, and stored it inside the pagoda. Unfortunately, the relics have already been lost.

Huzhubao Guang Pagoda is known as the "treasure" of the Tianma Shan Mountain because Song Dynasty Emperor Yuan Feng coins were once found in the cracks between the pagoda's bricks. Afterwards, many of the bricks were dismantled as people searched for money in the pagoda wall causing Huzhubao Guang to lean. According to a 1982 survey, the pagoda currently leans southwest at a 62 degree angle, and the pagoda roof's center has shifted 2.27 meters. Between 1984 and 1987, significant repairs were undertaken to prevent the tower from falling any further, preserving the 1982 measurements to this day. With a greater slant than even the Italy's Tower of Pisa, Huzhubao Guang claims to be the premier leaning tower of the world. Arboreal enthusiasts may take interest in the 700 year old ginkgo tree nearby.

Eight immortals slope
(bāxiānpō, 八仙坡)

As you head up the mountain, you will pass by a small slope of only eight small stones. Nearby, you can find a Taiji (yin-yang) diagram of the universe. People say that the diagram was arranged by the rustic Zhu Geliang (later to become a legendary Chinese tactician), in accordance with the famous Chinese eight tactical arrays.

Carp Rock *(lǐyúshí, 鲤鱼石)*

At the mountaintop you will see a carp-shaped rock that appears to be struggling to jump into the ocean. According to legend, the rock signifies this as a lucky place, and the underworld has blessed the people who live here.

Moyun Lansheng Scenic Area *(móyúnlǎnshèng, 摩云揽胜)*

White walls and green tiles, the Shangfeng Si Temple contrasts gracefully and delicately with the green bamboo and purple flowers of its surroundings. During World War II the Japanese stole the three meter Song Dynasty bronze Guanyin Goddess of Mercy statue from the temple, and the temple's main hall was burned to the ground. Today, the people of Tianma Zhen Town have replaced the old Guanyin with a newly cast bronze.

From Moyun Lansheng you can continue on two separate paths. One leads to the mountain's northern peak — an ideal place to watch the sunrise. The other leads to a small two-story pagoda. The pagoda's first floor has a statue of a wooden horse, Tianma Shan's "heavenly horse". The second floor is empty, but provides a bird's eye of the mountain. From the pagoda you can continue down two more paths. One path is marked with a sign that reads, "the back of the mountain is secluded and lonely, do not travel there by yourself," and the other has a sign that says, "explore the mystery of the stone cave". When you reach the front of

the cave you will see a large headless turtle and another sign marked with two Chinese characters. The characters read Mo Wang or "Prince of the Devils"! If you want to explore the cave, you definitely need to bring a flashlight.

Continuing on past the cave will take you into a mountainside covered with bluish green bamboo.

Address

Tianma Shan Mountian is located 10 KM to the southwest of She Shan Mountain, and 11 KM away from the Songjiang District prefecture. To get there, you can take the Hushekun Line from West Shanghai Bus Station, and the Tai Line from the Shanghai Indoor Stadium. Be warned that Tai Line usually has as long wait. You may also choose to travel first to Songjiang and change busses from there. In Songjiang, take the Tianmei Line from the Meilong Bus station (4 RMB). If you want to return directly from Tianma Shan to Shanghai, you can take the Tianmei Line from Tianma Zhen and get off at Jinjiang Amusement Park. From there you can take the subway to wherever else you need to go. Keep in mind that this bus does not run after 3:30pm. You can also wait at the Tianmei Line sign for the Hushekun Line bus and take it back to the West Shanghai Bus Station.

Tickets

10 RMB

Around Chongming Island (chóngmíngdǎo, 崇明岛)

Chongming Island is China's third largest island. Located on the frequently traveled "golden waterway" of the Yangtze River, Chongming is a major junction on China's gold coast. Heading inland from the island will take you past 18 cities and provinces off the Yangtze riverbank. Heading outbound will take you to the Pacific Ocean. Chongming Island is the world's greatest sandbar, and it is a great place to lie on the beach, go camping, and enjoy outdoor activities.

The 1,300 year old Chongming Island first emerged from the Yangtze river waters in 618 AD. Because the Yangtze deposits

large amounts of silt onto the island, every year, Chongming Island increases 487 hectares in area and stretches an additional 143 meters further east into the Pacific Ocean. Chongming Island's long history lends it a wealth of historical sites such as the Ming Dynasty Chongming Palace of Learning, Shou'an Si Temple, the Tang Yicen Mausoleum, and the Qing Dynasty Jin'ao Shan. It is also home to Eastern China's largest national forest park — Dongping Forest Park. A large pond called both "Chongming West Lake" and "Ming Pool" can be found near Chongming Island's western edge, and the fish that live there can grow as heavy as 50 kilograms. In the eastern part of the island,

Transportation

Ferrys to Chongming Island leave from three of Shanghai's wharfs: the Mouth of the Wusong River (吴淞, 8:45, 12:15, 16:00), the Baoyang Wharf (宝杨, 7:15, 10:30, 14:00; Speed boat at 7:10, 7:50, 8:45, 10:20, 12:00, 13:30, 16:00), and Shidong Kou (石洞口, 6:00, 6:15, 8:45, 10:30, 11:00, 12:40, 14:30, 15:00, 17:00, 18:00, 19:15).

A one-hour slow boat costs 10 RMB per person. The faster 40 minute boat costs 20 RMB per person.

Food and Drink

Chongming Island is large and its eateries are pretty spread out. Nevertheless, you will have a lot to choose from here. Not surprisingly, restaurants on the island are loaded with fresh seafood. You should be able to find some great local country-style food as well. **Dio Cafe** (迪欧咖啡) is located in Chongming's county seat at 308 Bayi Lu. The coffee here is okay, and the Hexiang Laweifan (a Cantonese dish of steamed rice and salted meat) is highly recommended. Expect to pay 30 RMB per person. Telephone: 021-59618977. **Yipinchuan** *(yìpǐnquán, 一品全)* is located in Chongming County's Nanmen Gang, and serves local Shanghai fare. Prices run about 50 RMB per person. Telephone: 021-59621177. **Guying Fanzhuang** *(gǔyíng fànzhuāng, 古瀛饭庄)* is located in the Qianwei Village. Local countryside dishes make up a large portion of the menu. The restaurant is large, made up of many different courtyards, and the portions served here are large as well. The Yangtze River mullet fish tofu is recommended. Expect to pay 50 RMB per person. Telephone: 021-59649177.

there is a migratory bird wilderness preserve where large numbers of birds choose to spend the winter. It goes without saying that winter is a great time for bird watching on Chongming Island.

Chongming Island has one other great natural treasure: the Narcissus Flower. Chongming is one of China's two famous narcissus flower cultivating regions. The other is Zhangzhou in the Fujian Province. Narcissus flowers grown on Chongming Island are famous for their ball-shaped stems with few branches, and their rich scent, which remains potent for a very long time.

Shou'an Temple
(shòuān sì, 寿安寺)

Shou'an Temple is the oldest of Chongming's four large monasteries. Located at the southern end of Jin'ao Shan, Shou'an Si was built in 1242 during the reign of Song Emperor Chun You. The temple you see today, however, was reconstructed in 1983. At the temple's front gate, you will notice a hanging scroll written by Zhao Puchu, the late President of the Chinese Buddhist Association. The scroll reads," Tathagata has infinite life, the Buddhism will bring peace for ten thousand years." Although the temple is not very large, there is still plenty of great architecture to see here including the imposing and magnanimous Precious Hall of the Great Hero, the San Sheng Hall, and Great Emperor Hall. One thing you definitely should not miss is the camphor wood sculpture of the Buddha, Siddhartha Guaṭama, and the colored gold Buddhist statues. The second floor of the temple's western wing has a giant jade reclining Buddha statue. Weighing in at 13 tons and measuring at six feet in length, this is Shanghai's largest reclining jade Buddha statue. It is a stirring sight.

Jin'ao Mountain
(jīn áo shān, 金鳌山)

Located inside Houjia Zhen Town's Ao Shan Village, the manmade mountain, Jin'ao Shan, sits right next to Shou'an Si Temple. As you walk in the front gate, you will see a Ming-Qing style arch over the gateway with Jin Ao Shan, three large vigorous characters, written by the hand of the late Zhou Gucheng, a former Fudan University professor and historian. Lower down on the arch, below Zhou Gucheng's inscription, you can see images of famous Ming and Qing Dynasty figures. Walk along Shou'an Si Temple's west wall and head up the mountain to see Jin'ao Shan's renowned Zhenhai Ta Pagoda. Zhenhai Ta was built in 1893 by one of the county's most wealthy and influential families. Located on Jin'ao Shan's highest peak (built in 1668), the pagoda's old Goddess of Mercy pavilion has been converted into a Sea Pavilion. With a total of nine floors, a wooden staircase will take you to the top of the tower. Each floor enshrines six small Bodhisattva statues. The higher you climb, the narrower the pagoda becomes. The top floor is so small that it can fit only one person. From the pagoda's

Accomodations

Chongming Bao Dao Vacation Village *(chóngmíng bǎodǎo dùjiàcūn, 崇明宝岛度假村)*: 021-59339898. Surrounded by both forest and grasslands, the Vacation Village's environment is quite swell. A standard room costs 528 RMB.

Dongping National Forest Park's Forest Vacation Cabins *(sēnlín dùjiàcūn xiǎo mùwū, 东平森林公园内的森林度假村小木屋)* cost 380 RMB a night. Telephone: 021-59338597. You would be wise to reserve a room in advance.

A room at **Qianwei Village's Nongjia Le** *(nóngjiālè, 农家乐)* costs between 70 RMB to 80 RMB, but the price goes up to 100 RMB when you turn on the air conditioner. You can choose to stay in any place you find appealing. Most of these hotels are established inside peoples' private homes and fees vary. You had best enquire about fees before deciding on a place. Of course, many of the hotel managers here do not speak English. If you cannot speak Chinese, you had better bring a Chinese speaking friend with you. Telephone: 021-59641861, 021-59649103

Special Note

In recent years, more and more people are taking part in bicycle tours around Chongming Island. You can start your tour from wherever you want. Circling the island takes about two days. If you want to camp on the eastern beach, you will need to bring your own tent and sleeping bag.

Chongming Island Information Center: 021-59625888, Website: www.tourinfo.sh.cn When you arrive on the island, be sure to buy both your return boat tickets and a map. If you try to buy your return tickets at the last minute, they might already be sold out.

top you can look out onto a panoramic view of the entire area. If the temperature is good and the air is clear, you can see all the way to the ocean — quite a refreshing sight.

Address

Houjia Zhen Town, Chongming County
Transportation: Take Tourist Line NO. 5

Telephone

021-59623200

Chongming Palace of Learning

(chóngmíng xuégōng, 崇明学宫)

One of Shanghai's three ancient schools of learning, Chengming Xuegong is known today as Chongming Museum. When you step out of Chongming's Nanmen Wharf and walk forward for two or three hundred meters, you should be able to see tier upon tier of Chongming Xuegong's architectural complex. Two simple and profound stone pillared archways stand in front displaying the words "Confucius paragon of virtue, the greatest man of past and present". At the gate, you will find two 350 year old gingko trees with trunks so wide that it would take three people to fully wrap their arms around one of them. A pair of stone lions stand guard in front of the entrance

The complex's largest structure is the main hall where sacrifices were traditionally offered to Confucius. Eastern and western verandas housed 72 dormitories for the institute's most distinguished students. Today, the main hall is an exhibition hall for old boats, and the eastern veranda is covered with pictures of Chongming celebrities and records of various achievements. There is also a collection of unearthed ancient tools on display. In the western veranda you will find the Huangpimo Art Exhibit. Housed in the two buildings behind the main hall, the Chongming Folk Museum has a lot of regional character.

Address

696 Ao Shan Lu.From urban Shanghai, take tourist line number 5, bus lines 51, 116, 522, 728, 848, 849, or the wharf line to Wusong Wharf. Alternately you can take tourist line number five,or bus lines 51, 207, 508, 541,728, the Pengjiang Line, or the Wharf Line to the Baoyang Lu Wharf. You must then travel by boat to the Chongming Nanmen Harbor.

Telephone

021-59623827

Hours of Operation

8am-4pm (closed Mondays)

Tickets

10 RMB

The Eastern Shore
(dōngtān, 东滩)

As Chongming's northern and eastern sections continue to collect silt at rapid rate, the islands shoals have continued to expand. Today these shallows are quite large, and have become a breeding ground and habitat for shihuang (local chickens), brackish water crabs, reeds, guancao, luzhu (a variety of edible bamboo) and other plants and animals. The shallows are also a store of abundant wildlife resources such as, reed marshes, collections of poplar and willow trees, and metasequoia. Scenery is not the most striking aspect of this place; however, it is the migratory bird preserve. Currently applying to be listed as an important world wetland, Dong Tan is home to 116 types of birds. This is especially true of small swans whose numbers increase to 3,000-3,500 in the winter. Even rarer birds such as white-fronted geese, striated herons, and black-faced Spoonbills can also be found here. Migratory birds from Australia, New Zealand, and Japan like to use Dong Tan as a transit point, and their total numbers can reach 3 million in peak season. During the apex of the bird watching season, blankets of birds move across the sky like clouds. It is a truly majestic sight.

If you want to go bird watching in Dong Tan, early morning is most ideal time. Dong Tan is the closest point in Chongming to the East China Sea, and if you make it early enough in the morning, you can catch the grand sunrise over the ocean waters.

Address

Take a boat from Wusong Warf (4 boats a day) or Baoyang Warf (10 boats a day) to Bao Zhen. From Bao Zhen you can take the Bao Qian Line to Dong Tan. If you want to drive, take the Yixian Elevated Road to Tongji Lu (Highway A30). Afterwards, take Baoyang Lu to the Bayang Lu Warf and than take Cheke Du to Bao Zhen Town. From Bao Zhen Nanlu drive to Bao Zhen Beilu and follow it to Chenhai Gonglu. Take Chenhai Gonglu to Beichen Gong Lu. Baichen Gonglu should take you directly to Dong Tan.

Special Note

After you finish bird watching at Dong Tan, take a trip to Chenjia Zhen, find a simple clean restaurant, and sit down to a plate of crabs and assorted seafood. Chenjia Zhen is China's biggest "Crab City," and a large portion of Shanghai's crab is fished from here. You will find some rare and unusual seafood dishes at Chenjia Zhen, and prices are reasonable.

Dongping National Forest Park

(dōngpíng guójiā sēnlíngōngyuán, 东平国家森林公园)

One of Shanghai residents' most loved local travel destinations, Dongping National Forest Park is packed on holidays with people who drive in to barbecue and enjoy the sunshine. The park is large and it has a lot of facilities. Here you can see a relatively large amount of manmade structures. Dongping is Eastern China's largest artificial flatland forest, and the largest forest park in Shanghai. Located in the northern-central region of Chongming Island, the park is 12 kilometers away from the Nanmen Harbor, and measures in at 3.55 square kilometers. Originally known as the Dongping Forestry Center, the area was established in 1959 after much of the land had been reclaimed with dikes, and was later transformed into a forest park. There are plenty of leisure activities to enjoy here such as rock climbing and sliding down grassy slopes. The park also has an environmentally friendly tram that you can ride around the forest. You can stop and get off the tram whenever you want to take in some of the sites. Rides cost 10 RMB per hour. If you want to camp, the best place to go is the Sweet Smelling Osmanthus Garden Beach (桂花园沙滩) between the artificial lake and the forest. It makes an ideal campsite. Bring your own tent. Camping fees run at 10 RMB per person. Barbecue supplies and food can be rented here as well although prices are high. A charcoal grill runs 30 RMB, a cup of cooking oil is 5RMB, and the grounds fees are 20 RMB. Bring your own supplies if you can. You can also buy camping supplies in the supermarket at Nanmen.

Bicycles are available for rent; there are single person bikes and bicycles built for two. A deposit fee of 100 RMB is required, or you can hand over your identification as a deposit. Rent runs at 10 RMB per hour or 50 RMB per day.

Adress

Dongping Forest Park is in the northern central part of Chongming Island. From Shanghai North Bus station take the Shenchong Line. You can also take the Nandong Line and the Nanjiang Line from Chongming's Nanmen. Both lines arrive at the Dongping Forest Park.

Hours of Operation

8:30 am- 4:30pm

Tickets

40 RMB, children under 1.4 meters tall are half price.

Around Qingpu Districts (qīngpǔ qū, 青浦区)

Located in Shanghai's Western suburbs, Qingpu was one of the origins of Shanghai's ancient civilization, and it is the definitely the oldest of all the nearby regions. Thirty years ago, archaeologists excavated the Songze site four kilometers east of Qingpu. Now known as the cradle of the Songze civilization, excavations have revealed 136 grave sites in the area. The grave owners are the oldest known residents of this region, dating back 6,000 years.

However, Song Culture is not what draws most people to Qingpu. People come here to see the ancient town, Zhujiajiao, and the spectacular lake and river scenery that this region is known for. Zhujiajiao is the pearl of Shanghai's suburbs. With its small bridges and flowing streams, Zhujiajiao is steeped in idyllic and poetic landscapes. Qingpu is a vast expanse of misty, rolling waters, and it has an incredible lake, Dianshan Lake, where the sky and water seem to merge. Dianshan Lake is Shanghai's largest freshwater lake. There are some newly constructed showplace gardens that can be found along the lakeside, but they are not entirely interesting as the lake itself. Natural countryside landscapes are the real attraction here, and a walk around the lake area is sure to make you feel happy and carefree.

Qushui Yuan Garden

(qŭshuĭ yuán, 曲水园)

Located inside Qingpu Zhen Town, the garden was originally a part of Qingpu's Chenghuang Miao (City God Temple). It is occasionally referred to as Ling Yuan or "Spirit Garden". Built in 1745, the garden is centered around the Ninghe Hall, and has 24 other attractions such as the Huanxian Building, Huanxi Pavilion, Jingxin Cottage, Tianguang Yunjing, Huangdui Feilai, Xiaohao Liang Bridge, Poxian Pavilion, Er Qiao Bridge, Huashen Temple, and Xiyang-

Transportation

You can take Tourist Line NO. 4, the Huzhu Line, Beiqing Line, and the special Yuling Line from urban Shanghai to Qingpu. If you want to go to Zhujiajiao, there is another bus line can take you there. (see text). If you want to drive, take the Yan'an Elevated road and Huqingping Expressway to the town before getting on Zhongchun Lu. Get on the Huqingping Highway, and then follow Qinghu Lu to Gongyuan Lu.

Food and Drink

Qingpu has a developed tourist industry and therefore plenty of restaurants. Not only does Qingpu Zhen town have a lot of independent eateries on their own, each tourist attraction also has its own restaurant.

Xiang Kai Ge *(Xiāngkāi gé, 香开格)*

Located at: 268 Gongyuan Lu; telephone: 021-69718646. This was once one of Qingpu's most famous establishments; though, in recent times it has fallen into slight decline. Xiangkaige serves local dishes, and the eel slices (鳗鱼段) are highly recommended. Expect to pay 60-80 RMB per person.

Nine Hundred Bowls and Pots Restaurant

(jiŭbăiwăn guōzhuāng, 九佰碗锅庄)

Located at: Pucang Lu 421 Nong 8; telephone: 021-59724809; This is a hot pot restaurant with great tasting food. At 35 RMB per person, the price is right too. They have fermented bean curd and peanuts, baked crispy corn, strong-smelling preserved bean curd, soy-braised pork, and a variety of mushroom dishes.

Located on the same street, you will find the Ronggang Seafood Tavern

(rónggăng hăixiān dàjiŭlóu, 榕港海鲜大酒楼)

Located at: 888 Pucang Lu near Yinggang

ban Lou. In 1798, the garden's name was changed to Qushui Yuan. Most of the scenery you see today underwent large-scale renovation between 1983 and 1986. Today, Qushui Yuan is one of Shanghai's five great gardens.

Address

612 Gongyuan Lu, Qingpu Zhen

Wanshou Pagoda
(wànshòu tǎ, 万寿塔)

Located in the south of Qingpu Zhen, the Wanshou Pagoda is also called the South Gate Pagoda. Constructed in 1743 during the reign of Qing Emperor Qian Long, this square-shaped wood and brick structure has four faces and seven levels. Originally called Wanshou Tayuan, in 1883 a coppersmith climbed to the top of the pagoda to steal tin. As he was melting the tin off the roof, the pagoda caught on fire and much of its original wooden structure was lost. Its roof, central structure, and eaves are now missing.

Ancient Town of Zhijiajiao
(zhūjiājiǎo gǔzhèn, 朱家角古镇)

Sitting on the western bank of Dianshan Lake, Zhijiajiao was once famous for its "three li (1.5 kilometer) street, and its thousand stores". Since the Song Dynasty, Zhijiajiao, has been known far and wide as the "Red Town", and in 1991 Zhujiajiao was declared one of China's notable cultural towns. Today, the ancient town is open for tourism, and a new town has been built right on its side. Walk straight ahead from the new town parking lot, turn right, and you

should arrive at the ancient town's main entrance, which is decorated with many recently-built faux ancient buildings. Continuing into the town, you will come upon the two small rivulets and large river that lend to Zhujiajiao's fame as Shanghai's best preserved ancient water town. Zhujiajiao is frequently referred to as the Venice of Shanghai, the Hollywood of the Shanghai suburbs, or simply, Jiaoli.

Fangsheng Qiao Bridge
(fàngshēng qiáo, 放生桥)

Walk in from the town entrance, pass the hospital, and you will arrive at Fangsheng Qiao Bridge. When the bridge was built, its builder, Xing Chao, a Buddhist monk, stipulated that the Fangsheng Qiao could be used only for freeing fish and turtles. He forbid anybody from catching fish there. The name Fangsheng Qiao or "the releasing animals bridge" stems from the bridge's fa-

Food and Drink

Lu; telephone: 021-69718888, 69718989. Ronggang has a great atmosphere and good food. Serving local cuisine, it is considered one of the best restaurants in the area. Recommended dishes include: hand torn chicken, Chongqing-style pickled vegetables and fish, and crispy radish cakes. Expect to pay about 90 RMB per person.

National Accounting Institute's Buffet Restaurant *(guójiā kuàijì xuéyuàn, 国家会计学院自助餐厅)*

Located at: 200 Panlong Lu inside the Accounting Institute. Telephone: 021-69768000. The buffet costs 20 RMB per person and has a large number of choices. There are also plenty of drinks, and every day has a new celebrity-themed dish. With food and prices like this, it is certainly worth a visit.

mous rule. Built during the Ming Dynasty, Fangsheng Qiao is a tall five-hole stone arch bridge. In the past, one could view the entire ancient town from the bridge's top arch, but new structures on both sides of the bridge have destroyed the view. Farmers on and underneath the bridge often peddle basins of small fish to tourists. Each basin costs one RMB. As they are selling fish, you can usually hear the farmers chanting: "Release the fish, make a wish, protect familial harmony."

Kezhi Yuan Garden *(kèzhíyuán, 课植园)*

Kezhi Yuan's name comes from the allegorical saying, "study hard, but do not forget to till the fields". Located at Zhujiajiao Beishou's Xijing Jie, the garden is quiet and secluded and its scenery is excellent and unique. Keshi Yuan has the town's largest manor-style garden architecture, and is frequently called "the Ma Family Garden". The garden's structure and arrangement is pleasantly asymmetrical, satisfyingly dense, and of innovative design.

Bei Dajia *(běidàjiē, 北大街)*

Also called Yixian Jie or "One Thread Street", Bei Dajie is over four hundred years old. A little over 1 kilometer in length, the road begins in the east at Fengsheng Qiao Bridge and runs west three hundred meters into Meizhou Nong alley. Bei Dajie's most representative and quintessentially Ming-Qing characteristic is its narrowness. Look up at the sky from Bei Dajie, and you will see only a narrow strip of blue. This is how the it came to be known as "One thread Street". Today, Bei Dajie is a tourist street lined with shops selling handspun cloth and tourist souvenirs.

Zhujiajiao still has plenty of other interesting things to see. Unlike the one-road villages that characterize other river and stream towns, Zhujiajiao has plenty of small tortuous alleys, leading you unaware from one tiny scenic spot to another. The people of Zhujiajiao are friendly, and will happily welcome you in to visit their family courtyards. You can admire the rich scenery of your surroundings from the top of Tai An Qiao and Lang Qiao bridges. Walking from one bridge to another, you will notice fishing boats at the river bank selling fish and shrimp.

Chenjia Nong *(chénjiā nòng, 陈家弄)*

Located at Xijing Jie's Caogang Tan, this is Zhujiajiao's most ancient alley. Building facades stretch up to the top of the alleyway, and its first forty meters are dim, secluded, and quiet. Concave holes are carved into the alley wall. In ancient times they were used to place oil cups and candles for light, making the alley seem both quiet and remote.

Zhujiajiao has a number of other interesting alleys including Caishen Nong and Yiren Nong. Each has its own special appeal.

Address

There are a lot of buses in Shanghai traveling to and from Zhujiajiao. You can take Tourist Line NO. 4 from the Shanghai Stadium. People's Square has buses to Zhujiajiao from the intersection of Chengdu Beilu and Da Gu Lu (6:30am-7pm); from the Puan Lu and the Jinling Lu intersection (7:30am-3:30pm); and from the Madang Lu -Jinling Lu intersection (7am-4pm). You can also take the Qingpu bus line direct to Zhujiajiao from the Western Bus station (5am-7pm). If you only buy one-way tickets on the way out, there might not be any seats available for the way back. Even if you buy return tickets though, there still may be no empty seats left on the bus. Be prepared to stand or sit on your bag.

Telephone

021-59240077

Accommodations

If you are here on vacation, it would be smart to find a hotel near the Dianshan Lake. The environment here is terrific and you can find all the vacation village facilities you could possibly need.

Dianshan Lake Forest Holiday Resort *(diànshānhú sēnlín dùjiàcūn, 淀山湖森林度假村)* is located at 8185 Huqingping Gonglu right next to the Lake. Telephone: 021-559291290. Standard rooms cost 400 RMB a night, and a private villa runs at 3,480 RMB per night. Villas can accommodate 6 people.

Dianshan Lake Riyue Island Resort *(diànshānhú rìyuèdǎo dùjiàcūn, 淀山湖日月岛度假村)* has standard rooms for 280 RMB to 380 RMB. A villa with one bedroom runs at 700 RMB per night. A two bedroom villa runs at 1400 RMB a night. Address: 8700 Huqing GongLu, telephone: 021-59262960.

Oriental Green Boat Holiday Resort *(dōngfāng lǜzhōu dùjiàcūn, 东方绿舟度假村)* Located at: 6888 Qingping Gonglu, Telephone: 021-59233000 ext. 6000. The greatest luxury here is fine greenery and the scent of flowers. During the spring and fall, you have to reserve a room at least one week in advance. There is a restaurant on the grounds that cooks great country-style food.

All of these establishments are well within reach of the lake and Zhujiajiao. There are no accommodations in Zhujiajiao itself, but you can find hotels outside the town. **Feiyuan Hotel** *(fēiyún bīnguǎn, 飞云宾馆)* is a five minute trip away from the ancient town (Zhujiajiao Zhen 21-32 Xiangning Bang Lu). It costs 100 RMB a night. Facilities in the rooms are neat and tidy. The service is also friendly.

Tickets

60 RMB (combo ticket includes 10 sites), entry fee 10 RMB

Special Note

In ancient Zhujiajiao the sweet smell of zongzi (glutinous rice dumplings wrapped in reed leaves) fills the air. Zhujiajiao is teaming with zongzi (粽子) and zharou (扎肉) sellers. Zharou is soy-braised pork wrapped in zongzi leaves. You will notice that when you eat them, the fresh taste of the reed leaves mingles with the meat. They are quite delicious. If you buy zharou in a restaurant, expect to pay 3 RMB for one. On the street you will pay 10 RMB for six, although the ones on the street are usually half the size of the ones in the restaurant.

There are a number of rickshaw drivers at the town entrance who will try to tell you that if you ride in on their car, you will not have to pay Zhujiajiao's entrance fees. This is a scam, so ignore them. Before leaving for Zhujiajiao you may want to visit the town's web page. Website: www.zhujiajiao.com

Grand View Garden *(dàguān yuán, 大观园)*

This is a large imitation ancient building complex and modern garden. Located on Dianshan Lake's eastern shore, Daguan Yuan is divided into eastern and western scenic areas. The eastern area is made up of the Shanghai Folk Culture Village, a Plum Blossom Garden, and Sweet-smelling Osmanthus Garden. The western section's ancient architectural complex was built using traditional Chinese landscaping techniques and arranged according to the gardens described in Cao Xueqin's classic, Dream of the Red Chamber. Qing Shang Lu road runs through the middle of the garden, separating it into its eastern and western sides.

Daguan Yuan *(dàguān yuán, 大观园)*

Located to the west of Dianshang Hu Lake, this architectural complex includes Daguan Lou, Xiaoxiang Guan, Yihong Yuan, Hengwu Yuan and over 20 other structures, forming Dianshan Hu's principle thematic area. In order to truly appreciate this place, it helps to be familiar with profound work, Dream of the Red Chamber. These modern artistic creations cannot compete with the beauty and majesty of China's ancient gardens.

Mei Yuan *(méi yuán, 梅园)*

Taking up 100 Hectares of Daguan Yuan Garden's eastern section, and with over 5,000 trees, the Plum Blossom Garden is a much more attractive spot. In March, when plum blossoms are in full bloom, the Mei Yuan is a stunning sight. One of Mei Yuan's scenic areas, Meiwu Chunnong, is already known as the best place in Shanghai to see plum blossoms. The concept behind the plum blossom garden comes from Cao Xueqin's Daguan Yuan. A rare "Yinhong Taige" Plum Tree can be found inside the park's Lengxiang Pavilion.

Adress

Daguan Yuan is located at 701 Qingshang Gonglu: You can get there by taking the tourist number four line from the Shanghai Stadium or the Qiangsheng Special Tourist Line from the intersection of Jinling Zhonglu and Madang Lu. These buses leave everyday at 7am, 8am, 9:20am, 1:50pm and 4pm. From the Qingpu Bus station, you can take the Qingshang Line or the Zhongba bus heading to Shangta and Zhouzhuang.

Telephone

021-69262831

Hours of Operation

8am-5pm

Tickets

60 RMB, Children under 1.2 meters tall receive a 40% discount. Seniors over 70 with proper ID receive a 50% discount. Groups of over 20 receive a 5% discount. Combo tickets that include entry to both the Folk Custom Village and Daguan Yuan cost 70 RMB.

Sun Island Golf and Resort

(tàiyángdǎo guójì lǚyóu dùjiàqū, 太阳岛国际旅游度假区)

Sun Island Resort can be found on Mao Island — a river island that formed where the Huangpu, Mao, and Taipu Rivers converge. Mao Island was historically the center of the Mao Lake. During the Tang Dynasty, a Buddhist monk named Ru Hai laid down a foundation, and built Mao Pagoda on the island. He also dug a well, built a pavilion, and called the entire complex Dengzhao Tayuan. Today, all that remains of the ancient complex is the five story brick and wood Mao Pagoda. The surrounding area has been converted into a holiday and leisure spot, which includes an international standard golf course, polo field, a go cart race car track, water park, and man made beach.

Address

Located in the Qingpu District at 2588 Shentai Lu. The Shangtai Special Bus line runs direct routes from Shanghai Indoor Stadium's Shuniu Station to Taiyang Island.

Telephone

021-69833888

Hours of Operation

All day long

Tickets

Adults 30RMB; Children 15 RMB; Groups of over 20 receive 10% discount .

Special Note

Taiyang Island Club Card: The gold card runs 588 RMB (Can be used on Friday and Saturday), and the silver card 388 RMB (for use on Sunday and Thursday). Cards purchases can be used with a standard double room at the resort, a Chinese-style breakfast, horse back rides, hot spring, wave pool, mini golf, line and hook fishing, beach volleyball, and other items.

The Bridge town Jinze

(jīn zé, 金泽)

If you are an ancient bridge buff, than this is the place for you. According to local Qing Dynasty records: "Jinze has water in all directions, many rivers, and more bridges than you can find anywhere else. In ancient times it was said to have had 42 arched bridges". With the help of supplemental records and the memories of local seniors, 28 ancient bridges can be identified today. Many others have disappeared due to severe damage and lack of proper maintenance. Nevertheless, bridge enthusiasts should still be excited to see the attractive and exquisitely constructed bridges that still remain, including: Wanan Qiao, Puji Qiao, Huanxiang Qiao, Tianhuangge Qiao, Ruyi Qiao, and Biansuihong Qiao.

Address

From the Zhixin long distance passenger bus terminal at 249 Zhijiang Xilu, get on the Pingwang bound long distance bus and get off at Jinze. The Tourist Number Four Line leaves from the Shanghai Indoor Stadium's meeting center. Tickets are 10 RMB. You can take the Huqing Special Line from the intersection of Pu'an Lu and Yan'an Lu at People's Square. Tickets are 6 RMB. The Qingjin Line leaves for Jinze from the Qingpu Bus Station. Ticket prices are 4 RMB. The first bus leaves at 5:10 am and the final bus leaves at 6:20 pm. The last bus from Jinze to Qingpu leaves at 6:30 pm.

Special Note

The Jinze bus station is located at the side of 318 Guodao, and many busses on their way to the Zhejiang Province make a stop here. One of them is the Shanghai — Nanxun tourist long distance bus.

language

It is difficult even for non-local Chinese people to understand the local Shanghai dialect. There is a large in pronunciation between Shanghai dialect and Mandarin Chinese. A part of the Han-Bai language family and the Wu language group, Shanghai dialect emphasizes clear articulation, short syllables, relaxed intonation, and rapid speech. When Shanghai locals argue their speech becomes even faster, sounding something like a super-fast rap. Shanghai locals are proud of their language and they never speak Mandarin unless they absolutely have to. Many travelers, including out-of-town Chinese travelers, have trouble understanding Shanghai locals talk. It may be useful to learn a phrase or two to help you out in a tight spot.

Basics

Hello	你好 *nŏng hō*
Good moring	你早 *nóng zao*
Yes	是 *sí e*
No	不 *wé sí*
Please	请 *qĭng*
Thank you (very much)	谢谢 *xiă xià*
You're welcome	不用谢 / 不客气 *wĕ ke qì*
Excuse me	请原谅 *nǚ liáng*
What's your name?	你的名字？ *nóng jiáo să mĭng sí*
My name is...	我的名字是…… *wŭ e mĭng sí jiáo…*
Do you speak English?	你会讲英语吗？ *nong wei gang yin wen wa*
I don't understand.	我听不懂。*Wŭ tĭng we dŏng*
How much is it?	多少钱？ *jĭ dí*
Goodbye.	再见 *zē wei*

Getting Around

When dose the...leave/arrive?	什么时间……出发 / 到达？

Bus	汽车 *qì cū*
Minibus	小公共 *mǐ bāo cū*
Train	火车 *hǔ cū*
plane	飞机 *fī ji*
bus station	公共汽车站 *gōng gōng qì cū zài*
road to	这条路去…… *ge diao lu qi...*
Go straight ahead.	一直向前走 *yi ze mang xi dou zou*
To the left.	左转 *zǔ zǎn*
To the right.	右转 *yóu zǎn*
Near/ far	近 / 远 *jín/yǔ*

Accommodation

I am looking for a...	我在找…… *wǔ lé lé xíng...*
Guesthouse	旅馆 *lǚ gān*
Hote	饭店 *wái dī*
Do you have any room available?	你们有空房间吗？*Nóng gé dē yóu kǒng wáng gāi wā?*
May I see the room?	我可以看一下房间吗？*wǔ kǔ yí kǜ yī kǜ wáng gāi wā?*
One night	一天 *yī tì*
Two nights	两天 *liǎng tì*
I'd like..	我想要…… *wǔ xiǎng yáo...*
a single room	单人间 *dāi níng gāi*
to share a room	和别人共用房间 *gēn bí níng góng yóng wáng gāi*

Around Town

Where is a/the...?	……在哪里？ *... Lé lé ǎ lí de?*
Bank	银行 *níng áng*
General store	商场 *sāng dì*
Market	市场 *sǐ sáng*
Post office	邮局 *yǒu jué*
Public telephone	公用电话 *gōng yōng dí wú*
Toilet	洗手间 *dǎ sōu gai*
What time does...	什么时间…… *sá e cóng guāng...*
open/close?	开放 / 关闭 *kāi mén/dáng yáng*

Food & Drinks

Breakfast	早餐 *záo wāi*
Lunch	中餐 *zōng wāi*
Dinner	晚餐 *yǎ wāi*
I'm s vegetarian.	我是素食者。 *Wú sí qī sǔ e*
Bread	面包 *mǐ bāo*
Butter	黄油 *wáng yóu*
Chicken	鸡肉 *jī nio*
Beef	牛肉 *níu nio*
Crab	螃蟹 *há*
Pork	猪肉 *zī nio*
Prawns	大虾 *hǘ*
Eggs	鸡蛋 *jī dai*
Fish	鱼肉 *éng*
Fruit	水果 *sǐ gū*
Milk	牛奶 *niǔ na*
Pepper	胡椒 *wú jiāo*
salt	盐 *yí*
sugar	糖 *dáng*
vegetables	蔬菜 *sú cai*
potato	土豆 *yǎng sāi yù*
water	水 *sī*
mineral	矿泉水 *kuǎng jǘ sī*
boiled water	开水 *kāi sī*
cold water	冷水 *láng sī*
tea	茶 *sú*
tea with sugar	茶加糖 *sú gà dáng*
tea without sugar	茶不加糖 *sú wě gà dáng*
coffee	咖啡 *kā fī*
beer	啤酒 *bí jiǔ*
red wine	红酒 *óng jiǔ*
orange juice	橙汁 *sěng ze*

Time & Days

What time is it?	现在几点？ *Yí zái jǐ dī zōng?*
It's one o'clock.	现在一点钟。 *Yǐ zái yī dī zōng*

Today	今天 *jīn zāo*
Tonight	今晚 *jīn zāo yá dāo*
Tomorrow	明天 *míng zāo*
Yesterday	昨天 *suó nié*
Monday	星期一 *lǐ bā yī*
Tuesday	星期二 *lǐ bā liǎng*
Wednesday	星期三 *lǐ bā sà*
Thursday	星期四 *lǐ bā sí*
Friday	星期五 *lǐ bā ěn*
Saturday	星期六 *lǐ bā ló*
Sunday	星期日 *lǐ bā tì*

Numbers

0	*lín*
1	*yē*
2	*liáng*
3	*sà*
4	*sī*
5	*ěn*
6	*ló*
7	*qī e*
8	*bē*
9	*jiǔ*
10	*sé*
11	*sé yē*
12	*sé ní*
20	*nié*
50	*ěn sé*
100	*yē bē*

Index

A

Accommodations 40
Ai Lu 213
Air 30
Airlines 31
Ambrosia 67
Ancient Town of Zhijiajiao 288
Architecture on the Bund 124
Around Chongming Island 278
Around Huaihai Lu 196
Around Huangpi Nanlu 180
Around Hengshan Lu 204
Around Jiading District 250
Around Jiangan Temple 174
Around Lujiazui 152
Around People's Square 144
Around Qingpu District 286
Around Sichuan Beilu 214
Around Songjiang District 266
Around The Bund 122
Around The City 226
Around The City God Temple 158
Around The Fengxian District 258
Art Archives and Warehouse — 50 Moganshan Lu 242
ATM 20

B

Banking 20
Bars and Nightclubs 87
Best Places to Shop 110
Boat 33
Books 119
Bringing your Money to China 20
Budget Hotels: 300 RMB and Less 57
Bund Sightseeing Tunnel and the Shanghai Wing of the Chinese Museum of Sex Culture 142
Bus 35

C

Cameras & Film 119
Cangbao Lou Antiques Market 116
Cangbao Lou Antiques Building 167
Cinemas 97
Changle Lu 119
Chenxiang Ge Temple 164
Chongming Palace of Learning 282
Classic Shanghai Favorites 81
Climate 18
Citywide Transport 34
Communications 21
Confucian Temple and Secondhand Book Market 168
Credit Card 21
Currency 19

D

Dimei Shopping Mall and Hong Kong Branded Street 116

Director of the French Concession Chamber of Industry Mansion 214
Downtown 121
Dongjiadu Catholic Church 171
Dongping National Forest Park 284
Dongtai Lu Antiques Market 116
Duolun Lu 218

E

East China University of Politics and Law 239
Eastern Paris Golf Village Club 254
Eastern Orthodox Church 198
Entertainment 86
Eryan Temple 262
Exclusive Luxury Hotels 41

F

Fahua Pagoda 257
Farces 101
Fengxian Bay Tourist Area 261
Food and Drink 60
Foreign Consulates in Shanghai 25
For the Children 104
Fudan University 236
Fuxing Park 189
Fuzhou Lu 139

G

Geography 17
Grand Hall 69
Grand View Garden 292
Go-cart Tracks 103
Guyi Yuan Garden 251

H

Healthcare 23
Heavenly Horse Mountain 276
Helpful Websites for Hotel Reservations 41
High-end Options 49
Histroy 12
Hongqiao International Airport 31
Huaihai Zhong Lu 112
Huangpu Park 142
Huatingdong Stone Embankment 264

J

Jade Buddha Temple 229
Jiading Confucian Temple 255
Jin'ao Mountain 280
Jingan Park 177
Jingan Temple 175
Jingan Xiaoting Market 118
Jin Mao's 88th floor Observation Deck 154

K

Kadoorie Residenc — Shanghai Children's Palace 177

L

La Villa Rouge 212
Little Peach Orchard Mosque 170
Local Services and Information 25
Local Shanghai Fare 71
Long Distance Bus 32
Long Distance Telephone Calls 21
Long Distance Transportation 30
Longhua Temple 233
Lovers Wall 142
Lu Xun Museum 224
Lu Xun's Residence 222

M

Massage 104
Markets 115
Middle Level Accomodations 55
M on the Bund 64
Moller Villa 201
Mu En Methodist Church 145

N

Nanjing Lu 137
Nightlife 86

O

Oriental Pearl Television Tower 153
Other Locations Worth Considering 114
Outside the city 249
Overview 8

P

Park Hotel 151
Paulaner Brauhaus 67
Pickpockets 24
Pool of Convergent Dragons 256
Pudong International Airport 31

Q

Qipu Lu Wholesale Clothing Market 115
Qiuxiapu Garden 256
Qushui Yuan Garden 287

R

Renting Houses and Apartments 59
Residence of Zhou Enlai 186
Rui Jin Guest House 192

S

Safety 24
Sasha's 66
Sens & Bund 65
Shanghai's Administrative Structure 17
Shanghai Art Museum 150
Shanghai Botanical Garden 245
Shanghai Film and Television Amusement Park 246
Shanghai International Convention Center 154
Shanghai Library 209
Shanghai Museum 147
Shanghai Natural History Museum 171
Shanghai Natural Wild Insect Museum 156
Shanghai Ocean Aquarium 156
Shanghai Zhan Railway Station 32
Shanghai Snacks 76
Shanghai Na Zhan 32
Shanghai to Putuo Shan Mountian Ferry Schedule 33
Shanghai Urban Planning Centre 150
Shanghai Zoo 245
She Shan National Holiday Resort 273
Shopping 108
Shou'an Temple 280
Songjiang Mosque 271
Song Qingling Residence 208
South Bund Cloth Market 115
Square Pagoda 268
St Nicholas Church 190
Staying Healthy 22
Subway 34
Sun Island Golf and Resort 293

T

Taxi 36

Taikang Lu Art Stores 118
Ten Things to do on a Shanghai day 7
Theaters and shows 96
The Bridge town Jinze 294
The City God Temple 160
The Dr. Sun Yat-sen Residence 184
The Dongtai Lu Curio Street 169
The Eastern Shore 283
The Maglev 37
The Marshall Residence 194
— The Taiyuan Villa
The Performing Arts 100
The Old City Wall 171
The Shanghai Community Church 210
The Shanghai Old Street 166
The Site of the First National 183
Communist Party Congress
The Toroni Sutra Stella 270
The Yongfoo Elite 68
Three on the Bund 62
Tickets 101
To DVD or not to DVD 96
Tongjin Bridge 263
Tongji University 239
Traffic 24
Train 31
Transportation 30
Travel Itinerares 8

U

Upscale Restaurants 62

V

Vegetarian Cuisine 83

W

Wanfo Ge Pavilion 259
Wanshou Pagoda 288

X

Xiangyang Park 201
Xintiandi 181
Xintiandi's Fine Cuisine 66
Xujiahui Catholic Church 206
— St. Ignacious Cathedral
Xujiahui Commercial Center 113
Xujiahui Library 207

Y

Yi Yuan Garden 272
Yu Yuan Garden 161
Yuyuan Shopping City 115
Yunxiang Temple 253

Z

Zhenru Temple 232
Zuibai Chi 267

责任编辑：王颖
图片摄影：达雅　张慧　陈启宇　刘国政　刘大冬　雅楠　国新办图片库
部分图片提供：上海松江区旅游局　上海青浦区旅游局　上海崇明岛区旅游局
书籍设计：马静
地图制作：咳嗽
责任印制：闫立中

图书再版编目 (CIP) 数据

上海旅游指南 = Shanghai Travel Guide / 达雅，
(美)继强(Giammarco. J.)编著 . –北京：中国旅游出版社，2007.1
ISBN 978-7-5032-2996-1
Ⅰ. 上… Ⅱ. ①达…②江… Ⅲ. 旅游指南—上海
市–英文 Ⅳ. K928.951
中国版本图书馆 CIP 数据核字 (2006) 第 127486 号

书　　名：上海旅游指南 = Shanghai Travel Guide

出版发行：中国旅游出版社
(北京建国门内大街甲 9 号　邮编：100005)
http: //www.cttp.net.cn　E-mail: cttp@cnta.gov.cn
发行部电话：010-85166504　85166517
印　　刷：北京盛通彩色印刷有限公司
版　　次：2007 年 1 月第 1 版　　2007 年 1 月第 1 次印刷
开　　本：889 毫米 × 1194 毫米　1/32
印　　张：9.5
印　　数：1-5000 册
字　　数：250 千
定　　价：98 元
ISBN　978-7-5032-2996-1 / K・1109
